# Death March
## Second Edition

# MISSION STATEMENT FOR YOURDON PRESS SERIES

In today's hectic, fast-paced economy, IT professionals and managers are under constant pressure to deliver new systems more quickly than ever before. One of the consequences of this pressure is that they're often thrown into situations for which they're not fully prepared. On Monday, they're given a new assignment in the area of testing, or risk management, or building a new application with the latest tools from IBM or Microsoft or Sun; and on Tuesday, they're expected to be productive and proficient. In many cases, they don't have time to attend a detailed training course; and they certainly don't have time to read a thousand-page *War and Peace* tome that explains the theoretical nuances of the technology, no matter how interesting those nuances may be.

Yourdon Press is aimed squarely at these busy professionals and managers. Our mission is to provide enough information for an experienced IT professional or manager to be able to assimilate the key aspects of a technology and begin putting it to productive use right away. We don't cover the historical background or the philosophical nuances of the technology; and in most cases, we don't cover all of the refinements, exceptions, and extensions that a Ph.D. student would want to know. Our objective is to provide pragmatic "how-to" information— supported, when possible, by checklists and guidelines and templates and wizards—that can be put to practical use right away. Of course, it's important to know that the refinements, exceptions, and extensions do exist; and the Yourdon Press books frequently provide references, links to Web sites, and other resources for those who need them.

Over time, we intend to produce books for every important aspect of IT systems development: from analysis and design to coding and testing. We cover project management, risk management, process improvement, and peopleware issues; and we plan to address several areas of new technology, from CRM to wireless technology, from enterprise application integration to Microsoft's .NET technology.

Perhaps one day life will slow down, and we'll be able to spend as much time as we want learning *everything* there is to be learned about IT technologies. But until that day arrives, we only have time for the most essential chunks of pragmatic information. And the place to find that information is the Yourdon Press series of computer books from Pearson/Prentice Hall PTR.

## ABOUT THE SERIES EDITOR

Edward Yourdon is an internationally recognized consultant, lecturer, and author/coauthor of more than 25 books, including *Managing High-Intensity Internet Projects, Death March, Time Bomb, The Rise and Resurrection of the American Programmer, Modern Structured Analysis*, and others. Widely known as the lead developer of the structured analysis/design methods in the 1970's and the popular Coad/Yourdon object-oriented methodology in the early 1990's, Edward Yourdon brings both his writing and technical skills as Series Editor while developing key authors and publications for the Yourdon Press Series.

Selected Titles from the
# YOURDON PRESS SERIES
Ed Yourdon, *Advisor*

ANDREWS AND STALICK  Business Reengineering: The Survival Guide

BOULDIN  Agents of Change: Managing the Introduction of Automated Tools

COAD AND NICOLA  Object-Oriented Programming

COAD AND YOURDON  Object-Oriented Design

COAD WITH NORTH AND MAYFIELD  Object Models, Strategies, Patterns, and Applications, Second Edition

CONNELL AND SHAFER  Object-Oriented Rapid Prototyping

CONSTANTINE AND YOURDON  Structure Design

DEGRACE AND STAHL  Wicked Problems, Righteous Solutions

DEMARCO  Controlling Software Projects

DEMARCO  Structured Analysis and System Specification

JONES  Assessment and Control of Software Risks

MOSLEY AND POSEY  Software Test Automation

PAGE-JONES  Practical Guide to Structured Systems Design, Second Edition

PUTNAM AND MEYERS  Measures for Excellence: Reliable Software on Time within Budget

RUBLE  Practical Analysis and Design for Client/Server and GUI Systems

RUSSELL AND FELDMAN  IT Leadership Alchemy

SHLAER AND MELLOR  Object Lifecycles: Modeling the World in States

SHLAER AND MELLOR  Object-Oriented Systems Analysis: Modeling the World in Data

STARR  How to Build Shlaer-Mellor Object Models

THOMSETT  Radical Project Management

THOMSETT  Third Wave Project Management

ULRICH  Legacy Systems: Transformation Strategies

YOURDON  Byte Wars: The Impact of September 11 on Information Technology

YOURDON  Death March, Second Edition

YOURDON  Managing High-Intensity Internet Projects

YOURDON  Modern Structured Analysis

YOURDON  Outsource: Competing in the Global Productivity Race

# Death March

## Second Edition

Edward Yourdon

PRENTICE
HALL
PTR

Prentice Hall Professional Technical Reference
Upper Saddle River, New Jersey 07458
www.phptr.com

Library of Congress Cataloging-in-Publication Data available

Editorial/production supervision: *Kathleen M. Caren*
Executive Editor: *Paul Petralia*
Editorial Assistant: *Michelle Vincenti*
Marketing Manager: *Chris Guzikowski*
Manufacturing Manager: *Alexis Heydt-Long*
Cover Design Director: *Jerry Votta*
Interior Design: *Gail Cocker-Bogusz*

 © 2004 Pearson Education, Inc.
Publishing as Prentice Hall Professional Technical Reference
Upper Saddle River, NJ 07458

Prentice Hall PTR offers excellent discounts on this book when ordered in quantity for bulk purchases or special sales. For more information, please contact U.S. Corporate and Government Sales, 1-800-382-3419, corpsales@pearsontechgroup.com. For sales outside of the U.S., please contact International Sales, 1-317-581-3793, international@pearsontechgroup.com.

ISBN  013143635X

9  1011121314 DOH   09 08 07

9th  Printing, August 2007

Pearson Education LTD.
Pearson Education Australia PTY, Limited
Pearson Education Singapore, Pte. Ltd.
Pearson Education North Asia Ltd.
Pearson Education Canada, Ltd.
Pearson Educación de Mexico, S.A. de C.V.
Pearson Education—Japan
Pearson Education Malaysia, Pte. Ltd.

To my first grandson, Liam;
and to his great-grandparents,
Marion and Ray.

There's nothing better than an extended family,
spanning four generations, to help put the demands and
priorities of a death march project in proper perspective.

# Contents

# Preface

Our achievements speak for themselves. What we have to keep track of are our failures, discouragements, and doubts. We tend to forget the past difficulties, the many false starts, and the painful groping. We see our past achievements as the end result of a clean forward thrust, and our present difficulties as signs of decline and decay.

—Eric Hoffer
*Reflections on the Human Condition*, aph. 157 (1973)

I know: You're intrigued by the title of this book, and you decided to peek inside to see what it's all about. But you're busy, busy, busy—and you don't know if you have the time to read yet another book about managing software projects. *Especially* if it's a book that tells you how things should be done in an ideal world where rational men and women make calm, sensible decisions about the budget, schedule, and resources for your software project.

You may have noticed that we don't live in an ideal world, and chances are that your project requires you to interact with people who seem anything but rational and whose decisions hardly seem calm or sensible. In other words, you're working on a *death march* project. The wonderful thing about the title of this book is that I don't even have to explain it: Every time I mention it to friends and colleagues, they just laugh and say, "Oh, yeah, you must be talking about *my* project!" Well, these days it's likely to be my project, and your project, and everyone else's project too—we're *all* working on death march projects, or so it seems.

The first question you should be asking yourself (though it may not occur to you until the end of your project) is: "Why on earth did I let myself get suckered into such a project?" I'll discuss this in the first chapter, because my experience as a consultant—visiting and observing many such projects from the sidelines—is that the world would be a healthier place if more of us had the guts to stand up and say, "Hell, no, I won't join this death march!"

But assuming there's no escape—e.g., there are no other jobs available or you've got some form of a "golden handcuff" relationship with your employer that strongly discourages you from leaving—the next question is: "How can I survive this project without ruining my health, my sanity, and my dignity?" If you're an optimist, you might even be wondering how you can conquer the obstacles before you and actually finish the death march project on time and under budget. But if you've been through a number of these projects before, you probably know that the odds are stacked against you and that survival is the best you can hope for.

Having worked in the software industry for over 30 years, I find that our profession has a rather interesting reaction to death march projects. In some parts of the industry, especially in Silicon Valley, such projects are glorified as a test of manhood, somewhat akin to climbing Mount Everest barefoot. I felt this way during my first few software projects back in the mid-1960s, and the fact that the same attitude prevails a generation later suggests to me that it's likely to be a permanent phenomenon, as long as technology continues to change as rapidly as it has been during my lifetime. Ours is not a mature industry: Every year there's a new Mount Everest to climb and a new crop of hotshot programmers who are convinced that they can run barefoot all the way to the top.

But another segment of our industry regards death march projects as embarrassing failures. We've all been bombarded with statistics about the prevalence of schedule delays, budget overruns, buggy software, disgruntled users, and outright project failures. We've been told repeatedly by consultants, gurus, and methodologists that the reason for all these embarrassments is that we've been using the wrong methods (or no methods at all), or the wrong tools, or the wrong project management techniques. In other words, death march projects exist because we're stupid or incompetent.

If you talk to battle-scarred veterans in the field—the ones who have gone through a couple of death march projects and have learned that it's really not fun to climb Mount Everest barefoot— you'll often hear them say, "Hey! I'm not stupid! Of *course* I would like to use the right methods and tools and project management approaches. But my senior management and my end-users won't let me. The reason we have such a ridiculous schedule for this project is that it was imposed upon us on the first day, before we had the faintest idea what the project was all about!" Conclusion: Death march projects occur because senior managers are Machiavellian bastards and/ or because our users are naive and unrealistic.

No doubt there's some truth to all this: We do make a lot of stupid mistakes managing our projects, our senior managers do indulge in ridiculous political games, and our end-users do make unreasonable demands on us. I'm convinced that much of this is due to the rapid pace of change, combined with the usual disrespect that each new generation has for the advice offered by the previous generation. Why on earth should today's generation of Java-oriented hotshots pay any attention to the advice offered by my generation, whose formative programming experience took place 30 years ago in Autocoder and assembly language? And how should today's generation of business users know what kind of Web-based application is reasonable to ask for, considering that their predecessors were asking for mainframe-based online systems, with character-based dumb-terminal interfaces?

Whatever the explanation for the phenomenon, I've come to a sobering conclusion: *Death march projects are the norm, not the exception.* I think that today's software developers and project managers *are* pretty smart and are eager to manage projects in a rational way; I also think that today's business users and senior managers are much more computer-literate than they were a generation ago and much less naive about what software developers can be expected to deliver with finite resources. That doesn't stop both groups of smart individuals from embarking upon yet another death march project—because the competitive business pressures demand it and the new technological opportunities invite it. The business managers may be fully aware that a rational schedule for their new system would require 12 calendar months, but they'll also tell you emphatically that unless it's available in six months, the competition will grab the entire market for its new product or service. And the technical staff may be fully aware that new technologies like the Internet are still quite risky, but they will tell you that if the new technology *does* work, it will provide a strategic competitive advantage that makes it well worth the risk.

To put it another way, industry surveys from organizations such as the Standish Group, as well as statistical data from metrics gurus such as Capers Jones, Howard Rubin, and Larry Putnam, suggest that the *average* project is likely to be six to 12 months behind schedule and 50 to 100 percent over budget. The situation varies depending on the size of the project and various other factors, but the grim reality is that you should *expect* that your project will operate under conditions that will almost certainly lead to death march behavior on the part of the project manager and his or her technical staff. If a project starts off with these high-risk factors, there's going to be a lot of overtime and wasted weekends, and there's likely to be a lot of emotional and physical burnout before the end of the project.

So the real question is: If you can't avoid death march projects, how can you survive them? What should you do to increase your chances of success? Where should you be willing to compromise—and when should you be willing to put your job on the line and plan to resign if you can't get your way? *That* is what this book is about. These issues are as relevant for the manager in charge of the project as they are for the technical staff that actually does the hard work of designing, coding, testing, and documenting the system. I'll address both groups in the chapters that follow.

A word about managers and technical staff members: Some of the comments you'll see in the following chapters will imply that management is "evil" and that the project team members are innocent, downtrodden victims. Obviously, this is not the case for all projects and all companies, though the very existence of a death march project is usually the result of a conscious management decision. While the project team members may be willing participants in such projects, they usually don't propose them in the first place.

If you've decided at this point that you don't have time to read this book, here's a simple word of advice that may provide some value for the time you've invested in reading the preface: *triage*. If you're on a death march project, it's almost certain that you won't have the resources to provide all the functionality or "features" requested by the end-user within the allotted schedule and budget. You'll have to make some cold-blooded decisions about which features to sacrifice and which ones to focus your resources on. Indeed, some of the frivolous features will *never* be implemented, so it's best to let them die on their own. Other features are important but also relatively easy to implement, e.g., because they're a by-product of the vendor-supplied class library or Computer-Aided Software Engineering (CASE) tools that you're using. To use the medical metaphor of triage, these features will survive on their own. The difference between success and failure on a death march project often lies in the project team's ability to identify the critical features of the system that would "die" without an investment of substantial resources and energy.

Of course, there's more to surviving a death march project than just triage. I'll cover triage in Chapter 3, but we also need to look at peopleware issues, "process" issues, and issues of tools and technology. I've tried to be as concise as possible , so you should be able to finish the whole book in a couple of hours; if nothing else, it should give you a more realistic assessment of your next death march project.

However, please don't get the impression that this book is a "bible," or that it will provide "silver bullet" solutions to all of your problems. There are no guaranteed "right answers" in this book; what works in some companies and in some situations may not work in others. Equally important: the compromises that some managers and technical staff members are willing to make will prove unacceptable to others. I'll make what I consider to be reasonable suggestions, but it's up to you to decide which ones will work in your environment.

I also intend, on an ongoing basis, to collect advice from the field on my Web site at http://www.yourdon.com —from real project teams that have some practical tips on best practices, worst practices, and "breathalyzer test" questions. Even if you don't have enough money in your project budget to buy this book (such penny-pinching budgets are an indicator unto themselves of the risk associated with a death march project!), it won't cost you a penny to check the Death March Web page.

Whatever you decide to do, best of luck on your next death march project. And remember the words of Samuel Beckett:

*Ever tried. Ever failed. No matter. Try Again. Fail again. Fail better.*

—Samuel Beckett
*Worstward Ho* (1984)

# 1 Introduction

*Happiness lies in being privileged to work hard for long hours in doing whatever you think is worth doing. One man may find happiness in supporting a wife and children. And another may find it in robbing banks. Still another may labor mightily for years in pursuing pure research with no discernible results.*

*Note the individual and subjective nature of each case. No two are alike and there is no reason to expect them to be. Each man or woman must find for himself or herself that occupation in which hard work and long hours make him or her happy. Contrariwise, if you are looking for shorter hours and longer vacations and early retirement, you are in the wrong job. Perhaps you need to take up bank robbing. Or geeking in a sideshow. Or even politics.*

—Jubal Harshaw, in *To Sail Beyond the Sunset*
by Robert Heinlein (Ace Books, reprint edition, 1996)

What is a death march project? What makes IT organizations create such things? Why would anyone in his right mind agree to participate in such a project?

To many grizzled IT veterans, these are rhetorical questions. *Everything*, in their experience, is a death march project. Why do they happen? Because corporations are insane and, as consultant Richard Sargent commented to me, "Corporate insanity is doing the same thing again and again, and each time expecting different results."[1] And why do we participate in such projects? Because, as consultant Dave Kleist observed in an e-mail note, "Death march projects are rarely billed as such, and it takes a lot of work when being hired from the outside to discover if your hiring company is prone to creating death march projects."[2]

If you think the answers to these questions are obvious, feel free to jump to the next chapter. I'm sometimes think they *are* obvious, since most people never ask me what I mean by "death march." But if you're one of the people who has no idea what I'm talking about, or wonder if this is a book about military campaigns from World War II, it may be worth the effort to pause for a moment and contemplate what this is all about.

## DEATH MARCH DEFINED

Quite simply, a death march project is one whose "project parameters" exceed the norm by at least 50 percent. In most projects, this means one or more of the following constraints have been imposed upon the project:

- The schedule has been compressed to less than half the amount estimated by a rational estimating process; thus, the project that would normally be expected to take 12 calendar months is now required to deliver its results in six months or less. Because of the competitive pressures of business competition in today's global marketplace, along with the concept of "Internet time" from the dot-com era of the computer industry, this is probably the most common form of death march project.

- The staff has been reduced to less than half the number that would normally be assigned to a project of this size and scope; thus, instead of being given a project team of 10 people, the project manager has been told that only five people are available. This may have come about as a result of someone's naive belief that a new programming language or application development environment will magically double the team's productivity—despite the fact that the team was given no training or practice with the new technology and probably wasn't even consulted about the decision to use the technology in the first place. Unfortunately, it's happening far more often, as this edition of *Death March* is being written in the spring of 2003, because of the ongoing economic recession and the associated cutbacks in IT budgets.

- The budget and associated resources have been cut in half. Again, this is often the result of downsizing and other cost-cutting measures, but it can also result from competitive bidding on a fixed-price contract, where the project manager in a consulting firm is informed by the marketing department that, "the good news is that we won the contract; the bad news is that we had to cut your budget in half in order to beat out the competitors." This kind of constraint often has an immediate impact on the number of project team personnel that can be hired, but the consequences are sometimes a little more subtle—e.g., it may lead to a decision to hire relatively inexpensive, inexperienced junior software developers, rather than higher-cost veterans. And it can lead to a pervasive atmosphere of penny-pinching that makes it impossible for the project manager to order pizza for the project team when they spend the entire weekend in the office working overtime.

- The functionality, features, performance requirements, or other technical aspects of the project are twice what they would be under normal circumstances. Thus, the project team may have been told that it needs to squeeze twice as many features into a fixed amount of RAM or disk space as its competitor; or it may have been told its system has to handle twice the volume of transactions that any comparable system has ever accomplished. The performance constraints may or may not lead to a death march project; after all, we can always take advantage of cheaper, faster hardware, and we can always search for a more clever algorithm or design approach to accomplish the improved performance. But doubling the functionality—i.e., the available features—usually means doubling the amount of work that has to be carried out; *that* does lead to a death march project.

The immediate consequence of these constraints, in most organizations, is to ask the project team to work twice as hard and/or twice as many hours per week as would be expected in a "normal" project. Thus, if the normal work-week is 40 hours, then a death march project team is often found working 14-hour days, six days a week. Naturally, the tension and pressure escalate in such environments, so that the death march team operates as if it is on a steady diet of Jolt cola.

Another way to characterize such projects is as follows:

A death march project is one for which an unbiased, objective risk assessment (which includes an assessment of technical risks, personnel risks, legal risks, political risks, etc.) determines that the likelihood of failure is ≥ 50 percent.

Of course, even a project without the schedule, staff, budget, or functionality constraints described above could have a high risk of failure—e.g., because of hostile politics between the IT department and the user community. But most commonly, the reason for the high risk assessment is a combination of the constraints described above.

# CATEGORIES OF DEATH MARCH PROJECTS

Not all death march projects are the same; not only do they involve different combinations of schedule, staff, budget, and functionality constraints, but they come in different sizes, shapes, and flavors.

In my experience, *size* is the most important characteristic that distinguishes one death march project from another. Consider four different ranges of projects:

- *Small-scale projects*—the team consists of three to six people who are working against nearly impossible odds to finish a project in three to six months.
- *Medium-size projects*—the team consists of 20–30 people, who are involved in a project expected to take one to two years.
- *Large-scale projects*—the project consists of 100–300 people, and the project schedule is three to five years.
- *Mind-boggling projects*—the project has an army of 1,000–2,000 or more (including, in many cases, consultants and subcontractors), and the project is expected to last seven to ten years.

For several reasons, the small-scale death march projects are the most common in the organizations that I visit around the world today; happily, they have the greatest chance of succeeding. A tightly knit group of three to six people is more likely to stick together through thick and thin, and this same group of highly motivated people is more likely to be willing and able to sacrifice their personal lives (as well as risk their health!) for three to six months if they know that the regimen of long nights, wasted weekends, and postponed vacations will come to an end in a matter of months.

The odds of successful completion drop noticeably with the medium-size projects and disappear almost completely with the large-scale projects. With larger numbers of people involved, it's more difficult to maintain a sense of cohesive team spirit; and the statistical odds of someone quitting, being run over by a beer truck, or succumbing to the various perils of modern society increase rapidly. What's crucial here is not just the number of people involved, but the time-scale: Working 80-hour weeks for six months may be tolerable, but doing it for two years is much more likely to cause problems.

As for the "mind-boggling" death march projects: One wonders why they exist at all. Perhaps the systems development efforts associated with the NASA project that landed a man on the moon in 1969 could be considered a successful example of a death march project; but the vast majority of such projects are doomed from the beginning. Fortunately, most senior managers have figured this out, and most large organizations (which are the only ones that could afford them in the first place!) have banned all such projects. Government organizations, alas, still embark upon them from time to time; along with potentially unlimited budgets with which to tackle truly mind-boggling projects, appeals to patriotic notions (e.g., "national security" in the post-9/11 era) may be sufficient to blind senior management to the futility of the task they've been given.

In addition to project size, it's also useful to characterize the "degree" of a death march project by such criteria as the number of user-organizations that are involved. Things are hard enough when the project team has to satisfy only one user or one group of homogeneous users within a single department. Enterprise-wide projects are usually an order of magnitude more difficult, simply because of the politics and communication problems involved in cross-functional activities of any kind. As a result, the systems development projects associated with business re-engineering projects often degenerate into a death march; even though the development effort is modest in terms of hardware and software effort, the political battles can paralyze the entire organization and cause endless frustration for the project team.

Finally, we can distinguish between projects that are incredibly difficult and those that are fundamentally impossible. As John Boddie, author of *Crunch Mode*, points out,

> The combination of excellent technical staff, superb management, outstanding designers, and intelligent, committed customers is not enough to guarantee success for a crunch-mode project. There really are such things as impossible projects. New ones are started every day. Most impossible projects can be recognized as such early in the development cycle. There seem to be two major types: "poorly understood systems" and "very complex systems."[3]

This still leaves unanswered the questions of why a rational organization would embark upon such a project and why a rational project manager or technical person would agree to participate in such a project. We'll deal with those questions below.

# WHY DO DEATH MARCH PROJECTS HAPPEN?

If you think about what goes on in your organization, it's not difficult to understand why death march projects occur. As Scott Adams, author of the incredibly popular "Dilbert" cartoons, points out,

> When I first started hearing these stories [about irrational corporate behavior] I was puzzled, but after careful analysis I have developed a sophisticated theory to explain the existence of this bizarre workplace behavior. People are idiots.
>
> Including me. Everyone is an idiot, not just the people with low SAT scores. The only difference among us is that we're idiots about different things at different times. No matter how smart you are, you spend much of your day being an idiot.[4]

Perhaps it's too depressing to imagine that you're an idiot and that you're surrounded by (and managed by!) idiots. Or perhaps you consider it an insult that someone would even make such a suggestion. In that case, Table 1.1 shows a more detailed list of reasons for the occurrence of death march projects:

**Table 1.1**   Reasons for Death March Projects

| Politics, politics, politics |
| --- |
| Naïve and/or devious promises made by marketing, senior executive, inexperienced project managers, etc. |
| Naive optimism of youth: "We can do it over the weekend" |
| The "startup" mentality of fledgling entrepreneurial companies |
| The "Marine Corps" mentality: *Real* programmers don't need sleep |
| Intense competition caused by globalization of markets |
| Intense competition caused by the appearance of new technologies |
| Intense pressure caused by unexpected government regulations |
| Unexpected and/or unplanned crises—e.g., your hardware/software vendor just went bankrupt, or your three best programmers just died of bubonic plague |

While the items in Table 1.1 may seem obvious, they do need to be discussed—because they may indicate that your death march project is *so* crazy and irrational that it's not worth participating at all. Indeed, even without an explicit rationale of the sort shown in Table 1.1, you should seriously consider whether you want to spend the next several months (or years) attached to such a project; we'll discuss that separately later in this chapter.

## Politics, politics, politics

Many software developers vow that they won't get involved in politics—partly because they've learned that they're not very good at playing political games, but also because they feel that everything about politics is repugnant. Alas, politics cannot be avoided: As soon as two or more people participate in some joint enterprise, politics are involved.

But when politics becomes the dominant "driving force" in a large, complex project, the project is likely to degenerate into a death march. Remember my definition of a death march project: It's one where the schedule, budget, staff, or resources are 50–100 percent less than what they should be. *Why are these constraints being placed on the project?* There are many possible explanations, as we'll see in the discussion below; but in many cases, the answer is simply, "Politics." It may be a power struggle between two ambitious vice presidents in your organization, or the project may have been set up to fail as a form of revenge upon some manager who stepped on the wrong toes at the wrong time. The possibilities are endless.

There is little chance that you'll get the politicians to admit what's going on; however, if you're a technical staff member, it's not unreasonable to ask your project manager whether the entire death march project is a political sham. Even if you don't like politics, and even if you think you're a political neophyte, listen carefully to the answer your manager gives you. You're not stupid, and you're not *that* naive. If you have a sixth sense that there's some ugly politics dominating the entire project, chances are you're right; and if your immediate supervisor gives a naïve, ambiguous, or thoroughly unconvincing answer to your questions, you should draw your own conclusions. To put it another way: If your project sounds like something straight out of a "Dilbert" cartoon, chances are that it will be the kind of death march project in which no rational person would want to be involved.

What if your manager openly agrees with you? What if he or she says, "Yes, this whole project is nothing more than a bitter power struggle between Vice Presidents Smith and Jones..."? If that's the case, then why on earth is your manager participating in the project? As we'll see in the section about why people participate in death march projects, there may be many reasons; but your manager's reasons are not necessarily *your* reasons. The existence of ugly politics doesn't necessarily mean that you should abandon the project or quit your job right away, but it does mean that you should keep your own priorities, objectives, and sense of ethics separate from what's going on in the project—for it's quite likely that many of the decisions that take place (beginning with the schedule/budget/resource decisions that defined the project as a death march in the beginning!) are not being made with the best interests of the end-user or the enterprise in mind. If the project succeeds at all, it's likely to be an accident—or it may be because the intended victim (who may be your project manager, but may also be a manager several levels above your immediate manager) is a more clever politician than the opposition counted on.

## Naive promises made by marketing, senior executives, naive project managers, and so on

Naiveté is often associated with inexperience; thus, it's common to see unrealistic commitments made by people who have no idea how much time or effort will be required to build the system they want. In the extreme case, this can lead to what my friend and colleague Tom DeMarco calls "hysterical optimism": Everyone in the organization desperately wants to believe that a complex project, which has never been attempted before but which has been realistically estimated to require three calendar years of effort, can somehow be finished in nine months.

The naiveté and optimism extends to the technical staff, too, as we'll see below. But for the moment, let's assume that it's your manager, or your marketing department, or the end-user who is responsible for the naively optimistic schedule or budget. The question is: How will they react when it eventually becomes clear that the initial commitments *were* optimistic? Will they extend the schedule, increase the budget, and calmly agree that things are tougher than they had imagined? Will they thank you for the heroic efforts you and your colleagues have made up to that point? If so, then it may turn out that the most important thing you need to do is avoid the classical waterfall life cycle, so that a realistic assessment of schedule, budget, and resources can be made after the first prototype version of the system is delivered.[5]

But in many death march projects, this kind of rational mid-course correction isn't possible. This can happen, of course, if a senior manager makes a naive promise to the customer, and then feels that the commitment has to be honored—no matter what. In the worst case, the person making the commitment knows full well what's going on: It's particularly apparent when the marketing manager confesses to the project manager over a beer after the celebrations accompanying a new contract from some gullible client, "Well, we wouldn't have gotten this contract if we told the client how long it will *really* take; after all, we knew that our competitors would be coming with some really aggressive proposals. And besides, you guys always pad your schedules and budgets anyway, don't you?"

The last comment is especially onerous if it comes from your boss, or from some manager two or three levels above you. Obviously, it suggests that the entire process of estimating schedules and budgets is a negotiating game, which we'll discuss in more detail in Chapter 3. But there is also likely to be some degree of naiveté, for the unspoken implication in your manager's complaint about "padding" the schedule and budget is that you *could* finish the death march project in time to meet the ridiculous deadline that has been imposed upon you. On the other hand, it could have something to do with the "Marine Corps" mindset that I'll discuss in that upcoming section. Similarly, the commitment to a ridiculous schedule and budget by the marketing department could turn out to be another form of politics, discussed earlier; that is, the marketing representative probably doesn't care whether the schedule and budget he proposed is ridiculous or not, because his primary objective is his sales commission, or meeting his quota, or pleasing his boss, etc.

Assume for the moment that the death march project has been created as a result of "pure" naiveté, absent of politics or other malicious influences. The question is: What should you do about it? As noted above, a key question is the probability that the decision-makers will revise their budgets and schedules when it becomes apparent that the original commitments can't be met. This is difficult to predict in advance, though it wouldn't hurt to check around and see what has happened to other death march projects in similar situations. (If this is the first such project that has ever occurred in your company, then you really are in uncharted territory!)

If you have the strong impression—either from your political instincts, or from the experiences from previous projects in your organizations—that management will hold fast to its original budget and schedule, no matter how much of a "denial of reality" is involved, then you need to make a much more fundamental decision about whether to proceed or not. Some of this involves the extent to which you can negotiate other aspects of your project—e.g., the technical staff that will be assigned to the project—which we'll discuss in Chapter 2.

## Naive optimism of youth: "We can do it over the weekend"

Though management is a convenient scapegoat for many of the idiotic decisions associated with death march projects, the technical staff is not entirely blameless. Indeed, in many cases senior management will happily admit its naiveté and lack of experience with the process of estimating and scheduling complex projects. "How long do you think it will take?" a vice-president will ask the technical hot-shot, who may have been promoted to the rank of first-level supervisor just last week.

And if the technical hot-shot is ambitious and filled with youthful optimism (which usually borders on the teenage delusions of immortality, omnipotence, and omniscience) the answer is likely to be, "No problem! We can probably knock it out over the weekend!" A really good software engineer—well, "hacker" might be a more appropriate description here—is firmly convinced that he or she can develop *any* system in a weekend. Minor details such as documentation, error-handling, editing of user inputs, and testing are so boring that they don't count.

If you're the naively optimistic software engineer responsible for making the death march estimate, chances are that you don't even know what you're doing. You probably read the paragraph above, bristled at the apparent insult, and muttered, "Damn right! I really *can* build any system over the weekend!" God bless you; maybe you'll succeed. In any case, nothing that you hear from an old fart like me is likely to change your mind.

But if you are a battle-scarred veteran, and you can see that you're about to be roped into a death march project because some naive young technical manager has made a ridiculously optimistic commitment regarding the project's schedule, budget, and resources—what should you do? The best advice, I think, is "Run!" When such technical managers realize that they are in over their heads, they often collapse into truly irrational behavior or paralysis. In most cases, they haven't dealt with anything before that was so big and complex that it couldn't be overwhelmed by sheer cleverness or brute force (e.g., 48 hours of nonstop coding over the weekend). In any case, they're certainly not in the mood to hear you say, "I told you so!" as their project falls behind schedule.

## The "startup" mentality of fledgling entrepreneurial companies

I've not only watched this occur, I've participated in such projects and have been responsible for initiating them in several cases. Shortly after the first edition of this book was published, it appeared that any startup company with "dot-com" in its corporate name or product name could get more venture capital than it knew what to do with. But as became clear to the venture capitalists and hopeful investors, startup organizations are generally understaffed, underfinanced, undermanaged, and hysterically optimistic about their chances of success. They have to be: A cautious, conservative manager would never dream of starting a new company without tons of careful planning and a large bank account to deal with unforeseen contingencies.[6]

So, almost by definition, a large percentage of the projects associated with startup companies comprises death march projects. And a large percentage of these projects will fail; a large percentage of the companies will fail with them. C'est la vie—that's what high-tech capitalism is all about (not only in the United States, but all over the world). Having been raised in this culture all my life, I think it's perfectly normal; my attitude is also biased by the fact that I've been lucky enough to succeed in a few such ventures. Indeed, this scenario is often one of the *positive* reasons for embarking upon a death march project, as I'll discuss in more detail in that section below.

But not everyone is familiar with the culture and environment of a corporate startup. If you've spent the past 20 years of your career working with brain-dead CO-BOL zombies in a moribund government agency (or in, for that matter, most banks or insurance companies or telephone companies) and you've just taken a job with a startup firm because you were downsized, outsourced, or given an early retirement, then you probably have little or no idea what you're in for. Death march projects occur in big companies, too, but they're often staffed by cast extras from *Night of the Living Dead*. The environment is completely different in startup-company death march projects; it's like a rush of pure adrenaline.

At the same time, the startup companies often suffer from the kind of naive optimism discussed earlier. Many startup companies are founded by technical hotshots convinced that their new technology will make them richer than Bill Gates; other such companies are founded by marketing wizards who are certain they can sell Internet-enabled refrigerators to gullible Eskimos. Optimism is important in any startup venture, and the success of the corporate venture may depend on doing what nobody has ever been able to do before; but even an aggressive, optimistic startup company has to obey basic laws of physics and mathematics. If you get involved in a startup-company death march project, check to see whether there is some kind of plan for success, or whether the whole venture is based on wishful dreaming.

## The "Marine Corps" mentality: *Real* programmers don't need sleep

Startup companies are sometimes vulnerable to the "Marine Corps" syndrome, but I've seen it most often in the consulting organizations like EDS and the Big-X[7] accounting firms. It may reflect the personality of the corporate founder(s), and it may reflect the corporate culture in its earlier days—the corporate behavior at Microsoft, for example, has often been attributed to these factors. In essence, you'll be told by the appropriate manager, "*Every* project is like this, because that's how we do things around here. It works, we're successful, and we're damn proud of it. If you can't handle it, then you don't belong here."

Whether an attitude like this is civilized, humane, or right is a topic for a separate discussion. Indeed, the question of whether it's even successful is something to be discussed elsewhere; the important thing is to realize that it's *deliberate*, not accidental. If you're a martyr or a revolutionary, you might decide to attack the corporate culture, but the chances are that you won't succeed. It's quite possible that there will be some negative long-term consequences of the overall death march culture, for example, the best people may slowly drift away and the company may fail. But when it comes to *this* death march project, there's no point questioning why it has been set up with a nearly impossible schedule and budget. As the prototypical manager of such companies says, "If you can't handle it, then you don't belong here."

Sometimes there's an official rationale for such corporate behavior—for example, "We compete in a tough marketplace, and all of our competitors are just as smart as we are. The only way we succeed is to work twice as hard." And sometimes the death march projects are set up to weed out the younger (weaker) junior employees, so that only the survivors of the death march projects will reach the exalted status of "partner" or "vice president." Whatever the rationale, it's usually fairly consistent; there's not much point complaining about it for the sake of a single project.

That doesn't necessarily mean that you should accept an assignment on such a project; after all, just because every other project within the organization is a death march doesn't necessarily mean that yours will succeed, or that you will survive. It simply means that the decision to create such a project has an understandable origin.

## Intense competition caused by globalization of markets

Organizations that might not have tolerated death march projects in the past are some-times forced to do so in the 21st century, simply because of the increased level of competition associated with the global marketplace. The secondary factors here are the Internet and the Web, as well as governmental decisions to open previously pro-tected markets or eliminate tariffs and quotas.

For some organizations, this is not a new phenomenon; the automobile and elec-tronics industries, for example, have been facing stiff competition since the 1970s. But for other organizations, the appearance of European or Asian competitors in the North American marketplace can come as a rude shock. Once senior management has accepted the reality of serious competition, it may decide to embark upon a variety of radical moves, ranging from downsizing to outsourcing the entire IT organization to the other side of the world; it may also decide to compete head-on with a new product or service that requires a new, ambitious system to support it. *Voila!* A death march project has begun.

A relatively recent version of this globalization phenomenon is the outsourcing of software development projects to "offshore" organizations in India, China, Russia, or other countries. Having visited software organizations in several of these countries, I can testify that such organizations are typically *not* "sweat shops" that engage in the kind of death march projects that require their programmers to work 16 hours a day, seven days a week. Nevertheless, the presence of lower cost offshore programming re-sources may cause domestic software companies and IT departments to respond by making their higher priced programmers in the United States work longer hours. As one reader suggested to me in a recent email message:

"I see things getting worse. With the trend of outsourcing software development work overseas to dramatically cut labor costs, the remaining domestic software hous-es will suffer tremendous competitive pricing pressures. The only way to compete will be to get your product on the market first and cut costs. 'Deathmarch' may become standard procedure for many companies. An improving economy won't change these market realities."[8]

## Intense competition caused by the appearance of new technologies

Competition from an expanded marketplace is often perceived as a defensive issue, but it can also be perceived as an aggressive, proactive opportunity—"If we build this new system, with double-byte characters, then we can offer our company's products for sale in Japan." Similarly, the introduction of radically improved technology may cause a defensive response from a company that was reasonably happy with products built around an older technology; or it may lead to a proactive decision to utilize the new technology for competitive advantage. At the time this book was being written, technologies such as wireless computing and Web services were obvious examples of this phenomenon; but the amazing thing about our industry is that new examples appear every couple of years.

If the corporate response to the new-technology situation is essentially defensive in nature, then the death march project may be one that seeks to exploit the company's *old* technology far beyond its normal limits. Thus, if the organization has too much invested in the old technology (and the infrastructure surrounding it) to abandon it entirely, it may embark upon a rewrite of its old systems, with demands that the programmers find a way to make it ten times faster and sexier.

But many death march projects in this category are the ones that involve first-time usage of the new technologies. Think back to the first client-server projects, object-oriented projects, relational database projects, or Internet/Java projects in your organization; some of them may have been modest experiments to explore the potential benefits of the technology, but some of them were probably created as a competitive response to some other company's introduction of the same technology. And in the latter case, these projects can be huge, as well as being saddled with outrageously aggressive schedules and budgets.

But what really contributes to the death march nature of such projects—beyond the obvious characteristics of size, schedule, and budget—is the attempt to use bleeding-edge technology for an industrial-strength application. Even if the technology is basically usable, it often does not scale up well for large-scale usage; and nobody knows how to exploit its strengths and avoid its weaknesses; and the vendors don't know how to support it properly; and on and on...

While all of this may be perceived as an unpleasant experience by the older technical project team members (the ones who remember the "good old days" of FORTRAN II and assembly language), it's important to remember that the younger technicians and project managers *prefer* these new technologies, precisely because they *are* new. And these are the same folks whom I characterized above as naively optimistic about the schedule and budget constraints within which they're working. Is it any wonder that things degenerate into a death march project, with everyone working late nights and long weekends in order to coax the experimental new technology into some semblance of working order?

## Intense pressure caused by unexpected government regulations

As noted above, one of the reasons for death march projects associated with globalization of markets is the decision by governmental authorities to reduce tariffs, eliminate import quotas, or other such decisions to "open" a previously closed market. But this is just one example of governmental influences that can lead to a death march project; deregulation of controlled industries, or privatization of government agencies are two other obvious examples. Indeed, many of the death march projects taking place today around the world are a direct result of a government decision to deregulate the telecommunications industry, the financial services industry, the airline industry, and so on.

However, there are also many instances of *increased* regulatory pressure from governmental authorities—especially in the areas of taxation, reporting of financial details to stock-market authorities, environmental regulations, and so forth. In any kind of democratic society, there's likely to be a great deal of advance notice about such regulations, because the legislative body argues and debates and fusses over details for months or years before the relevant legislation is enacted. But the details often aren't clear until the last moment, and the typical reaction from senior management is to ignore the whole thing until it become an unavoidable reality. And then, boom! Another death march project is created.

The particularly onerous thing about many of these government-mandated death march projects is the deadline: The new system *must* be operational by some arbitrary date such as January 1st, or fines of a million dollars a day will be imposed. There may be an opportunity to ask for an extension or a waiver, but in most cases, the deadline is absolute. And the consequences are usually as dire for the organization as those mentioned above: Layoffs, bankruptcy, or other calamities will occur if the new system isn't finished on time.

Notice that in projects like these, technology is usually not the issue; what characterizes the projects as death march in nature is the aggressive timetable. Of course, management sometimes complicates the situation by understaffing the project or hobbling it with an inadequate budget.

## Unexpected and/or unplanned crises

Your two best programmers have just marched into your office to inform you that (a) they're getting married, (b) they're joining a missionary group building hospitals in the jungles of Africa, and (c) today is their last day on the job. Or your network services manager calls you to say that your vendor has just gone bankrupt and you'll have to reprogram everything in the next 30 days in order to use another vendor's network protocol. Or your legal department calls to say that the company has been sued by ten zillion dollars because the company is not in compliance with Sub-paragraph 13(b) or Regulation Q of some arcane tax code that nobody even knew about.

Of course, you could argue that, in a well-managed company, the impending departure of your two best programmers would have been anticipated and planned for; and you wouldn't have been so silly as to be wholly dependent on one telecommunications vendor; and management would have had the foresight to check into the details of Regulation Q. Such crises, according to the purists, are the result of poor planning and poor management; an "unplanned crisis" is therefore an oxymoron.

Perhaps so; but as a practical matter, it's becoming increasingly difficult to anticipate and plan for all the crazy things that can happen in the business world today. For better or worse, we live in a world of chaos, and death march projects are a natural consequence of such chaos.[9] Indeed, even if we have a general idea that chaotic things *could* occur in the future, we may still have to respond to them in a death march fashion. Everyone in the vicinity of the San Andreas fault in California, for example, knows that a truly massive earthquake will occur sooner or later; but that won't prevent a rash of death march projects from starting up the day after the "big one" drops the western half of the state into the Pacific Ocean.

Indeed, even when we know *precisely* when a crisis will occur, it often leads to a death march project—because management's tendency is to avoid dealing with the situation until the last possible moment. How else could we explain the panic that crept into many IT organizations as the Y2K problem loomed ahead of them? We had known for a *long* time that January 1, 2000, was coming, and it was obviously a deadline that could not be postponed. We knew precisely what the nature of the problem was, and it didn't require newfangled technologies such as Java. So why did so many Y2K death march projects get launched in 1998 and 1999?

In any case, unforeseen crises can lead to all kinds of death march projects. In the worst case, they create projects for which the deadline is "yesterday, if not sooner"—because the crisis has already occurred and things will continue to worsen until a new system is installed to cope with the problem. In other cases, such as the unplanned departure of key project personnel, it can turn an otherwise rational project into a death march exercise because of the shortage of manpower and the loss of key intellectual resources.

For various reasons, these often turn out to be the worst kind of death march projects, *because nobody anticipated that they would turn out this way.* For the Marine Corps situation discussed above, there are no surprises: Everyone knows from the first day of the project that this one, like all previous projects, is going to require extraordinary effort. And for the startup companies, the death march project is anticipated with excitement; not only will it be exciting and challenging, but its success could make everyone rich.

# WHY DO PEOPLE PARTICIPATE IN DEATH MARCH PROJECTS?

The theme of the discussion in the previous project is that organizations create and/or tolerate death march projects for a number of reasons. We may agree or disagree with those reasons, and we may sympathize with the ones caused by truly unexpected crises—but ultimately, as individuals, we have to accept them as a fact of life.

But that doesn't mean we have to participate in them. Most of this book presumes that you *will* participate in a death march project, though I will specifically suggest that you resign under certain circumstances. But the best time to do so, in most cases, is at the beginning. When told that you have been assigned to such a project (either as a leader or a technical staff member), you should consider saying, "No, thanks! I'll pass on this one." If that's not an acceptable response within your corporate culture, you almost always have the option of saying, "No, thanks! I quit!"

Obviously, some developers—and probably a larger number of managers—will argue that this is not a practical choice for them. I'll discuss this in more detail below, but for now it's sufficient to note that it's one of several possible "negative" reasons for participating in a death march project; it may not be fun, but perhaps it's not as bad as the alternatives. On the other hand, some developers (and some managers) *gladly* sign up for such projects; aside from the issue of naive optimism discussed above, why would any rational person volunteer to participate in a project that's likely to require 14-hour days, seven-day weeks, and a year or two of postponed vacations?

The most common reasons are summarized in Table 1.2; I'll discuss them in more detail below.

**Table 1.2**    Reasons for Participating in Death March Projects

| |
|---|
| The risks are high, but so are the rewards |
| The "Mt. Everest" syndrome |
| The "buzz" of working intensely with other committed people |
| The naiveté and optimism of youth |
| The alternative is unemployment |
| It's required in order to be considered for future advancement |
| The alternative is bankruptcy or some other calamity |
| It's an opportunity to escape the "normal" bureaucracy |
| Revenge |

By the way, this is not intended as a complete list; Kevin Huigens[10] asked his project team to do a little brainstorming at one of their recent staff meetings, and they came up with the following list (Table 1.3):

**Table 1.3**  *More Reasons for Participating in Death March Projects*

| | |
|---|---|
| Everybody wants to feel wanted | Perceived opportunity |
| Perceived money gain | Can't afford to lose job |
| Brought in from the outside to lead the project | Willing suspension of disbelief |
| Don't care whether project fails, get to work with cool technology | On-the-job-training on new technology |
| Eternal optimism | Challenge |
| Plain stupidity | Chance to prove yourself |
| To get the job done | It's the only project |
| Your friend is running the project | Your brother is running the project (It'd take more than friendship) |
| Your boss said so | You have no other life |
| Nothing better to do | Stock options |
| Existing pay vs. expectation of raise | Love is blind |
| Resumé-building | Ignorance |
| Camaraderie | Expectations for how long it will take are too low |

Of course, all of this assumes that you know in advance that it *is* a death march project. As consultant Dave Kleist[11] observed to me, that's not always so easy when you're interviewing for a new job:

> ...it's rarely printed as part of the want ad. Not much sense in saying, "Are you interested in working incredible hours for no additional benefit beyond your hiring salary?"... Seriously, death march projects are rarely billed as such, and it takes a lot of work when being hired from the outside to discover if your hiring company is prone to creating death march projects.

And, as Steve Benting[12] pointed out to me, sometimes you get taken by surprise:

...it seems to be a well-thought-out project this time. You've got someone leading who has a real sponsor in management, the project plan appears to be solid, the people involved all appear to be good. Hell, you *want* to work on this thing. Then it collapses because your sponsor gets taken out in a political struggle, the project plan turns out to be built on assumptions that are incorrect, and one or two key people turn out to be flaky. You can learn to watch out for them, but sometimes you misjudge. And you don't want to believe that it's happening again.

## The risks are high, but so are the rewards

The startup-company scenario discussed in an earlier section is a good example of this situation. If you tell project team members that the success of their project will mean the company can go public, and that their stock options will make them instant millionaires, they'll happily work until they drop from exhaustion. They realize—at least in an intellectual way—that there are risks associated with the venture; but since many of them still believe that they're immortal and omnipotent, they don't pay much attention to the risks.

Indeed, considering the influences of Western culture (especially in the United States), it's not at all surprising to see young software developers voluntarily sign up for death march projects. We've been told in countless ways that the success of movie stars, rock singers, sports heroes, and Olympic athletes, as well as business executives and software entrepreneurs, depends largely on tireless energy, enormous commitment, long hours, and personal sacrifice. We never hear about the guile and duplicity, the shady deals and illegal activities, that are sometimes associated with success. And we rarely hear anything about luck and the importance of being in the right place at the right time; Bill Gates, for example, certainly exhibits all of the textbook characteristics of a successful business executive, but if a group of IBM executives hadn't shown up in Seattle in 1980 to look for a PC operating system, and if Gates hadn't been available when IBM was unable to meet with its originally intended OS contractor ... well, who knows where Microsoft would be today?

And one more thing: We don't hear enough about the real consequences of the "sacrifice" that a death march project usually requires—sacrifices, that is, in the area of personal health, mental health, and personal relationships. None of this is likely to matter very much to a 22-year-old technical person; and it often doesn't matter to the introverted, anti-social people who are attracted to the computer field. On the other hand, it's small wonder that you'll find fewer people in their mid-40s and 50s volunteering for death march projects; not only have they learned that most such projects really *are* doomed to fail, but they've also learned (usually the hard way!) that it's not worth sacrificing their marriage and their relationship with their children.

Ultimately, this is a personal choice, based on personal values; I'm no position to tell anyone else what's right or wrong. I should emphasize, though, that I'm not as negative as one might think from the comments above. Though I'm much less naive than I was when I entered the computer field in the mid-1960s, I'm still attracted by entrepreneurial opportunities. Show me a sufficiently exciting risk/reward formula, and I'll sign up for yet another death march...

By the way, sometimes the rewards are psychological, not financial. As Sharon Marsh Roberts[13] observed to me,

> The "heros" are needed, wanted, desired. They are certain of their place in history, if only they can keep this project from outright sinking under its own weight.

> The same people take on EMT work and enjoy firefighting (literally). If you only win once in ten times, but everybody else lost all ten, wouldn't you be a hero, too?

And as Paul Neuhardt[14] put it,

> For me, it was ego, pure and simple. They told me that they just *knew* I could help prevent the project from becoming a death march. I was made the "technical project manager," given ego boosts on a regular basis, then hung out to dry along with the rest of the team. Left, right, left, right, left, *plop!*

## The "Mt. Everest" syndrome

Why do people climb dangerous peaks like Mt. Everest, despite the pain and the risk? Because it's there. Why do people run a marathon and drive themselves to the point of physical collapse in triathlons? Because of the challenge. It's all the more exciting if the challenge is one that has never yet been successfully accomplished; of the six billion people on the planet, for example, only one can stand before us and say, "I was the first to walk on the moon." Some may think it's crazy, egotistical, and selfish to even try; but others are willing to brave the odds and deal with horrendous obstacles for the private thrill and the public glory of succeeding. As consultant Al Christians[15] remarked to me in a recent e-mail note,

> I am somehow prompted to reply "testosterone," which is about the same as "because it's there." There are plenty of jobs that raise the 'why?' question. Underground mining, cowboying, logging, smoke jumping, jet fighting, submarining, even high-rise window washing all have serious drawbacks far beyond what you describe for software

projects, and yet all these have practitioners whose sense of self is linked to their profession.

And so it is with death march software projects. I had the chance to visit the original Macintosh project in the fall of 1983, a few months before the product was officially unveiled, and was humbled by the intensity of the team's commitment to its challenge. In addition to whatever other reasons the members might have had for working long hours and dealing with Steve Jobs' megalomaniacal ego, the team was utterly convinced (partly as a result of Jobs' charisma) that the Macintosh would revolutionize personal computing. They were lucky—they turned out to be right.

From this perspective, even the death march projects that fail can be *noble* failures. Countless projects in Silicon Valley have fallen into this category, often after burning tens of millions of dollars of venture capital; while most of the dot-com startups had no substance at all, some of them really did seem awe-inspiring and revolutionary until they went into bankruptcy. But even though they failed so badly that entire companies went bankrupt, and though they caused divorces, ulcers, and nervous breakdowns—even though they did all of this and more—the people who worked on those projects still speak of their experiences in hushed tones. "I worked on the Toys.com system," a grizzled veteran will tell her awe-struck apprentice. "Now *that* was a revolutionary piece of software!"

Though it may never reach the front pages of *Computerworld*, there are also numerous death march projects with lofty ambitions buried within large organizations—with application developers signing up gladly because the "corporate Mt. Everest" seems such a worthy challenge. Sometimes these projects fail because the marketplace or the corporate end-users don't want and don't need the glorious, revolutionary systems being developed; and sometimes they fail because the project team bit off more than it could chew and promised more than it could deliver.

There are two things to watch for if you find yourself being swept up in the hysteria of a Mt. Everest-style death march project. First, watch out for the projects that are predetermined failures. Suppose, for example, that someone told you that you could be on the first manned mission to Mars, and that you would even have the honor to be the first person to plant a foot on Martian soil. "Of course," your project manager goes on to say, "you won't have any oxygen tanks, because we won't have enough room on the space craft for all that extra weight. So it's a guaranteed fact that you're going to die—but think of the honor and the glory!" I'll discuss these projects in more detail in Chapter 3, under the heading of "kamikaze" projects; for now, the scenario speaks for itself.

The second thing to watch out for is that the challenge being described by your corporate management (or by the entrepreneurial founder of your software company) may not turn out to be such a big deal after all. This is a particularly insidious danger if the challenge is technical in nature, for example, "We'll be the first people on earth to put an operating system with the functionality of Windows XP into 128K of ROM!" Granted, that would be an amazing technical accomplishment—but so what?

It's a good idea to ask the "So what?" question two or three times—in other words, *continue* asking the question in response to each successive answer you get from your corporate management. If the response to the Windows XP scenario posed above is, "Well, that means we could put *all* of Windows XP onto your wrist watch!", then ask, "So what?" again. In some cases, the answers will eventually become silly and you'll be jerked back into the real world. For example, suppose your boss answers the second "So what?" question above with the explanation, "Well, if we can also squeeze in a full voice-recognition system, that means you'll be able to write Visual C++ programs while you're walking down the street, by talking to your wrist-watch!"

No doubt there are a few dozen programmers who would say, "*Cool!*" and volunteer to spend the next three years of their lives on such a project. The fact that nobody in his right mind would ever use such a project is irrelevant to them; the technical challenge is a sufficient justification. Putting Windows XP, full voice recognition, and Visual C++ into 128K of ROM would give you supreme bragging rights at any convention of hackers and programmers; if that's what you live for, then by all means go ahead and sign up for the project.

It's also a good idea to explain the project in simplified non-technical terms to your spouse, or your "significant other," or your parents—or, even better, your children. *They* will ask the "So what?" question, without the burden of being tempted by the technical challenge. "You're going to give up your nights and your weekends and your vacations for the next two years in order to put Windows XP on a wrist-watch?" your spouse will ask incredulously. And your children will ask, "Yeah, but Mom/Dad, why would anyone *do* that?" If you can answer those questions without feeling utterly foolish, then you can sign up for the project with a clear conscience.

A worse form of Mt. Everest project is the one where the challenge matters *enormously* to corporate management, but not at all to anyone who stops and thinks about the situation for a second. "Why are we signing up for this death march project, boss?" the young programmer asks innocently. "Because," the boss thunders righteously, "it will increase our corporate earnings per share by a full 3.14159 cents!!" This means that if the programmer was lucky enough to have options on a hundred shares of the company's stock, and if every penny of increased earnings was paid out in dividends, the programmer would get a whopping $3.14; and if Wall Street traders got so excited by all of this that they boosted the price of the stock by a dollar, the programmer's net worth would increase by another hundred dollars. "And what else would I have to show for the thousands of hours of overtime you're asking me to sign up for, boss?" the young programmer asks. The boss is silent, for he knows that the honest answer is: *nothing*. The project is intrinsically boring, involves no interesting technology, and has a 75-percent chance of failing anyway.

But the very worst death march projects, in my opinion, are the ones where the boss deliberately manipulates the innocent project team into believing that a Mt. Everest-style challenge is involved, when the boss knows full well that it's not. Imagine the project team member who asks, "Why are we trying to build this batch, mainframe, COBOL airline reservation system in six months, boss?" The boss is likely to respond, "Because *nobody* in the entire airline industry has ever tried to do it in less than three years before!" I suppose that one could argue that there *is* a technical challenge involved in creating a batch-mode airline reservation system, but it's not the kind of technology that I would want on my resumé in the 21st century. In any case, what makes this scenario a death march project is not the technical challenge, but the ridiculous schedule imposed on the project. Why is the project manager doing it? Who knows—but it's not likely to be the sort of thing you'll want to brag about to your friends a year from now.

## The naiveté and optimism of youth

Ours is a young industry, and many of the most exciting and challenging projects are being performed by, and led by, people in their twenties. It's not at all uncommon to see death march projects where the entire technical team is under 25, and where the majority are in the 21–23 age range. As such, they remind me of the fighter pilots and bombing crews recruited by the Air Force in the Gulf War: like Tom Cruise's character in *Top Gun*, they are young, idealistic, and absolutely convinced that they could do *anything*. As David Maxwell[16] put it:

> …projects are like a marriage. We tend to start off naively and full of hopes and slowly as reality sets in, we have to re-assess our expectancies within the relationship. There are many reasons apart from *logic* that attract people together into a marriage and it is the same case with projects. With a predominantly youthful workforce, it is likely that the "death march" project will occur again and again as a training ground for managers and developers alike. And, as I know from personal experience, I often repeat the same mistake many times before the penny drops.

Indeed, it's this supreme confidence that enables a death march team to succeed where traditional project teams have failed before. Part of the folklore of our industry is that the most successful products—ranging from Lotus 1-2-3 to the original Netscape Navigator Web browser—have been developed by a handful of people under conditions that no "rational" project team would have accepted. When these projects succeed, they often bring fortune and fame to the project team; and when they fail, they often provide some valuable lessons to everyone involved (though the corporate consequences may still be disastrous!).

It's important to note that the naiveté and optimism of youth are usually combined with enormous energy, single-minded focus, and freedom from such distractions as family relationships. Obviously, youth doesn't have a monopoly on any of this, but it's a lot more common to see a 22-year-old programmer willing and able to focus on the technical demands of a death march project for 100+ hours per week continuously for a year or two, than a 35-year-old programmer with a spouse and two children and a moderate passion for mountain climbing. The young programmer who signs up for a death march—as well as the relatively young project manager who optimistically promises success to the corporate chieftains—is implicitly saying, "Of *course* I'll succeed with this project; I'll overwhelm the obstacles with sheer energy!"

I won't make any value judgments about all of this, because it's pointless. As noted above, ours is an industry that attracts young people, and I don't think that will change in the next few years. I also think it's unlikely that young people will abandon their optimism, energy, and ability to focus single-mindedly on a problem. As for their naiveté ... well, it doesn't help much for battle-scarred veterans to accuse their younger colleagues of this disease.

## The alternative is unemployment

Because we *do* have an industry populated by young, optimistic people, and because it's a vibrant industry that has been growing steadily (and sometimes rapidly!) for the past 30-40 years, I'm sometimes surprised to hear this explanation for participation on death march projects.

But even our industry has its downturns and recessions. As this edition of *Death March* was being written in the spring of 2003, the high-tech recession had been underway for roughly three years—with no obvious indication of when it would end. And for those too young to remember, there were also downturns in the early 1990s, the early 1980s, and the mid-1970s.

We're also an industry where rapid change renders some veterans obsolete. Indeed, there has been such enormous change during this decade that our profession—like so many other white-collar professions—has experienced significant downsizing, re-engineering, and outsourcing. Aggregate employment in the software industry may be rising steadily, but we sometimes forget that this means only that the C++ programming jobs are increasing more rapidly than the COBOL jobs are declining. In addition, the large IT shops that have expanded into bureaucracies of several thousand people have been particularly vulnerable to downsizing and outsourcing; senior management may not be ready to reduce the ranks of technical staff, but they're often eliminating the middle managers, administrators, and staff people.

All of this becomes a factor in death march projects. The reason your project team has only half as many people as it should have is that management has cut the entire software organization in half. And the reason that your project schedule is twice as demanding as it should be is that management is attempting re-engineering by edict: It has announced that the entire organization needs to be twice as productive as before, which translates into simple commands of "Work harder! Work faster!"[17]

This is not a book about re-engineering, and I don't want to comment on the re-engineering strategies employed by management. The significant issue here is that many technical staffers and many project managers feel an implied threat when projects are created in this kind of environment: If they don't agree to the death march project parameters, they'll be the ones to lose their job. For the 22-year-old, unmarried programmer, this shouldn't be a problem; for the 35-year-old project supervisor with a family and a mortgage, it can be a more serious problem. And for the 45-year-old programmer whose only skills are COBOL and CICS, it can be a serious problem indeed. Even though we do have a young industry, it's been around long enough that there are even some 55- and 60-year-old programmers who are grimly holding on until their pension is fully vested.

It's also common for middle-aged or older people to find that they're locked into a community, because their spouse has a job in the same town, or their children can't be pulled out of the local schools, or because the prospect of leaving behind aging parents and other family members is too painful. None of this seems a problem when the job market is growing, but anyone who lived in Poughkeepsie, New York, in the early 1990s knows exactly what I'm talking about. People living in Redmond, Washington, could conceivably find themselves faced with the same kind of rude shock five, 10, or 20 years from now.

I'm generally sympathetic to the middle-aged and older software professionals who find themselves in this position, though the re-engineering/downsizing phenomenon has been around long enough that I'm amazed to find technical people who ignore the possibility that it could happen to them. But this, too, is a subject for a different book; I've discussed it at length in *Decline and Fall of the American Programmer* and *Rise and Resurrection of the American Programmer*, and I'll confine my remarks here to the *reality* of such death march projects.

If your company has told you—either explicitly, or by innuendo—that your job will disappear unless you sign up for a project with a ridiculous schedule, budget, and resource allocation, what should you do? Obviously, this depends on your assessment of your financial, physical, emotional, and psychological situation; you also need to accurately assess the situation within your company. In some cases, the real threat is that your promotion, bonus, or salary increase will be withheld if you don't participate; I'll cover this separately below. But even if the threat is termination of employment, big companies can't usually carry out their threat right away; you may have two or three months before your job disappears, and that may be enough time to find a job elsewhere.

What if the threat is more immediate and blunt? "Sign up for this death march project right now, or pack up your things and get out!" says your boss. It's inconceivable to me that a rational person would choose to work in such an environment, but let's assume the environment had been reasonably friendly until the latest re-engineering craze turned your boss into a raving lunatic. So here you are: Sign, quit, or be fired. What can you do?

If at all possible, my advice is: Quit now, because it's just going to get worse. You may have to live off your savings for a few months, and you may even have to take a pay cut while you gain experience in some newer technology; but chances are you'll be a happier person than if you knuckle under and continue on in a situation that has little or no upside potential. Sometimes you can accomplish this by volunteering for the death march project while simultaneously updating your resumé and starting the job search; however, this can create some ethical dilemmas if you feel that quitting in the middle of the death march project would leave your teammates stranded and helpless.

If you feel that you are truly stuck—because of imminent pension vesting, or because of unmarketable technical skills, or because personal commitments keep you locked into a one-employer town—then you might be tempted to take a more positive approach to the death march project. "By gosh, I'll show them that there's still some bark in this old dog," the middle-aged veteran will say. "I'll show management that I'm still just as good as those young whippersnappers, and we'll get this project done on time!" Your courage and positive outlook are admirable indeed, but just remember one thing: If your death march project succeeds, there will another one. Remember the theme at the beginning of this book: *Death march projects are not the exception, they have become the norm.*

## It's required in order to be considered for future advancement

As noted above, there are times when the "invitation" to join a death march project carries with it a threat that future promotions and raises will be contingent upon (a) acceptance, and (b) success in the project. This is often associated with a re-engineering initiative—for example, "The people who lead the Megalith Bank into the 21st century will be the ones who have led us through this incredibly complex and challenging Total System 2020 re-engineering project!" If you find yourself in this situation, remember that politics is a key factor: The people who take credit for the success of the death march project may or may not be the people who participated in it. And the manager who proposes the death march project may be using the re-engineering "crisis" solely as an opportunity to advance his or her career, with little or no concern for whether the project team members survive in the process.

If you've memorized every word of Machiavelli's *The Prince*, and if you enjoy playing political games, then such death march projects might sound like great fun. But most software professionals haven't seen *The Prince* since their college days (if ever) and, in addition to admitting their political naiveté, they'll also express disgust at the whole concept of politics and enormous disrespect for those who indulge in it. If that's the case, why would anyone sign up for the Megalith Bank's Total System 2020 project? The only plausible answer: because you sincerely believe that it's a one-time death march project, and because you really believe that it will help advance your long-term career within the Megalith Bank. And if you believe this, chances are pretty good that you also believe pigs can fly.

In the majority of cases I've observed, the threat of withholding promotions and raises is part of the "Marine Corps" culture discussed earlier in this chapter. Whether it's right or wrong doesn't matter at this point; what counts is that it's fairly consistent. If you receive such threats on your first death march project, you'll probably get them on your second, third, and fourth. You may have been too innocent or naive to contemplate the long-term implications of such a policy when you first joined the company, but sooner or later it will sink in. There are really only two options in this case: Accept it, or quit.

## The alternative is bankruptcy or some other calamity

As mentioned earlier, some death march projects have been caused by the re-engineering, downsizing, and outsourcing decisions made by senior management, which in turn have often been caused by global competition, unexpected government regulations, and so forth. Whatever the cause, the results are the same: The employee signs up for the project because he sincerely believes that the alternative is bankruptcy or some other dire calamity. And the situation is often exacerbated by blunt statements from management that anyone unwilling to participate in the death march should resign forthwith, so that those who remain can concentrate on saving the company.

Again, the issue here is not whether the situation is right or wrong, or whether management should have taken earlier steps to avoid the crisis. The point is that once the crisis has arrived and management has initiated the death march project, you need to make a rational decision about whether or not to participate.

From the discussion in earlier sections of this chapter, you can anticipate my advice here: Step back and ask yourself whether this death march project is a one-time exception or the beginning of an ongoing pattern. Even if you win the battle, your company may have lost the war; indeed, your success with your death march project may have the ironic consequence of delaying the final demise of the company just long enough to sustain a *second* death march project.

Again, this is a personal decision, and it may be colored by feelings of loyalty, sympathy, or a Hollywood-inspired desire to "win one for the Gipper"—a last hurrah to show the world that you and your company are not going to give up without a fight. And who knows: Maybe a tremendous success with your death march project will turn things around, as appeared to be the case when Borland delivered its Delphi product to the marketplace. None of us has a crystal ball when it comes to predicting the outcome of a death march project, nor can we accurately predict what the consequences of a death march success or failure will really be. Some companies die quickly, others die a long, lingering death; still others are acquired before the terminal rot sets in.

As you consult your own crystal ball, seek advice from as many people as possible, especially from those who have no vested interest in the outcome. You may find some honest, objective managers in your company who will candidly discuss the consequences of the death march failure/success; but you should also remember that the same managers have their own career and paycheck to worry about, and that their ego and political instinct may prevent them from sharing the really vital information you need to make an informed decision.

## It's an opportunity to escape the "normal" bureaucracy

Technical staffers and project managers often complain that their corporate bureaucracy stifles productivity and introduces unnecessary delays into the software development process. But the larger the organization, the more entrenched the bureaucracy—especially in organizations where the methodology police enforce strict adherence to SEI-CMM or ISO-9000 processes. Similarly, the human resources department may have elaborate procedures that must be followed before new people can be hired, or before external contractors can be used on a project.

Death march projects often provide the opportunity to circumvent some, if not all, of the bureaucracy—and this is reason enough for frustrated software developers to sign up for such projects. In the extreme case, the effort takes on the characteristics of a "skunk works" project: The project team members move out of the corporate facility into a separate building, where they can carry out their work without the distractions of the normal bureaucracy. But even in a less extreme situation, a death march project can often get permission to use its own tools and programming languages, to try new technologies such as object-oriented programming, and to short-circuit much of the ponderous procedures and documentation that would otherwise be required.

Equally important, the death march project manager is often given far greater latitude when selecting team members than would normally be the case.

In the best case, all of these changes can transform a death march into a civilized experience—that is, the very procedures (and technology and people) that turned the project into a death march have been removed or replaced. And if the death march project is eminently successful, it can serve as a catalyst to make permanent changes to the technology, peopleware, and processes used in other development projects throughout the organization. Conversely, if the death march project fails, it might serve as an affirmation that the "standard" policies aren't that bad after all.

In any case, a situation like this is a perfectly plausible reason for working on a project that might otherwise seem uncivilized. In some organizations, certain software developers make a point of *always* signing up for such projects because it's the only way to avoid getting sucked into the bureaucracy.

## Revenge

Revenge may not seem like a rational explanation for working on a death march project, but it's real nonetheless. The success of the death march project might be sufficient to wrest power away from an incompetent vice president, or it might serve to humiliate an obnoxious critic who continually tells you "it can't be done" within the schedule and budget constraints of the death march project. Revenge is a powerful emotion, and it is particularly evident in the senior management ranks of large organizations, where insults are remembered forever, and where crafty politicians will sometimes wait months or years to wreak revenge upon their enemies.

Revenge can be a very powerful personal motivator, but it's usually somewhat more difficult to imbue an entire project team with the emotion. And when it happens, it often creates a situation where the team loses track of the "official" objective of delivering a working system within a specified budget and schedule—after all, their first and highest priority is revenge.

If revenge is *your* motivation, then there's not much for me to say: This is another personal judgment call. But if you're signing up for a project in which it's the manager's revenge, or the team's revenge, fueling the project (and causing it to accept deadline and budget constraints normally unacceptable), then you should be very careful indeed. "The vice president is an idiot," your project manager might tell you, "and if we finish this project in six months, he'll be so humiliated in front of the Board of Directors that he'll have to resign!" Well, that's fine—maybe the VP really is an idiot, but do you really want to sacrifice your personal life for the next two years in order to bring about his demise? After all, the next VP is likely to be just as much an idiot as the last one.

On the other hand, if everyone perceives the Vice President to be the personification of Darth Vader, and if the project manager is seen to be a combination of Luke Skywalker and Yoda, then a death march project can be very invigorating indeed. In this case, the entire project is re-cast into a battle of Good versus Evil, and that's enough to make people accept incredible sacrifices without complaint.

## SUMMARY

If the discussion in this chapter seems pessimistic and cynical, remember: It hasn't stopped death march projects from taking place. Companies both large and small are filled with politics and are staffed by managers and technical developers who suffer from hysterical optimism as well as the usual gamut of emotions such as fear, insecurity, arrogance, and naiveté. And the combination of re-engineering, downsizing, outsourcing, and global competition—together with the opportunities provided by new technologies such as object orientation, client-server, and the Internet—suggests to me that death march projects are likely to be a common occurrence for years to come.

And that's the primary point of this chapter. You may not agree with any of the rationales suggested here; you may not like any of the reasons for initiating such projects or joining such projects—but they're real nonetheless. The key point is to recognize and understand your own motivations at the beginning of a death march project, so that you can make a rational decision to join the team or look elsewhere for your next job. Since many of these projects are initiated during periods of great corporate stress and emotion, rational decisions are not as easy as you might think; it's all too easy to be swept away by the emotions of your fellow colleagues or your manager.

It's worth noting that some observers have a more optimistic outlook than what I've suggested; they believe that there will actually be *fewer* death march projects during the remainder of this decade. For example, when I asked in an online discussion forum during the spring of 2003 whether death march projects were likely to diminish, Erik Petersen responded by saying:

Hopefully going down. Two reasons.

The culture of the ever expanding IT budget has gone, and management wants projects to succeed (even if they still try to run them lean). From what I have seen, sub project deliverables are becoming more common and highlighting death march issues earlier, and projects are killed sooner.

Better education should reduce the naiveté of newbies. Most graddies now learn about testing and quality as part of their studies. Some even learn project mgmnt. Agile methods are popular at universities as well, with test first development, etc. XP is becoming

*more popular, complete with no overtime mantra. I think this will*
*help to empower teams, both delivering better software, and stand-*
*ing up to unrealistic schedules and targets.*[18]

Whether there are more or fewer of them in the future, I should emphasize that I'm not necessarily opposed to death march projects; I agree with my colleague Rick Zahniser[19] that such projects can be an educational experience even if they fail:

*I've told you before, I think everyone should be on at least one of*
*these projects. However, there are some other things that you*
*should do at least once:*

*+ Spend a night in jail.*

*+ Get commode-hugging drunk*

*+ Raise a boy*

*+ Raise a girl*

*+ Start your own business*

*+ Climb Mount Fuji*[20]

In any case, for the remainder of this book I'll assume that you *have* made a rational decision to join the death march project—though I'll remind you from time to time, in later chapters, that you always have the option of quitting during the project. But we'll assume that your primary objective at this point is to succeed, or at least survive, the death march project. In subsequent chapters, we'll see how that can be done.

# NOTES

1. From: Richard Sargent, 72762,3342
   To: Ed Yourdon, 71250,2322
   Topic: Ed's new book project, Msg #159427, reply to #158778
   Date: Mon, Jun 24, 1996, 2:22:20 AM
   Ed,
   A colleague of mine passed along this paraphrased quote. I think it applies here.
   The definition of (corporate) insanity is doing the same thing again and again, and each time expecting different results.
   I have no idea who originally framed the assertion, but it's gold!
   Richard Sargent
   5x5 Computing Solutions Inc.
2. From: Dave Kleist, 70730,1613
   To: Ed Yourdon, 71250,2322
   Topic: Ed's new book project, Msg #158064, reply to #158015
   Date: Tue, Jun 4, 1996, 7:28:03 PM

Ed,

>> 1. Why would anyone in his right mind agree to work on a "death march" project (defined in the terms above)? <<

Because it's rarely printed as part of the want ad. Not much sense in saying, "Are you interested in working incredible hours for no additional benefit beyond your hiring salary? Does the idea of working endlessly on obsolete technology while 'waiting' for a slot to open up on that exciting GUI/DSS/warehouse/HTML subproject really entice you? Do you define three-tier architecture as an opportunity to hear what other project members will work on without your help?"

Seriously, death march projects are rarely billed as such, and it takes a lot of work when being hired from the outside to discover if your hiring company is prone to creating death march projects. In addition, death march projects only look that way. While they demand the hours, every hour is not productive. After a while, people find ways to do the things they being deprived of (pay bills, run errands). It just isn't billed that way. The environment still sucks, people hate it.

And, how accurate are those hours that are being billed? Where do they come from? Got any contractors? Ever heard of "nuisance hours" or "annoyance hours"? You know, where a contractor overbills because they can't stand some of the people they are working for. (Let me say right now that I've never done it and never will do it, but know people who have). The lead or manager does what the contractor thinks is stupid, and the contractor takes revenge (in their own quiet way). And, what about overhead? Are all hours to be marked to the project, including corporate and department meetings, training, etc.?

>> 2. If a colleague of yours was about to take on the task of managing a death-march project, what is the ONE THING you would advise him/her to do? <<

Try to craft an exquisite exit clause in the contract <VBG>. Seriously, one of the reasons for a runaway is the inability of someone to hear reality, usually upper management (either side, IT or business). Someone taking over a death march has got to find an angle for them to get some manuevering room (functionality, cost, time) in at least one aspect or they are doomed.

>> 3. Conversely: what is the ONE THING you would advise your colleague NOT to do, under any circumstances, when embarking upon such a project? <<

Acknowledge that it is going to be a death-march. Doesn't sound honest but admitting that it's going to be a killer can be demoralizing for two reasons: one, people don't like to hear that the next 6-12 months could be hell; two, management usually underestimates the negatives. Not much hope if you know right out of the gate that it's going to be ugly. I had friends who worked on one project that

had management openly admitting that there was going to be roadkill on the project. Oddly enough, they had trouble recruiting
internal replacements once the turnover kicked in.
Seriously, admitting upfront that it's out of control is already
saying very little for one's management skills. If you ask, sometimes staff will volunteer ways to help keep it from becoming a
death march. In the death marches I've seen, the one thing that
I've seen common to them all is a lack of empowerment among the
staff.
- Dave

**3.** John Boddie, *Crunch Mode* (Englewood Cliffs, NJ: Yourdon Press/Prentice Hall, 1987), page 20.

**4.** Scott Adams, *The Dilbert Principle* (New York: HarperBusiness, 1996), page 2.

**5.** We'll discuss this idea in more detail in Chapter 4.

**6.** It should be emphasized that while the dot-com startups are probably the most recent, and perhaps the most extravagant, examples of this phenomenon, they are by no means the only ones. The software industry has spawned startup companies since the 1960s, if not earlier, and it will continue spawning them as long as smart people have intriguing ideas for exploiting new technology.

**7.** "X" used to be eight for many years, then it shrank to six. With the Enron/Worldcom scandals, the number seems to be shrinking steadily. Perhaps one day there will be only a "Big-One" accounting firm!

**8.** Email from "Ought-Six," June 17, 2003.

**9.** See my book, *Byte Wars: the Impact of September 11 on Information Technology,* for more discussion of this point.

**10.** From: Kevin Huigens, 74762,2726
To: Ed Yourdon, 71250,2322
Topic: Ed's new book project
Msg #158577, reply to #158015
Date: Mon, Jun 10, 1996, 9:13:16 AM
Ed:
At our weekly staff meeting, my team and I had a brainstorming ses-
sion on your 3 questions. Here's our answers:
1. Why would anyone in his right mind agree to work on a "death
march" project (defined in the terms above)?
Everybody wants to feel wanted  Perceived opportunity
Perceived money gain Can't afford to lose job
Brought in from the outside to lead the project
Willing suspension of disbelief
Don't care whether project fails, get to work with cool technology
On-the-job-training on new technology  Eternal optimism
Challenge  Plain stupidity  Chance to prove yourself
To get the job done  It's the only project
Your friend is running the project  Your brother is running the
project (It'd take more than friendship)

Your boss said so  You have no other life  Nothing better to do
Stock options  Existing pay vs. expectation of raise  Love is blind
Resumé-building  Ignorance  Comeraderie
Expectations for how long it will take are too low
2. If a colleague of yours was about to take on the task of managing
a death march project, what is the ONE THING you would advise him/
her to do?
Leave me out  Run!  Keep your eyes open
Ask "What's the pay?"  Get a lot of rest before you start the
project
Make sure you can trust all of your co-workers
Realize the developers aren't your enemy, the managers are
Try to get management to understand the ramifications of the
project
Communicate. Communicate. Communicate.
Keep the team small  Hire new graduates  Keep the team intact
Manage scope  Review the design  Focus is a substitute for time
Make sure testing plan is ready when it's time to test
Make sure you have a test plan  Make sure everybody knows what to do
Documentation is critical  Don't rush to code
Keep documentation updated and current
Everyone should have access to documentation
Have regular weekly progress meetings  Have daily progress meetings
All code works before you leave at the end of the day
Keep plenty of good coffee on hand  Make sure team is happy
Make sure team has everything they need
Use management by walking around
Make sure everyone understands what they're doing
3. Conversely: what is the ONE THING you would advise your col-
league NOT to do, under any circumstances, when embarking upon such
a project?
Don't plan a wedding  Don't have unclear areas of responsibility
Don't allow design changes lightly  Don't assume 1st version is
final
Don't become irritated or angry  Don't lose your cool
Don't let others lose their cool  Don't forget to back stuff up
Don't expect everyone on the team to be dedicated
Don't get too personally involved in success or failure of the
project
Don't rely too heavily on 1 member of the team
Don't allocate resources lightly
Don't assume team members understand the entire project
Don't overcommit  Don't underestimate
Don't refrain from asking questions when you don't understand
Don't start the project
Don't start the project if you haven't got the money to finish
Don't commit to unreasonable dates

Don't be afraid to quit if you feel management is unreasonable
Don't be too hard on overworked, underpaid workers
Don't let meetings last > 1.5 hours
Don't be afraid to bend the rules
Don't forget to have a life  Don't sweat the small stuff
Don't be afraid to let management know you need something
Don't be afraid to stand up to management
Don't forget to keep your resume updated
Don't accept as gospel info from so-called experts
Don't forget that management doesn't understand how to develop
software
Don't forget that shortcuts just defer work, they don't eliminate
it
Is that enough for you?
Kevin

**11.** From: Dave Kleist, 70730,1613
To: Ed Yourdon, 71250,2322
Topic: Ed's new book project
Msg #158064, reply to #158015
Date: Tue, Jun 4, 1996, 7:28:03 PM
Ed,

>> 1. Why would anyone in his right mind agree to work on a "death
march" project (defined in the terms above)? <<
Because it's rarely printed as part of the want ad. Not much sense
in saying, "Are you interested in working incredible hours for no
additional benefit beyond your hiring salary? Does the idea of
working endlessly on obsolete technology while 'waiting' for a slot
to open up on that exciting GUI/DSS/warehouse/HTML subproject
really entice you? Do you define three-tier architecture as an
opportunity to hear what other project members will work on without
your help?"
Seriously, death march projects are rarely billed as such, and it
takes a lot of work when being hired from the outside to discover
if your hiring company is prone to creating death march projects.
In addition, death march projects only look that way. While they
demand the hours, every hour is not productive. After a while, people find ways to do the things they being deprived of (pay bills,
run errands). It just isn't billed that way. The environment still
sucks, people hate it.
And, how accurate are those hours that are being billed? Where do
they come from? Got any contractors? Ever heard of "nuisance hours"
or "annoyance hours"? You know, where a contractor overbills
because they can't stand some of the people they are working for.
(Let me say right now that I've never done it and never will do it,
but know people who have). The lead or manager does what the contractor thinks is stupid, and the contractor takes revenge (in
their own quiet way). And, what about overhead? Are all hours to be

marked to the project, including corporate and department meetings, training, etc.?

>> 2. If a colleague of yours was about to take on the task of managing a death march project, what is the ONE THING you would advise him/her to do? <<

Try to craft an exquisite exit clause in the contract <VBG>. Seriously, one of the reasons for a runaway is the inability of someone to hear reality, usually upper management (either side, IT or business). Someone taking over a death march has got to find an angle for them to get some manuevering room (functionality, cost, time) in at least one aspect or they are doomed.

>> 3. Conversely: what is the ONE THING you would advise your colleague NOT to do, under any circumstances, when embarking upon such a project? <<

Acknowledge that it is going to be a death-march. Doesn't sound honest but admitting that it's going to be a killer can be demoralizing for two reasons: one, people don't like to hear that the next 6-12 months could be hell; two, management usually underestimates the negatives. Not much hope if you know right out of the gate that it's going to be ugly. I had friends who worked on one project that had management openly admitting that there was going to be roadkill on the project. Oddly enough, they had trouble recruiting internal replacements once the turnover kicked in.

Seriously, admitting upfront that it's out of control is already saying very little for one's management skills. If you ask, sometimes staff will volunteer ways to help keep it from becoming a death march. In the death marches I've seen, the one thing that I've seen common to them all is a lack of empowerment among the staff.

- Dave

12. From: Steve Benting, 72410,477
To: Ed Yourdon, 71250,2322
Topic: Ed's new book project
Msg #158362, reply to #158015
Date: Fri, Jun 7, 1996, 12:59:21 AM
Ed,
As long as you're asking...

>>1. Why would anyone in his right mind agree to work on a "death march" project (defined in the terms above)?<<

  Because it seems to be a well-thought-out project this time. You've got someone leading who has a real sponsor in management, the project plan appears to be solid, the people involved all appear to be good. Hell, you *want* to work on this thing. Then it collapses because your sponsor gets taken out in a political struggle, the project plan turns out to be built on assumptions that are incorrect, and one or two key people turn out to be flaky. You can learn to watch out for them, but sometimes you misjudge. And you

don't want to believe that it's happening again. (I'm assuming some
things here. I've only been involved on one large project, but it
certainly went down hard. Delivery date was October, '94 and later
moved to March '95. I was working on the contingency plan towards
the end and left after most of the team in January '95. The new system still does not exist. The company is now in the process of pur-
chasing someone else's system that doesn't have half of the
functionality they originally required.)

>>2. If a colleague of yours was about to take on the task of man-
aging a death-march project, what is the ONE THING you would advise
him/her to do?<<

I would say to take care of his/her people as much as possible.
Kick them all out of the office on Friday nights and try to make
sure they're getting sleep. (Those months of 12-hour days six days
per week can just burn out the developers, making them either quit
or make too many mistakes.) No matter how badly the work needs to
be done, you've got to take care of your people. Sometimes getting
the most out of them requires sending them home. (If you know the
project's in trouble when you start, you've got a long haul ahead
during which you'll need good people.)

Also, make sure that you've got the best salary scale possible. It
won't make all the difference, but it should be cheaper than attri-
tion if it's enough to keep some people on.

>>3. Conversely: what is the ONE THING you would advise your col-
league NOT to do, under any circumstances, when embarking upon such
a project?<<

Don't let anyone put serious pressure on the employees besides
you. Run interference to keep the developers free from others who
are trying to ask them to run that 2-minute mile. (We had a developer working for us when I was the IS Manager -- and before the
aforementioned project was started -- who was writing a new commis-
sions system. The Sales VP came down to tell her that until she
completed this system, her  -- the sales manager's -- salespeople
couldn't pay their mortgages. My VP quite rightly threw her out to
let the developer work in peace.) That's not to say that you can't
push those employees yourself, but you have to have some control
over the stress levels in the organization if you're going to keep
them going.

>> I'd like to solicit input, feedback, war stories, case studies,
good jokes, etc.<<

This must be where I tell you about how, on that infamous project,
the new President explained to me why he wouldn't sign off on
requirements when asked to. (Needless to say, scope creep was a
major factor in its death.) He was a down-home type who thrived on
people taking his southern drawl as a sign that they were dealing
with a country bumpkin. He had also just orchestrated the removal
of our sponsor -- the previous President -- by killing the project.

His reason for the management group's refusal to sign off on requirements was that my VP was "going to hold our feet to the fire" with that document. In other words, he wouldn't agree to sign the document because he would have to live with it later! At this time, I knew I really needed to get out of there, and quickly...
Steve

13. From: S. Marsh Roberts [ICCA], 70007,4251
To: Ed Yourdon, 71250,2322
Topic: Ed's new book project
Msg #158111, reply to #158015
Date: Wed, Jun 5, 1996, 5:31:15 AM
Ed--
>> 1. Why would anyone in his right mind agree to work on a "death march" project (defined in the terms above)? It's understandable that an inexperienced software developer (or someone who hasn't had the pleasure of reading Scott Adams' "The Dilbert Principle") might be bamboozled by management's claim that the death march is an anomaly, and that the superhuman efforts are going to revolutionize the human race, defeat Communism, cure cancer, etc. But after you've heard this pitch two or three times, it sounds like a broken record. So why do we get sucked into this again and again?<<
The "heros" are needed, wanted, desired. They are certain of their place in history, if only they can keep this project from outright sinking under its own weight.
The same people take on EMT work and enjoy firefighting (literally). If you only win once in ten times, but everybody else lost all ten, wouldn't you be a hero, too?
>>2. If a colleague of yours was about to take on the task of managing a death-march project, what is the ONE THING you would advise him/her to do? (The "one thing" motif was suggested by Jack Palance in the wonderful movie "City Slicker", starring Billy Crystal)<<
I'd encourage him to keep his sense of humor. It may be gallows humor, but it's all that such a group has. <sigh>
>>3. Conversely: what is the ONE THING you would advise your colleague NOT to do, under any circumstances, when embarking upon such a project? <<
I would encourage him (and excuse me, it would be a him in 99/100 attempts) to not invest in options or get a large mortgage. You can only take high risk in one arena at a time, without risking a total wipeout of personal assets.
I once said that I would be willing to take a certain job whose incumbent tended over a seven year period to last no longer than a year. I figured that three months' salary would provide enough savings to recover from the inevitable.
Sharon

14. From: Paul Neuhardt, 71673,454
To: Ed Yourdon, 71250,2322

Topic: Ed's new book project
Msg #158349, reply to #158015
Date: Fri, Jun 7, 1996, 12:20:19 AM
Ed,

<< 1. Why would anyone in his right mind agree to work on a "death
march" project (defined in the terms above)? >>

For me, it was ego, pure and simple. They told me that they just
KNEW I could help prevent the project from becoming a death march.
I was made the "technical project manager," given ego boosts on a
regualr basis, then hung out to dry along with the rest of the
team. Left, right, left, right, left, PLOP!

(The really embarassing thing is, I let these same people do it to
me AGAIN just one year later. Once I began to feel myself falling
into the step of the death march, I ran like hell for the door. Me,
and about 60% of the rest of the staff. BTW, It's been four years
now since I first got suckered in, and neither system has ever seen
the light of day, nor will they.)

<< 2. If a colleague of yours was about to take on the task of man-
aging a death march project, what is the ONE THING you would advise
him/her to do? >>

To quote those mad englishmen in "Monty Python and The Holy Grail"
I would say "RUN AWAAAAAYYYYYY!!!". It sounds like a flip answer,
but it isn't really. Some of the most damaging effects of a death
march project are psychological. Lower self esteem, depression,
anxiety and sudden mood swings are all behaviors I have witnessed
(and sometimes experienced) during these projects. I've seen at
least one marriage break up in no small part because the partner
involved in a death march let it consume her so totally that she
bacame an entirely different person, one whom her husband (and most
of the rest of us) had no desire to be around. I know another woman
who, when a three year "death march" ended with the project being
cancelled, said that it was the only experience in her life that
even approached the heartbreak she felt when she miscarried during
the sixth month of pregnancy. Now that's trauma. If you can get
out, go.

<< 3. Conversely: what is the ONE THING you would advise your col-
league NOT to do, under any circumstances, when embarking upon such
a project? >>

If you can't beat 'em, this is one case where you do NOT want to
join 'em. Do not let yourself become too emotionally attached to
the outcome of this project. Like POWs on death marches, think
about anything else but the march in order to survive. Try to go to
work, grind out your day's brick for the wall, and go home. If you
want stimulation and personal reward, read a book, join a social
club, volunteer at the local animal shelter or buy a kiln and throw
some clay pots. Do anything to keep your mind off of work as much as
possible. The moment you get to attached to the project, the guards

with the rifles win and you, the lowly POW, lose.
Paul

**15.** From: Al Christians, 74031,316
To: Ed Yourdon, 71250,2322
Topic: Ed's new book project
Msg #158029, reply to #158015
Date: Tue, Jun 4, 1996, 12:04:05 PM
Ed

Sounds like you are going to have a lot of fun this summer.
1. Why would anyone in his right mind agree to work on a "death
march" project?
Since you mentioned "City Slickers", the movie that used such
regrettable sexual stereotypes, I am somehow prompted to reply
"testosterone", which is about the same as "because it's there."
There are plenty of jobs that raise the 'why?' question. Under-
ground mining, cowboying, logging, smoke jumping, jet fighting,
submarining, even high-rise window washing all have serious draw-
backs far beyond what you describe for software projects, and yet
all these have practitioners whose sense of self is linked to their
profession.
But if you really think that reasons are needed, here are a few:
 a. We think we learned so much in the last experience that it would
be a waste to not find a project on which it could be applied.
 b. We know that some of our colleagues are going to be suffering,
and we don't mind doing our part to lessen their burden.
 c. It's like a lottery ticket -- despite the odds, we can imagine
the possibility of large rewards if we win big.
 d. The high level of urgency that arises during these difficult
projects redistributes power to those who know how to resolve the
crises, i.e., us, and we like power.
> 2. If a colleague of yours was about to take on the task of man-
aging a death march project, what is the ONE THING you would advise
him/her to do?
Remember that the people who love him/her, love him/her for reasons
that have nothing to do with the project.
> 3. Conversely: what is the ONE THING you would advise your col-
league NOT to do, under any circumstances, when embarking upon such
a project?
Since "this is the way it's been for a long time, and this is the
way it's gonna continue to be," don't try to work at a pace that you
can't sustain healthfully for a long time.
Al

**16.** From: David Maxwell, 100342,3620
To: Ed Yourdon, 71250,2322
Topic: Ed's new book project
Msg #158991, reply to #158015
Date: Mon, Jun 17, 1996, 4:53:16 AM

Ed

As I talked on another thread the other day, projects are like a marriage. We tend to start of naiively and full of hopes and slowly as reality sets in, we have to reassess our expectancies within the relationship. There are many reasons apart from \*logic\* that attract people together into a marriage and it is the same case with projects. With a predominantly youthful workforce, it is likely that the "death-march" project will occur again and again as a training ground for managers and developers alike. And, as I know from personal experience, I often repeat the same mistake many times before the penny drops.

Niezche, the German philosopher in the last century said that "society is governed by mediocrity". What he was presumably imply-ing here is the central, conservative-stream will tend to dominate behaviour and control events. This central-stream is hell-bent on preservation from the extremes and will draw the blinds on anything that threatens their positions. What we are really asking for in IT is a radical re-shaping of the way projects are managed, with open vertical and horizontal communication.. and an openness to radical-ism. This is very threatening for the central core of the typical task, role, club organisational culture. An Organisation with a cuture of existentialism has a much better chance of developing good projest on a regular basis but these Organisations are still a rarity.

An old girl-friend of mine who is in a leading position in one of the Major Business Schools regularly seeks advice from me as to how to overcome the deluge of internal politics and methods that are stifling their practices, certainly a case of not practicing what they preach! In addition, Computer Science departments the world over are paying scant regard to People and Management issues as the Lecturers themselves are, in general, inept outside of the techno-logical framework.

So perhaps it is inevitable that, with an inappropriate education and cultural backdrop, we can expect "death march" projects to con-tinue to be the norm... But looking at it from another perspective, these "death march" projects are the essential grist-for-the-mill for the few success stories that make the whole show worthwhile.

David

17. This scenario is *far* more common in North America than it is in Western Europe or the Pacific Rim countries that I've visited. While companies all around the world have engaged in re-engineering projects, it's less common, outside North America, to see the "radical" re-engineering projects that eliminate large numbers of employees. And for the same reasons—cultural traditions, social policies, government regulations—there are fewer death march projects in these countries. The work force, especially in Western Europe, is far more likely to be shielded from excessive overtime, and is far more likely to adamantly refuse to give up sick days, vacation days, holidays, per-

sonal days, and other forms of time off. Whether this is a good thing or a bad thing is outside the scope of this book.

**18.** Erik Petersen email, June 20, 2003.

**19.** 
```
From: Rick Zahniser (SL), 70313,1325
To: Ed Yourdon, 71250,2322
Topic: Ed's new book project
Msg #158437, reply to #158015
Date: Fri, Jun 7, 1996, 10:57:25 PM
Ed,
>>why do they do it??<<
I think they do it because, as Al, suggests, they think they're
better than others who have tried. And, sometimes they really are!
(That doesn't eliminate the death march. In fact, it probably pro-
longs it.)
I've told you before, I think everyone should be on at least one of
these projects. However, there are some other things that you
should do at least once:
 + Spend a night in jail.
 + Get commode-hugging drunk
 + Raise a boy
 + Raise a girl
 + Start your own business
 + Climb Mount Fuji
(The Japanese have a saying:
"He who fails to climb Fuji-san is a fool. He who climbs Fuji-san
twice is an even greater fool.")
One thing to do:
Get a good manager, who is empowered to do the right things.
One thing not to do:
Kill yourself when the project goes south.
Sr. ric
```

**20.** Science fiction *aficionados* will recognize the similarity between Zahniser's advice and the wonderful aphorism from Robert Heinlein in *Time Enough for Love: the Lives of Lazarus Long* (Ace Books, re-issue edition, 1994): "A human being should be able to change a diaper, plan an invasion, butcher a hog, conn a ship, design a building, write a sonnet, balance accounts, build a wall, set a bone, comfort the dying, take orders, give orders, cooperate, act alone, solve equations, analyze a new problem, pitch manure, program a computer, cook a tasty meal, fight efficiently, die gallantly. Specialization is for insects."

# 2 Politics

You are never dedicated to something you have complete confidence in. No one is fanatically shouting that the sun is going to rise tomorrow. They know it is going to rise tomorrow. When people are fanatically dedicated to political or religious faiths or any other kinds of dogmas or goals, it's always because these dogmas or goals are in doubt.

—Robert Pirsig, *Zen and the Art of Motorcycle Maintenance*

Politics is more difficult than physics.

—Albert Einstein

Politics is a factor in *every* software development project, no matter how much we might want to deny it; the difference with death march projects is that the politics is so intense it can overwhelm the effort to get any work done. Thus, while the *process* associated with politics, namely, the political process of negotiation, will be discussed in a separate chapter, it's important to acknowledge the existence of politics in this chapter and to offer some general advice.

Many software developers will argue that while politics exists, they would prefer to steer clear of the whole ugly mess. That's understandable: Many of us who gravitate to the software field are socially inept and politically naive; not only do we find political "games" nauseating, but we know that we won't do well if we try to play the "game" of politics. That's fine, as long as *someone* (typically the project manager) can handle the politics. But if everyone participates in a death march project on the assumption that "because this project is so important, they'll leave us alone and spare us the usual messy political negotiations," then the project has almost no chance of success.

I'll discuss four aspects of politics in this chapter:

- Identifying the political "players" involved in the project
- Determining the basic nature of the project
- Identifying levels of commitment by project participants
- Analyzing key issues that lead to political disagreements

## IDENTIFYING THE POLITICAL PLAYERS IN THE PROJECT

The key point to remember here is that your chances of success in a death march project are effectively zero if you don't know who the key players are. Some of them will be noisier than others, and some will be your supporters and friends; but some will be vocal opponents of the project, and others will be waiting for the chance to stab you in the back. It's easy to forget this while juggling a thousand other management crises and technical problems, but it's essential.

I believe that it's also imperative for *everyone* on the project to know who the key players are—even if it's the project manager's job to interact with all the players on a day-to-day basis. On rare occasions, a "skunk works" project will manage to isolate all of the project team members from the rest of the human race while the work is being done, but that's unusual. Indeed, in today's world even a skunk works project isn't completely isolated—because everyone is connected to everyone else via email and the Internet.[1] And in normal working environments, everyone is bound to have some interactions with other technical colleagues, as well as managers above and outside the project, and various members of the user community during the course of the project. It's inevitable: We bump into them in the hallway, in the cafeteria, or in the restroom.

Thus, if a project team member receives an apparently innocent phone call, email message, or casual question in the hallway from an apparently friendly middle-level manager asking, "So, how's the project coming along?", it's important for that team member to know whether the message is from a friend or foe, and whether it's thus likely to have political overtones. Whatever answer you provide to the casual question is likely to be carried back to other parts of the organization, and it's not uncommon to see the information amplified, distorted, or buried. As Dale Emery observed in an email message to me:[2]

> In general, I've observed that if there is a constituency whose input is relevant, the developers will often get it anyway, though perhaps in a more expensive, more distorted way than if the manager weren't trying to keep it from them. Other times, the developers will simply make assumptions about what each stakeholder needs.

The typical "players" in a death march project are the following:

- Owner
- Customer
- Shareholder
- Stakeholder
- Champion

I'll discuss each of these below.

# Owner

The *owner* is traditionally the person who accepts, authorizes, or pays for the system and/or the results of the project. It's obviously important to identify this person and do everything possible to keep him or her happy during the course of a death march project.

It's amazing how many software projects take place without anyone having the faintest idea of who the owner is; this is particularly common in organizations where projects are spawned by ambitious and overly eager IS/IT professionals who reassure one another with statements like, "I'll bet the marketing department will be really ecstatic when they see this new system we're building for them." Obviously, well-managed organizations would never let such projects get started—but the major point to keep in mind here is that you won't see many death march projects initiated without a clear command from an owner. The reason is simple: Such projects involve extraordinary expense and/or risk and/or schedule constraints. The IS/IT department is unlikely to invent such projects on its own initiative, and the normal bureaucracy in the organization would prevent it from being scheduled and funded unless a strong, vocal command is issued by someone willing to take authority.

This raises another interesting point: The owner of a death march project often turns out to be a much higher level manager than would be the case for a normal software project. Indeed, it sometimes turns out to be the president or CEO of the organization, because the project affects the very survival of the company. Even if it's only a vice president, the owner of a death march project often has much more clout and latitude when it comes to authorizing expenditures and exceptions to bureaucratic restrictions, than might the case for a normal project.

On the other hand, this doesn't mean that the rest of the political hierarchy has disappeared; indeed, one of the problems with many death march projects is that the project manager has little or no direct contact with the owner. Authorization for the project, as well as periodic demands for status reports, may be filtered down the chain of command from the high-level owner to the middle-level manager who sits just above the death march project owner. And all of these intermediate managers between the *real* owner and the project manager may be, in the terminology discussed below, either customers, shareholders, stakeholders, champions—or political enemies of the project.

The reason it's important to keep this in mind is that the owner's original demand for a death march project can be easily distorted before the project manager receives his or her marching orders. Most often, the nonnegotiable aspect of the death march project is the deadline: The new Super-Widget system absolutely, positively *must* be finished by January 1st or the world will come to an end. But as that order is transmitted down the chain of command, the organizational bureaucracy will tack on its own list of additional constraints: The project must be programmed in a combination of

Ada and RPG; and the team must include George, Harriet, and Melvin (because they're so incompetent that no other project manager will take them); and it must use the organization's newly created (but never-before used) object-oriented methodology; and it must suffer weekly visits from the methodology police; and the project team members must fill out the 17-page form XJ13 in triplicate at the end of each work day; and... the list goes on.

In situations like this, a face-to-face meeting with the high-level project owner can often result in all of these idiotic constraints being eliminated, by executive fiat— all except one: the deadline. But if the project manager has a written authorization that exempts him or her from the other ridiculous rules (which may well be the reason no other project has even been finished on time!), then it may be possible to finish the death march project within its required schedule constraint. And if the high-level owner can be convinced that some extra money is needed in the budget for equipment, tools, or even a slush fund for weekly pizzas for the project team, the project manager can usually obtain it, even if the bean-counters and penny-pinchers elsewhere in the organization would normally do their best to prevent it.

Obviously, not all high-level owners are so cooperative, and not all project owners occupy lofty positions within the organization. But the point remains: While it's important for *any* project to identify its owner, it's doubly important for death march projects. And my experience has been that in a majority of cases, the high-level project owner is far more likely to be a friend than a foe: It's in the owner's interest to cut through the red tape and eliminate the bureaucratic constraints, which is almost always a blessing for the project manager.

However, keep in mind that the project owner may not be the person who actually uses the system when it's installed; nor is the owner the only one who has a political impact upon the project. The other players, discussed below, also have to be kept in mind.

## Customers

The *customer* is the person—or, in many cases, the *group* of persons—who will use the system when it is finished by the death march project team. It's common, in organizations around the world, to refer to this person as the "user." Customers may also be owners of death march projects; but a far more common scenario is the one where the customers are administrative or clerical users who will interact with and operate the system developed by the death march project team.

The politics associated with project customers are discussed in most project management textbooks, so I won't cover the subject in much detail; suffice it to say that all of the politics are magnified in a death march project. We know, for example, that the customer is usually the source of detailed requirements for a system, because the owner (and various other high-level managers) has little or no experience with the actual operation of the business application and tends to view the operational terrain from a height of 30,000 feet. But despite the necessity of communicating directly with the customer/users to elicit the detailed requirements of the system, we know that in many projects, the owner (or other managers) will tell the project team *not* to talk to the users because "they're too busy" or because "I can tell you everything you need to know about their requirements," or will give various other excuses. Finally, we know that in normal projects, the customers can ultimately sabotage the project by refusing to use it or by complaining that it doesn't meet their needs.

All of this is true for death march projects as well, with one additional caveat: the customer(s) may not be aware of the extraordinary politics, constraints, or pressures associated with the death march project. This can create a disaster if someone on the project team marches up to a customer and says, "Hi—I'd really appreciate it if you could interrupt your work now to describe your requirements, because if our project is late, the entire company will go bankrupt. But of course, if the project *does* succeed, you'll be out of a job, too, because the whole point of our new system is to facilitate a massive downsizing effort that will eliminate the entire 700-person clerical department you belong to."

A particularly important example of a customer/user is someone I like to call the "loser user"—that is, the person whose interests would be harmed or decreased if the project succeeds. Typical examples of a negative impact would be a loss of power, prestige, compensation, convenience, etc. Some typical examples of loser users are:

- The vendor whose legacy system will be replaced by the new system

- The end-users who will lose their jobs when the new system is installed

- The end-users who are perfectly happy with their existing system, and who believe that the new system will be *less* functional or convenient

- The end-users who worry they may not have the skills required to use the new system

- The manager whose budget will be reduced in order to provide funding for the development of the new system

- The manager who believes that the project is so ambitious that it will fail—and who is determined to make his prediction come true!

- The manager whose influence, prestige, power, and overall "empire" will be diminished if the new project succeeds

As with other roles discussed in this chapter, the loser-user may change during the course of the project—for example, some of the loser-users may come to see the benefits of a project success and may gradually begin supporting the project. But others may gradually realize the implications of the project success, in terms of their own personal "stake," and may gradually become less enthusiastic, supportive, or cooperative.

## Shareholders

Shareholders are effectively "co-owners" of the system; while they may not have the authority to initiate the project, to accept its results, or to approve the budget, they have a vested interest in its outcome. Indeed, they *do* share the budget in many cases, along with all of the other benefits and risks associated with the project. Think of them as members of a "Board of Directors" with the owner as "Chairman of the Board." The shareholders may or may not get together on a regular basis, and they may not have any explicit contact with the project team; but they're shareholders nonetheless.

Thus, to a large extent, the project team and the project manager can treat the shareholders in much the same way they treat the owner—but the key point here is that the shareholders must not be forgotten or ignored. It's hard to overlook them, for they tend to throw their weight around and make their voices heard; they're also present at many of the meetings and presentations associated with the death march project. On the other hand, there's a tendency on the part of some project managers to avoid these individuals if possible, on the theory that the project owner can speak for the group—and, understandably, the project manager feels that every moment spent coddling a shareholder is a moment that could have been spent working on the project. But just as the shareholders can participate in the decision to authorize, approve, and pay for the death march project, they can be involved in decisions to cancel the project. If they feel they are being ignored, they are that much more likely to do so.

Consultant Dave Kleist identified an interesting form of shareholder in a recent email communication:[2]

> In several of the death march projects I've experienced, I believe that there is a variation of shareholder that is very important to identify: the vendor, especially if they have people on site to work on the project.

Actually, if vendor(s) are involved, there may be several categories of shareholders. The vendor's market representative is often more concerned about making the sale and earning a commission than about whether the vendor's products actually work and the project succeeds. If the vendor has installed consultants, technicians, or other individuals who will work with the project team, then a slightly different set of political agendas will emerge.

## Stakeholders

The distinction between shareholder and stakeholder may seem academic, but it's an important one. Stakeholders are people whose interests are affected by the success or failure of the project—and who thus have a "stake" in the outcome of the project. Even if they don't have an explicit decision-making role in its conduct or progress, they typically have some degree of influence and can thus become an ally or obstacle to project success. Customers, in the sense discussed above, are obviously stakeholders; and so are the owner and the other shareholders.

But the *other* stakeholders might be members of the management hierarchy who will have to abandon their old information systems if the new system is finished on time. Or they might be members of unions, or suppliers, or customers, or competitors. They might even be other members of the IS/IT organization, for if the death march project succeeds, it could have an impact on methods, tools, or other aspects of the way "normal" projects are conducted. Paul Neuhardt pointed out another common form of stakeholder in a recent email message to me:[4]

> You missed "the inner circle." These are the people who have no direct stake in something yet they have influence with those who do, an opinion on what should be done and a burning need to inflict their opinion on others. Also known as "the closest advisors," these people often spend time whispering in the ears of decision makers in soft, subliminal tones and can turn a friend into a foe overnight without you even knowing that it happened.

Erik Petersen identified another important group of stakeholders: the people who test the newly-developed system:

> The test team are often the hardest done by stakeholders, especially if the project manager regards testing time as contingency for development overruns. A possibly OK project could be a death march once it finally hits testing because of the reduced testing time and poor quality delivered late to test.[5]

And another important group of stakeholders was highlighted by a reader who identifies himself as "OughtSix":

> A deathmarch project manager had best be on good terms with his IT Support Department. New employees will need network access, new PCs will need to be set up, network problems will need to be fixed, and server access, password & space allocation issues will need to be addressed. If a project manager can't get these things done immediately, he will have his people sitting on their thumbs, waiting, unable to do their work. The most valuable currency a

> deathmarch project manager has is man-hours, and lack of response
> from an IT Support Department can make a bonfire of that currency.[6]

This sounds like stakeholders are "enemies" of the death march project, and I don't mean to imply this; stakeholders can be allies and valuable supporters, too. They can put in a good word during the kibitzing that inevitably takes place behind the backs of the project team members; and they can supply all kinds of assistance—tangible and intangible—to the project team if they feel it's worthy of support. Indeed, if the death march project is regarded as an "underdog" that somehow got involved in a "David-versus-Goliath" battle, even those members of the organization who have no stake at all in the outcome of the project will step forward and offer support.

Notwithstanding the possibility of this kind of support, there is a higher likelihood that the stakeholders will be critics and enemies of the project. The reason is simple: A death march project is more likely than a normal project to represent a severe change in the status quo; and one of the basic principles of politics is that individuals and organizational cultures automatically resist a change in the status quo, even if they can be convinced intellectually that the change is important and necessary. So, while the project team obviously wants to welcome stakeholders who turn out to be friends of the project, it needs to be alert to the possibility of stakeholders who will throw road-blocks into the schedule and the project plan.

One other point to keep in mind: The existence and identity of the stakeholders are not always obvious, because they're not part of the formal organization chart. If the system has an explicit impact on the labor union, or on the clerks in the order-entry department, then it isn't hard to identify them as stakeholders. But if there's a crusty old project manager who plays golf with the vice president of information systems, and if that project manager is muttering to himself, "If that death march project succeeds, then we'll *all* have to learn Smalltalk, and I'm still convinced Smalltalk is a Communist plot," then you've got a silent stakeholder who could have a subtle but important impact on the project.[7]

## Champions

Just as there are potential enemies for the death march project, there are also friends—including friends so powerful and so helpful that they come to be known as *champions*. The best of all worlds is the champion who is also the project owner; champions may also come from the ranks of customers, shareholders, or stakeholders. But champions are often outside the normal set of political players in the project: The champion might be rooting for the success of a young project manager that he or she considers a protégé. Or the champion might be concerned about the overall success of the project because of the impact on the reputation and credibility of the IS/IT department or the entire organization. Most often, the champion is intrigued by the technology "silver bullet" with which the death march project manager hopes to accomplish miracles—whether it's Java or OO technology, or a new client-server development tool, the champion may have seen earlier demonstrations of it, and may even have been the one who suggested that the project manager use it for the death march project.

Every project can use a champion or two, but death march projects *really* need them. The reasons should be obvious from the discussion above: Projects like this already have plenty of critics and enemies, along with those who will second-guess every decision that the project manager makes. Another reason is because the death march projects usually break several rules along the way—rules that are near and dear to the human resources department, or the methodology police, or the accounting department. There will be numerous occasions throughout the project when someone in a management meeting will complain that, "Those hotshot techno-nerds on the Titanic Project have ordered seven copies of Visual Basic Enterprise without going through proper channels. Not only that, the project manager took $32.98 out of petty cash to buy MacDonald's hamburgers and French fries for the project team last Friday. Why, I could smell the French fries all way down the hall in *my* office![8] We can't let them get away with this blatant disregard for company policy!" The champion is the one who can stop all of this nonsense by saying, "Trust me; these kids might be a little feisty, but they'll get the job done. Leave them alone."

This won't work, of course, unless the champion has a great deal of respect and credibility within the organization's political circles—without this, he/she is not a champion at all. But it often means that the champion will be a veteran within the organization, deemed older and wiser than the hot-headed project manager and the death march volunteers who still have the stamina to work 18-hour days for months on end.

Bottom line: A project champion is more important than the latest methodology or razzle-dazzle programming language. A death march project without a champion to defend the team's disregard for bureaucratic rules and to support the team's decision to use risky techniques and technology, is a lonely, miserable experience. I don't recommend it. If your champion is also the project owner, *and* if there aren't any other shareholders to worry about, *and* if your owner/champion is persuasive enough and involved enough to deal with the stakeholders, then you may have the luxury of ignoring all of these political issues. But unfortunately, most death march projects don't have that luxury; while it's usually the project manager who takes on most of the burden of dealing with the situation, everyone else on the team needs to be at least minimally aware of the cast of political characters.

# DETERMINING THE BASIC NATURE OF THE PROJECT

In the previous chapter, I described several characteristics of death march projects: They can be big or small; they can involve one homogeneous set of customers or an incompatible, heterogeneous group; and they can be affected by different combinations of schedule, budget, and resource constraints.

But there's another way of characterizing these projects which is likely to have a significant political impact on all concerned. As illustrated in Figure 2.1, there are two key issues that can be mapped on a two-dimensional grid; the horizontal axis represents the chances that the project will succeed, while the vertical axis represents the satisfaction or happiness that the project team members feel while the project continues. One way of determining where the team members would place themselves on the vertical axis is to ask, "When this project is over, would you consider taking on another death march project again?" Or, more simply, "Are you in pain?"

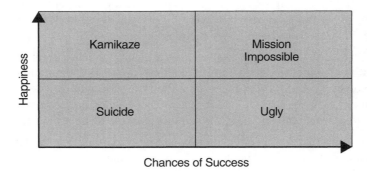

**Figure 2.1**   Chances of Success

There's no particular scale on this chart, and the boundaries among the four quadrants are rather arbitrary; even so, I have yet to find a death march project team that can't identify which quadrant they're in (though they may not have thought about it before I ask the question and draw the picture for them). It's highly doubtful that anyone initiated the death march project with the explicit intention of placing it into a specific place on the chart, but the combination of politics and project constraints (budget, schedule, etc.) will push the project in one direction or the other.

The descriptions of the four quadrants are also rather arbitrary, and you should feel free to change them to fit your organization's cultural idiosyncrasies. Here are the basic characteristics of the four quadrants:

- *Mission-impossible projects*—These are the projects glorified by the old (vintage 1970s) TV series and the new (vintage 1996) Tom Cruise movie. The odds are heavily stacked against the project's success, and there are all manner of villains and traitors plotting the demise of the team. But the project manager is a handsome Hollywood hero, the technical hackers are clever geniuses, and the team has God on its side. The team members are fanatically loyal to one another (notwithstanding the twist in the Tom Cruise movie), and it's clear that each individual thrives on the challenge and the thrill of "living on the edge." And while it's rarely indicated in the old TV series, the real-world mission-impossible project teams typically do dream of fame, glory, and riches if they succeed. And their mission *is* to succeed; they are convinced that a combination of hard work and technical virtuosity will make that possible.

- *Ugly projects*—These are the projects whose team members are sacrificial lambs that will be slaughtered by a cold-blooded project manager in order to bring the project to a successful end. Projects of this kind usually have the "Marine Corps" mentality discussed in Chapter 1—for example, the project manager will be constantly haranguing his or her team that "*Real* programmers don't need sleep!*" The implication is also that "real" programmers don't have to go home to their families, nor do they have to visit their aging parents in the hospital, nor do they have to do anything else that would distract for a moment from the demands of the project. In projects like this, it's not uncommon to see one or two of the project team members collapse from exhaustion, suffer ulcers or a nervous breakdown, or experience a divorce. And when it happens, the project manager chuckles and tells the other team members that the unfortunate victim is a weakling who deserved his or her fate.

    The key characteristics of the ugly project are that (a) the project manager is determined to succeed, (b) the project manager is determined to survive and thus profit from the success of the project, and (c) the project manager is willing to (and indeed *expects* to) sacrifice the health and happiness of the project team members in order to accomplish his or her goals.

- *Suicide projects*—In these projects, everyone is doomed and everyone is miserable. The team members *and* the project manager have typically agreed to work on the project only because the alternative is to be fired; and they know from the outset that there is no chance at all of succeeding. They can't afford to quit, they have no project champion, they have all the cards stacked against them...

- *Kamikaze projects*—These projects are doomed, too, but everyone agrees that it will be a glorious failure, one they will be proud to be associated with. The technical members of the project team sometimes derive their happiness from the opportunity to work with advanced technology they've never had before and which they assume they'll never see again after the project collapses. The project manager hopes that the project will be an inspirational lesson to future project managers. Sometimes the kamikaze projects are associated with a doomed company whose glorious past has created such fierce loyalty on the part of the team members that they feel it is an honor and a privilege to be allowed to sacrifice themselves in a doomed project whose failure will be the company's last hurrah. Of course, there is a small chance that the project *will* succeed, and the company may survive; and even if the project team members utterly destroy themselves in the course of bringing about such a miracle, they will feel good about it.

From the comments above, you can probably tell that I'm in favor of mission-impossible projects, and I admire kamikaze projects; I sympathize with those who have ended up on suicide projects; and I detest ugly projects. But that's *my* value system, which may not be the same as yours. More important, it may not be the same as your project manager's value system; or if you *are* the project manager, you may find that your value system is different from that of your team members. For obvious reasons, it's a good idea to have everyone in the same quadrant: it's hard to succeed with a mission-impossible project if one or two key members think they're on a suicide mission.

Also, remember that public assurances from the various shareholders, stakeholders, and miscellaneous managers surrounding the death march project may or may not be honest indications of the *real* situation. One would like to hope that a project owner would not create a suicide-mission style of death march project, but stranger things have happened in big companies: it may be part of a larger political battle that the project owner is fighting. Quite often, senior management has a broader scope of information which provides a more realistic picture of the project's chances of success. Your vice president, for example, may be fully aware that a merger/acquisition is going to be publicly announced a week before the deadline of your death march project, and your project is going to be canceled at that point, no matter how well or poorly it's doing. *C'est la vie.*

The most common danger, though, is getting involved with an ugly-style death march project in which the project manager refuses to acknowledge that he/she plans to sacrifice team members whenever it's expedient. Fortunately, it's usually easy to spot these situations, even when the manager refuses to acknowledge it: The "macho" behavior, and the denigrating references to weakling team members who can't keep up with the performance of "real programmers" is a dead give-away to the manager's attitude. Obviously, if you have a Marine Corps mentality—that is, you are both willing and able to meet any physical, emotional, political, and psychological demands—then this won't matter to you.

Managers of ugly-style death march projects are often brought in from the outside, either at the beginning of the project or after the first project team manager has quit or been fired. The new manager often has no past history or personal relationship with anyone in the company, and thus has less hesitation than might be expected when pushing the team members to work harder and longer. Indeed, I've seen several situations where the project manager is a "hired gun" who moves from company to company to take on the challenge of such projects. The manager typically delivers a successful project result—that's why he's got the reputation that allows him to charge hefty consulting fees—but the project team members are so disgusted and exhausted that they all quit at the end of the project (if not before), and the project manager has made so many enemies that he, too, has no choice but to pack his bags and move on to the next death march project. It's a perfect role for Clint Eastwood, and it's a situation to watch out for if someone bearing his likeness rides into town to take over the death march project you've just signed up for.[9]

The best time to deal with these issues is *before* the project begins; as part of choosing the team members, the project manager should provide an assessment of what kind of death march project he or she expects it to be and then ask prospective team members (a) how they assess the project, and (b) how they feel about occupying one of the quadrants in the diagram above. As I'll discuss in Chapter 4, I feel very strongly that the manager of a death march project *must* have the freedom of choosing the members of his or her team; and in addition to choosing the appropriate technical skills, it's also crucial to choose individuals who have a compatible assessment of the "style" of the project.

The situation is different, of course, if you're a prospective member of a death march project team, and you're being interviewed by the project manager. As discussed in Chapter 1, sometimes you don't have a choice about participating in the project, and contrary to the advice given in the previous paragraph, sometimes the project manager doesn't have a choice about whether to accept you as a member of the team; in this case, it's at least helpful to know how your manager assesses the project. If you *do* have the option of saying "No, thanks!" to the death march project, then it's all the more important to ensure that your assessment of the project is compatible with that of your manager. As discussed above, it's doubly important if your manager intends to carry out an ugly-style death march project; you need to ask yourself whether it's likely that you will be one of those sacrificed during the course of the project.

Remember also that the situation can change dynamically during the course of the project—either because of the progress (or lack of progress) made by the team, or because of the political situation outside the team, or because of physical or emotional exhaustion on the part of team members, and so on.

# LEVELS OF COMMITMENT BY PROJECT PARTICIPANTS

One last item needs to be discussed: the level of commitment the various project team members are willing and able to make to the project. To understand the concept of "commitment," recall the old parable about the argument between the chicken and the pig as to whose contribution to a bacon-and-eggs breakfast was most important.

"I work incredibly hard to produce those eggs each morning," the chicken says. "And they are the centerpiece of the breakfast meal."

"Well, there's no question that you're involved," replies the pig. "But I provide the bacon. I'm *committed*."

Paul Maskens responded to this parable with the following observation:[10]

> I'm not sure you will find any old pigs in development, perhaps more chickens. I think that kind of commitment continues until (inevitably?) you get into the first death march project—then there is a rude awakening. Either the pig realizes what's happening, this is the slaughterhouse! RUN!! Or the pig is making bacon...

The level of commitment by team members is usually strongly influenced by the overall "style" of the project, as discussed above; for example, if everyone realizes he or she has been assigned to a suicide project, then he or she will probably exert no more effort and emotion than absolutely necessary. For example, even if management insists on large amounts of involuntary overtime during the project, you'll find that the team members are spending the evening hours and weekends (times when the high-level managers who imposed the overtime are virtually certain *not* to be present) catching up with personal phone calls, writing letters to their family, or sitting around the coffee machine shooting the breeze with one another.

Similarly, an ugly-style project will have a level of commitment dictated, or at least strongly influenced, by the demands of the project manager. My experience has been that the ugly-style project manager *is* willing and able to make the same level of physical and emotional commitment to the project that he or she is asking of everyone else; thus, if the project team is in the office on Saturday and Sunday, the ugly-style project manager will be cracking the whip over them.

But what about the kamikaze project and the mission-impossible project? And what about a death march project that nobody wants to characterize as being in one of the four quadrants suggested in Figure 2.1? It's essential that the project manager get a realistic assessment of the limits that the team members have placed on their commitment to the project; and for any of the project team members who are contemplating making an enormous sacrifice to their personal life for the next several months, it's important that they know whether they can expect a similar level of commitment from their colleagues.

In the best of all cases, everyone will provide an honest assessment of his or her commitment and constraints. "I'm 100-percent committed to this project," someone might say, "but my sister is getting married just before the deadline in June, and I'll be gone for three weeks, no matter what. I'm sorry the schedule worked out that way, but her wedding is the most important thing in my life." Since the rest of the project team doesn't even know the sister, this might be regarded as a frivolous excuse to disappear during the crucial final weeks of the project development effort—but at least the team member is being honest about his or her level of commitment.[11]

Unfortunately, not everyone is able to announce a schedule of his or her personal commitments. A typical team member might promise a 100-percent commitment to the project, but if he or she has a child that has to be taken to the hospital, all bets are off. And of course, there's always the chance that a team member will win the grand prize in a lottery and receive a once-in-a-lifetime opportunity to take the entire family to Tahiti...and who knows what other unpredictable events might pose a challenge to an otherwise sincere promise to devote oneself to the death march project on a 100-percent basis?[12] It's unrealistic to ask everyone to anticipate all the possible situations that might arise, but it *is* realistic for the project manager to provide an explicit and realistic picture of the level of commitment he or she expects from the team members. If a two-week absence to attend your sister's wedding is going to be considered an act of treason, far better to know about it in advance.

Brian Pioreck reminded me in a recent email message that it's also crucial for the team members to be aware of each other's level of commitment, which the project manager can also accomplish through appropriate communication:[13]

> I think you also have to make their commitments public through the use of a project plan. Everyone sees the total involvement of all team members this way and what their own involvement means to the project. It is up to the project manager to communicate this and make their commitment match their effort.

# ANALYZING KEY ISSUES THAT LEAD TO POLITICAL DISAGREEMENTS

Inevitably, politics plays a role in every IT project and in virtually every interaction between two or more individuals. But in the best of all cases, it's a minor factor—

either because the various individuals and parties find a way to negotiate and reach a compromise, or because one individual (or an allegiance of several individuals) overwhelms the other(s) and imposes his or her decisions on the group.

In the context of a death march project, the most obvious source of political discussions, debates, and knock-down/drag-out battles is the schedule, budget, and resource restrictions discussed in Chapter 1. After all, if the project team was given a relaxed schedule, a generous budget, and as many technical staff members as it wanted, this would take away most (though probably not all) of the reasons for objecting and complaining.

But aside from disagreements about time, money, and resources, there are usually some additional sources of nasty political disagreements. Some of these are fairly obvious and fall within the scope of normal systems development experiences—for example, the debate about whether "requirements specification" actually describes what the end-users need and want, or whether it describes a garbled, inadequate, and unacceptable version of what they want. This is particularly relevant in a death march project where there is limited time to interview the end-users, document their requirements in a formal manner, and then go through the time-consuming process of review and approval.[14] And most IT professionals today realize that this can be a serious problem even in a non-death march project; hence the growing interest in prototyping, iterative development, and other development processes that we'll discuss in Chapter 5 of the book.

*A related, but often more severe, problem is that of determining which subset* of the user's requirements can actually be implemented within the pre-ordained schedule and budget. As we'll discuss in later chapters of this book, a realistic estimating/planning activity often makes it unmistakably obvious to the project manager that even if the project team members work 24 hours a day, seven days a week, they simply cannot implement all of the user-requested functionality within the allocated schedule and budget. But confronting that reality is a major political issue in itself; and negotiating an acceptable compromise—in other words, reducing the amount of functionality, extending the schedule, increasing the budget, or agreeing to compromise the quality expectations—can sometimes make the Middle East peace negotiations look simple by comparison.

A more fundamental political dispute—and one that may take the project manager entirely by surprise—is the basic question of whether the new system is needed or wanted in the first place. In some cases, external forces (e.g., government regulations) are responsible for launching the project; the key stakeholders may understand this to be the case, but they may still be annoyed and resentful. In other cases, the new system may have been mandated by a senior executive, despite the disagreement of his or her peers, and over the complaints and objections of his or her subordinates. In some cases, the project manager was an active participant in the political battles that preceded the official managerial approval to initiate the project; and in that case, the project manager should expect to deal with the political consequences throughout the entire development and installation process. In other cases, though, the project manager is an unwitting pawn (indeed, he or she may have been hired to run the project *after* the fateful decision was made), and doesn't understand why he or she has so many enemies among the key stakeholders. Of course, there's no easy solution to this problem—but at the very least, it's crucial to be *aware* of the problem as early as possible.

Aside from these issues, there's one other source of political disputes: disagreements about the status of the project, the likelihood that it will finish successfully, and the appropriate actions that should be taken if the project is visibly behind schedule and/or over budget.

We'll discuss several of these issues in subsequent chapters of the book; but for now, you should study these questions from a political perspective—not only to anticipate and prepare the answers that you'll be asked to provide, but also to anticipate how the various stakeholders are likely to line up to either support or attack your position.

**What are the realistic chances for success at various stages?**

- At the very beginning of the project
- At the end of various life-cycle activities: analysis, design, "code complete," unit testing, and so on
- Halfway through the originally designated project schedule
- A month (or a week, or a day) before the deadline

***When*** **should it become evident to a reasonably intelligent observer/participant that the project is in trouble?**

**Who is the person who should** *know* **whether there's a realistic chance of success, or whether there are serious problems?**

- The project manager
- The user/customer
- Senior management
- Others

**What should the project manager** *do* **when it becomes obvious that the project is in trouble?**

- Work 24 hours a day to "save" the project?
- Escalate the problem to higher levels of management?
- Gather together key stakeholders to find a consensus solution?

The key point about many of these political disagreements is that they can lead to significant project delays—thus exacerbating what is *already* a problem in a death march project. One possible solution, particularly for the disagreements about functionality and other requirements-oriented issues, is the use of "Joint Application Development" (JAD) sessions, in which all of the stakeholders are brought together with a trained facilitator in order to reach a consensus in a brief but intense series of collaborative meetings.[15]

If that's not possible, the project manager should try to get a commitment from key stakeholders that all issues requiring their approval, consent, or review will be resolved in *no more than 24 hours*. For a good example of this strategy, see the discussion of "extreme software engineering" in the 100-day projects carried out by Shoulders Corp, located on the Internet at www.shoulderscorp.com/.

## CONCLUSION

The discussion in this chapter doesn't provide any *operational* advice about managing or planning or carrying out a death march project. But style and substance are inextricably entwined in many aspects of life: Even if a death march project is following all of the "rules" about designing, coding, and testing a software system, the "style" issues discussed in this chapter can kill it.

However, once we've identified the key players in the project, determined the "style" of the project, and communicated the level of commitment that the manager expects and the team members can realistically promise, then it's time to move on to the real work of the project. That begins with an even larger issue of politics: *negotiation*. I'll discuss that in Chapter 3.

## NOTES

1.  There are some rare exceptions to this situation, especially the so-called "clean room" project environments, in which the project team is deliberately cut off from Internet-based contact in order to minimize the chances the members will access "tainted" material associated with a litigious competitor. In this same context, it's worth remembering that if the project fails, and if for any reason the failure could lead to a lawsuit, then the lawyers on both sides will pounce on all of the email messages as potential "evidence" to support their clients' arguments.

2.  From: Dale Emery, 72704, 1550
    To: Ed Yourdon, 71250,2322
    Forum: CASE - DCI
    Date: Sun, Jul 14, 1996, 1:31:14 PM

Ed,
>>Are there any significant constituencies that I've missed?<<
Yes. Developers, the people whose death is referred to in your
title.
>> How important do you think it is for _all_ of the project team
members to be aware of the existence of these constituencies and
whether or not they can be viewed as a "friend" or "foe" of the
death march project? I personally believe that everyone on the team
_should_ know this information, but I have manager friends who
believe that this is too distracting, and that the developers
should be spending every ounce of their energy on the project
itself, while the project manager (who presumably is more politically adept) spends his or her time dealing with the outsiders.
What's your opinion? <<
I agree with your manager friends that the developers should be
spending every ounce of energy on the project itself. But I also
believe that information about each constituency is part of the
project, so it's better for everyone (the constituencies, the managers, the developers) if the developers have that information. Any
information that's relevant to the project but is hidden from the
developers brings the project one step closer to the edge of failure.
If the project manager were extremely talented at knowing what
information was relevant, that might make a difference. I haven't
seen managers who were very good at that.
In general, I've observed that if there is a constituency whose
input is relevant, the developers will often get it anyway, though
perhaps in a more expensive, more distorted way than if the manager
weren't trying to keep it from them. Other times, the developers
will simply make assumptions about what each stakeholder needs.
>> mission impossible, kamikaze, ugly, suicide <<
I like these terms. I'm not sure how to know which kind of project
I'm involved in until after the project succeeds/crashes. I think
developers involved in a death march always believe (or are trying
desperately to hold on to the belief) that they are in a mission
impossible project.
>> How important do you think it is for the project manager to get a
really good assessment of each team member's level of commitment? <<
"Level of commitment" is way too vague to be useful to me. If I want
to know what kind of "commitment" I can expect from someone, I
would want to know what things in particular are more important to
them than this project, and what things are less important.
I've always like Watts Humphrey's ideas about "commitment discipline." He describes them in section 5.1 of "Managing the Software
Process."
>> Is the project manager just kidding himself/herself by believing
the team member's sincere statement of commitment, given that

things can change drastically during the project? <<
Any statement of commitment can only describe how the team member
feels right now, given what they know right now.
If a manager asking about commitment really wants to know, "How
committed will you be, regardless of what happens on the project,
regardless of what happens in our outside life, regardless of what
demands I may make of you?" then any answer the team member gives
is likely to be useless.
I've been asked many times to commit to achieving some result that
is not completely within my control. I can tell you what actions I
can commit to, but commit to a result and there are factors beyond
my control, what would my statement of commitment do for you?
Dale

3. From: Dave Kleist, 70730,1613
   To: Ed Yourdon, 71250,2322
   Topic: Death March Ch2 Queries
   Date: Wed, Jul 10, 1996, 11:05:26 PM
   Ed,
   >>1. Are there any other significant constituencies that I've
   missed? <<
   In several of the death march projects I've experienced, I believe
   that there is a variation of shareholder that is very important to
   identify: the vendor, especially if they have people on site to
   work on the project.
   Depending on who bought the project or software from the vendor,
   you may have some difficulties right away. A golf game sale for a
   package (my president plays golf with your president) is a big pre-
   dictor for a deathmarch, since the requirements process is typically shorted severely. Don't be the first company to buy anything.
   Once the vendor staff and client staff start banging heads, things
   rarely improve. It makes progress that much slower since position-
   ing and putting spin on project news takes precedence over real
   project status. Makes it that much harder to manage if you don't
   know who is telling you the truth or when they are doing it.
   - Dave

4. From: Paul Newhardt, 71673, 454
   To: Ed Yourdon, 71250,2322
   Msg # 160615, reply to # 160484
   Section: The Cutter Edge [14]
   Forum: CASE - DCI
   Date: Fri, Jul 12, 1996, 12:10:13 AM
   Ed,
   << [Stuff about identifying the key political players in a project]
   Are there any other significant constituencies that I've missed? >>
   Unfortunately, yes. You missed "the inner circle." These are the
   people who have no direct stake in something yet they have influ-
   ence with those who do, an opinion on what should be done and a

burning need to inflict their opinion on others. Also known as "the closest advisors," these people often spend time whispering in the ears of decision makers in soft, subliminal tones and can turn a friend into a foe overnight without you even knowing that it happened. It happens in any political organization from the White House to the Congress to any company with more than 3 people. Even if they have no apparent stake, you had better have The Inner Circle on your side if you want to make a of it. These people can be old college buddies, the VP of Sales who has an opinion on everything and the chutzpah to believe he is always right or the faithful secretary of 20 years' service who has "seen it all" and knows "what really works for us."

To put it another way, if you want to get anywhere with Mr. Clinton you had better not make an enemy out of Mrs. Clinton.

<< How important do you think it is for *all* of the project team members to be aware of the existence of these constituencies and whether or not they can be viewed as a "friend" or "foe" of the death march project? >>

Essential. Yes, lot's of people hate getting into politics and want to be left alone to "do their jobs." My response to that is, "It's your job to get this software written, and these people can keep you from doing that just as easily as any compiler fault or hardware crash will. If you don't keep them happy, your job evaporates."

<< I've identified four fundamental types of death march projects in this chapter from the perspective of the political climate that will prevail during the project: >>

I've seen another type of death march, but it sort of screws up your quadrant concept. I would call it "the lost squadron": We set out to go somewhere, but the destination changed in mid-trip. And then it changed direction again and again and again until finally we started wandering around without knowing where we are or how to get home. If we actually ever get finished it will only be because we stumbled on the destination by accident.

<< How important do you think it is for the project manager to get a really good assessment of each team member's level of commitment? >>

Vital. Commitment breeds both efficiency and quality, and if you can't get a reasonable handle on commitment, it makes estimation and quality control that much harder.

<< Is the project manager just kidding himself/herself by believing the team member's sincere statement of commitment, given that things can change drastically during the project? >>

Probably. At the outset, every one tells you they are commited, and they may even believe it themselves. The trick is to continually re-assess the team members' commitment levels because they will almost certainly change over time and thus the efficiency and quality of death march work will change (almost certainly for the worse) over time as well. It helps to be able to read minds <g>.

**5.** Erik Petersen email, June 23, 2003.

**6.** OughtSix email, June 16, 2003.

**7.** For another perspective on this, see "Project clarity through stakeholder analysis," by Larry Smith, *Crosstalk: the Journal of Defense Software Engineering*, Dec. 2000.

**8.** For some reason, politicians (other than Bill Clinton) hate French fries and seem to regard the odor as a direct challenge to their authority. I began noticing this on consulting engagements in the mid-70s, when members of a project team I was working with told me in hushed tones that they had to keep the conference room door closed lest the highly feared Vice President smell the odor. I was delighted to see that Scott Adams remarked upon the problem in *The Dilbert Principle*. Could it be that university business schools are teaching fledgling MBAs that French fries are a communist plot? Or could it be that the managers most offended by the practice grew up before MacDonald's started its enterprise in the mid-1950s, and never got over their rage at having missed out on one of the important American childhood experiences?

**9.** One such manager, whom I observed operating in the Wall Street financial services community in the early 1990s, did have an interesting strategy for calibrating the physical stamina and emotional strength of his team: he would create a "false crisis" at the beginning of the project and *immediately* throw the entire team into a double-overtime level of effort. Then he would stand back and watch to see what happened; one or two of the team members might quit, one or two might have a nervous breakdown, and one or two "quiet heroes" might emerge to solve the artificial crisis through hard work or a clever technical strategy. Having thus calibrated his team, the cold-blooded manager would then relax the pressure and get on with the real work of the project—confident that once the *real* crises began to occur (which they inevitably will in a death march project), he would have a good understanding of how his team would behave.

**10.** From: Paul Maskens (UK), 104074,3277
To: Ed Yourdon, 71250,2322
Topic: Death March Ch2 Queries
Date: Mon, Jul 15, 1996, 6:12:03 PM
>> How important do you think it is for the project manager to get a really good assessment of each team member's level of commitment? <<
I'm not sure you will find any old pigs in development, perhaps more chickens.
I think that kind of commitment continues until (inevitably?) you get into the first death march project - then there is a rude awakening. Either the pig realises what's happening, this is the slaughter-house! RUN!!
Or the pig is making bacon...
To my mind this fits in quite nicely with the death march theme.
Paul 104074,3277
 100012,3274
 on 15-Jul-96 at 22:57:43 OzWin v2.01

**11.** The manager of an ugly-style project would probably pounce on this situation, and loudly complain that it was unacceptable. That's okay, too, if it happens at the beginning of the project: The project team member is thus made aware of the need to make a binary choice; if the sister's wedding has the higher priority, it's better for the team member to resign gracefully at the beginning of the project than to be involved in an ugly personal crisis later on.

**12.** This is one good reason for having small project teams and short project schedules. A five-person team working on a six-month death march project is far less likely to be interrupted by unpredictable distractions than a 30-person team slaving away for three years. People *do* get married, they *do* have children, and they *do* have to attend to the other demands of a personal life; sometimes these events can be postponed for a few weeks or a few months, but it's almost impossible to block everything out of your life for three years.

**13.** ```
From: Brian Pioreck, 74224,611
To: Ed Yourdon, 71250,2322
Topic: Death March Ch2 Queries
Section: The Cutter Edge [14], Forum: CASE - DCI
Date: Mon, Jul 15, 1996, 6:39:30 PM
Ed
>>1.... Are there any other significant constituencies that I've
missed?<<
I also include anyone who might be affected/involved by the imple-
mentation of the project. People who are not exactly stakeholders
but whose cooperation is required for success. Say, the DBA group
for example.
>>2. How important do you think it is for _all_ of the project team
members to be aware of the existence of these constituencies and
whether or not they can be viewed as a "friend" or "foe" of the
death march project?<<
It is critical to developing the kind of group consciousness among
team members that helps to compress time during a project. It will
help the requirements process be more accurate, cut down on the
number of meetings required, and deliver better information from
the meeting you do have.
>>...I have manager friends who believe that this is too distract-
ing, and that the developers should be spending every ounce of
their energy on the project itself, while the project manager (who
presumably is more politically adept) spends his or her time deal-
ing with the outsiders.<<
The whole concept of "outsiders" has to be abolished. It feeds the
myth that developers are some kind of different family of the human
species. Without the other team members involvement the developers
could be spending every ounce of their energy building a project
that is off target.
>>3. I've identified four fundamental types of death march
projects...
```
```

The premise is that none of these are worthwhile outcomes, right? I
think it would be interesting to present these types without any
death march explanation and let people pick which type of project
they'd be willing to work on. The point is that so many projects
are like these and people are so used to them they might not even
question the categories.
>>4. ...How important do you think it is for the project manager to
get a really good assessment of each team member's level of commitment?<<
It is critical. Without commitment you don't really have a project.
Why is this person involved? What are they hoping to get out of
this project? I think you also have to make their commitments public through the use of a project plan. Everyone sees the total
involvement of all team members this way and what their own
involvement means to the project. It is up to the project manager
to communicate this and make their commitment match their effort.
Brian

14. A particularly unpleasant form of this problem occurs in the case where the development team has inadequate time or resources to identify detailed user requirements,
and where the project team uses a "waterfall" methodology that postpones the political disagreement until the very end of the development effort, when the project is
likely to be over budget and past its deadline. As Tom DeMarco observes in *The
Deadline* (Dorset House, 1997), an incomplete, ambiguous specification is often a
sign of irreconcilable disagreements among stakeholders that occurs *early* in the
project, rather than incompetence on the part of systems analysts that gradually
becomes apparent *late* in the project, during acceptance testing.

15. There are several excellent books on JAD techniques, on of which is *Joint Application
Development*, by Jane Wood and Denise Silver (2nd edition, John Wiley & Sons,
1995).

# 3 Negotiations

Only free men can negotiate. Prisoners cannot enter into contracts.

—Nelson Mandela
Statement from prison, Feb. 10, 1985,
refusing the terms offered for his release
by South African President P.W. Botha
Quoted in *Higher than Hope*, Part 4, Chapter 30, Fatima Meer (1988)

If you're the manager of a death march project, it's very easy to predict the outcome of negotiations over budget, schedule, and resources: *You lose.* This is almost inevitable, because such negotiations take place at the beginning of the project (or even before the project is formally initiated), when the project owner/customer has neither the intellectual ability, the emotional stamina, nor the political necessity to accept the unpleasant counter-offers of the project manager. More rational negotiations sometimes take place a month or two before the deadline, when the first project manager has quit or been fired, and when a new project manager demands (as a condition of accepting the assignment) that everyone face up to the reality that the original deadline, budget, and required functionality will never be achieved.

But none of us seems willing to accept this sad state of affairs. Thus, even though this chapter probably *could* focus on rational negotiating strategies for the replacement project manager, I'll nevertheless confront the question most of us wrestle with: How can we negotiate a tolerable set of conditions at the *beginning* of a death march project? Alas, there are no magic secrets to be revealed in this chapter; the sad reality is that at the end of the process, you lose. Still, it's useful to be aware of the devious political games by which you're likely to be outmaneuvered, as well as the options that should be explored when you have been presented with a completely unrealistic schedule, budget, and/or staffing constraint.

My assumption throughout this chapter is that *you* are the one involved in the negotiations about death march projects, schedules, and so on. If you're a technical staff member, you may be indirectly involved—for example, providing advice and estimating data to the project manager, so that he or she can carry out the negotiating battles with higher levels of management. But in an email communication with Doug Scott[1] recently, I was reminded that in some projects, even the project manager has only an indirect role, because all of the negotiations are being made on his or her behalf by the next higher up manager:

> ...my biggest single obstacle in deathwatch projects has been my own management. I came to the UK in 1972, and moved on to big projects almost immediately. I don't think I learnt anything about running projects since that date (I learnt a lot about politics, but that's

*something else).* You need to understand your own management's negotiating stance, and if they love to play roll over, you have to keep them well away from the project.

# RATIONAL NEGOTIATIONS

The suggestion that we really *do* know how to accurately estimate the required schedule, budget, and resources for a nontrivial project will set off an emotional debate among any group of software professionals and managers. Our track record over the years certainly hasn't been a very good one; on the other hand, many would argue that the problems have been the result of political games associated with the very death march projects that we're discussing in this book.

But most large organizations can point to dozens of projects where the software team made its own schedule, proposed its own budget, and expressed supreme confidence that it would deliver a fully functional system within those constraints; the team then proceeds to hoist itself on its own petard and fails to deliver anything, any time. So it's no wonder that in many of these organizations, the user community and senior management have given up on the negotiating process and have instead begun imposing "do-or-die" deadlines and budgets. Such is the genesis of many a death march project.

Still, that doesn't mean that we should abandon all efforts to derive a "rational" estimate that we can use in the preliminary negotiations for a project. Indeed, it's crucial that the project manager avoid the temptation to give up and simply accept the initial death march project constraint as an edict. One of the common signs that a project team has adopted what I called a "suicide-style" behavior in Chapter 2 is the attitude—expressed by the project manager and echoed by the team members—that "we have no idea how long this project will really take, and it doesn't matter since they've already told us the deadline. So we'll just work seven days a week, 24 hours a day, until we drop from exhaustion. They can whip us and beat us, but we can't do any more than that..."

I'm not going to discuss estimating techniques at length in this book; if the project manager has no skill or experience in estimating, then a death march project is no place to begin learning. But let me point out some of the obvious resources that we have available in this field:

- *Commercial estimating tools*—Products such as SLIM and CHECK-POINT are available from Quantitative Systems Management and Software Productivity Research (SPR). SPR's Chairman, metrics guru Capers Jones, estimates that there are some 50 commercial project estimating tools. None of them are perfect, and all of them require intelligence on the part of the user (garbage-in/garbage-out applies in this field, too!), but in the best case, they can produce estimates that are accurate to within ± 10%. Even if they're only accurate to within ±50%, it's better than the political demands that the project manager is coping with, which are often 1,000% beyond the ability of the team to deliver.

- *System dynamics models*—Numerous simulation models have been developed to explore the nonlinear interactions between various factors that affect a project's behavior. For example, if part of the strategy of a death march project is to impose a demand for heavy overtime on the part of the project manager, what will be the effects over a period of weeks or months? The natural assumption is that more "output" will be produced than would be the case with a normal eight-hour working day, but most experienced project managers will also point out that productivity (measured in function-points per day, or lines of code per hour, etc.) gradually decreases as exhaustion builds up. Error rates also begin to increase, which have an obvious impact on testing and debugging effort. And if the overtime continues long enough, the project team eventually collapses from exhaustion. Of the simulation models that I've seen in this area, the best is Tarek Abdel-Hamid's [1], which has been implemented in languages such as DYNAMO and iThink.

- Dozens of articles and books have been written on the topic of project estimating. Barry Boehm's *Software Engineering Economics* [2] is a good place to begin; it's important to note that Boehm's COCOMO model from the early 1980s has been updated to COCOMO-2 [3]. Another classic is Brooks' *The Mythical Man-Month* [4]; this has also been updated recently to reflect modern technology and software practices. More recent books on software estimating include Jim McCarthy's *Dynamics of Systems Development* [5].

- The *process* of estimation has been studied and documented, and organizations like the Software Engineering Institute have published useful guidelines and checklists for improving the process of estimation [6,7]. Even if we aren't very good at it, we know how to get better.

- Familiar techniques such as prototyping and time-boxing can be used to get an accurate picture of how feasible or infeasible the project constraints are for the overall system being developed. This is by no means a foolproof approach, but it can inject a dose of reality into the project team and the surrounding layers of managers and customers. If management is demanding a system that will require a team of three to write a million lines of code in 12 months, then it should be possible to define a skeleton version of the system that can be built within the first month; this will provide at least a rough calibration of the team's level of productivity, as well as a rough idea of the overall feasibility of the project.

# IDENTIFYING ACCEPTABLE TRADEOFFS

Let's assume that the project team has prepared a "rational" estimate of the schedule, budget, and personnel required for a death march project; and let's assume that management is prepared for some kind of give-and-take process of negotiation before the final decisions are made. The most common situation is that management will declare the initial estimates "unacceptable" and make counter-demands that are far more stringent. What should the project manager do?

As author/consultant John Boddie[2] pointed out to me in a recent email message to me, the crucial thing is to ensure that everyone agrees that there is more than one possible "scenario" for the project:

> Some useful questions during negotiations,
>
> "If the system is ready on the fifth of September rather than on the first, will we already have declared bankruptcy September second?"
>
> "Is there an 80/20 rule here? If we deliver the critical 20 percent that gives eighty percent of the value, do we need the twenty percent at initial roll-out?"
>
> "Everybody wants things good, wants them fast, and wants them cheap. Everyone knows that you can actually achieve any two of the three. Which two do you want?"
>
> The principle at work is to make those who are demanding the death march look unreasonable if they are unwilling to consider more than one possible outcome. Unless there is an acceptance of more than one way to approach the problem, then there is no negotiation. All the manager can say is, "We'll give it our best shot, but there are no guarantees."

If the counter-proposal from senior management or the customer involves only one "variable," then the project manager can estimate the impact on the other variables. For example, if the manager's first estimate is that the project will take 12 months with three people and a budget of $200,000, it's possible that senior management's first response will be, "Baloney! We need to have that system up and running in *six* months!" The obvious way to accomplish this is to add more people and/or spend more money (e.g., to pay higher salaries to hire more productive programmers).

But Fred Brooks told us nearly 30 years ago that the relationship between time and people on a software project is not a linear one; the term "man-month" (which would probably be expressed as "person-month" in today's politically correct organizations) was thus exposed as a myth. Indeed, the relationship between *all* of the key variables in a project is likely to be nonlinear, and it's likely to be time-sensitive as well: Because of the "feedback effect" of many management decisions, a change in one variable (such as adding more staff) will not only have an impact on other variables (such as productivity) over time, but will eventually have an impact on the original variable—for example, the hiring of additional staff could lower morale, which raises the turnover rate within the project, which ultimately reduces the size of the staff.

The nonlinear, time-sensitive nature of these interactions is the essence of the systems dynamics models mentioned above; but it's also the reason for using the various commercial estimating tools described earlier. There is a key point here: The mathematics behind the systems dynamics models is typically based on nonlinear differential equations, and most of us aren't very good at doing that level of mathematics in our heads. Similarly, the commercial estimating tools carry out elaborate calculations involving dozens of parameters; trying to do this intuitively, based on a "gut" feeling for the situation, is likely to be quite error-prone.

Unfortunately, that's exactly the situation many death march project managers find themselves in. Sometimes this is because of the nature of the negotiating process (particularly a game called "Spanish Inquisition," which I'll discuss below); but it's also caused by the lack of estimating tools and expertise in many organizations. Again, this is not a problem you're going to be able to solve in a death march project if it hasn't been addressed already: If the organization is accustomed to deriving its project estimates by scribbling numbers on the back of an envelope, the death march project manager probably won't get away with spending $10,000 on a sophisticated estimating tool.

So what should the manager do in a situation like this? In the extreme case, the manager should recognize the futility of the situation and respond appropriately; I'll discuss that in more detail in a section below. But in the less extreme case, here are two guidelines:

- If the negotiating demand from users or senior management involves a change of less than 10% in one project variable, then you can compensate by increasing one of the other variables in a direct, proportional fashion. Thus, if management wants the schedule reduced by 10%, then add 10% to the size of the project team. This isn't entirely accurate, but it's a good first-cut approximation, and is about all you'll be able to get away with from a negotiating perspective.

- If the change involves more than 10% in one dimension, then you should assume it will have an "inverse square law" impact on any other single dimension. Thus, in the scenario above, management wants to reduce the project schedule from 12 months to six. Rather than responding by doubling the size of the project team, the manager should *quadruple* the team—or quadruple the budget, in order to hire super-programmers who can code with both hands at the same time. Without a formal estimating model, there's no way to know whether this crude heuristic will be accurate for any specific situation, but at least it's better than falling into the trap or negotiating a "linear" exchange of time for people. Unfortunately, the inverse square law is difficult to negotiate, and there's a good chance that the project manager's "outrageous" demands will be beaten down; but with luck, the manager will still end up in a better position than with a linear exchange.

# NEGOTIATING GAMES

Negotiating *is* a game, and it takes place on all software projects; what's different about death march negotiations is that the stakes are much higher, emotions are much more highly charged, and the demands of the other side (in terms of schedule, budget, etc.) are usually so extreme that they overwhelm any "safety factor" that we might have used in the past. The most obvious safety factor in a traditional project, for example, is overtime: even if the project manager has been browbeaten into a tight schedule and restricted budget, success can still be achieved by asking the project team to work 10-20 hours per week of overtime for the final few months of the project. The additional effort doesn't show up in the official records, because the programmers aren't paid for overtime work; thus the manager ends up looking like a hero.

But in a death march project, modest amounts of overtime are typically inadequate to achieve the dramatic results that are being demanded. Besides, the users and senior management aren't naive: they *know* that overtime effort can be requested, and they've factored that into their own estimate of the "required" schedule for the project—thus pre-empting the manager's opportunity to hide that free resource. But project managers who are veterans of such negotiations have a few tricks up their sleeves, and the bargaining sessions begin.

The neophyte project manager is at a terrible disadvantage; in the extreme case, the neophyte isn't even aware that his past successes may have occurred *only* because the project team voluntarily contributed sufficient overtime effort to compensate for a ridiculous project schedule. And the ridiculous schedule may have been imposed upon the team precisely because of the manager's naiveté in the area of estimating negotiations.

Management consultant Rob Thomsett has described the most common negotiating games in a wonderful article [8]; I've summarized the more familiar games below:

- *Doubling and add some*—This is a ploy that has been used on projects dating back to the Pyramids, if not earlier. Use whatever estimating techniques you have available, then double the "rational" estimate; for added safety, add three months (or three weeks, or three years, depending on the overall size of the project). The major problem with this strategy is that it runs head-on into the most pressing constraint associated with death march projects: schedule compression.

- *Reverse doubling*—As noted earlier, management hasn't been oblivious as software project managers have attempted to "pad" their estimates by the doubling strategy discussed above. One reason for this political astuteness is that the senior managers in many organizations today are former IS/IT project managers—so they're intimately familiar with the games involved. As a result, they take the initial estimate given to them by the project manager and automatically cut it in half. Pity the poor neophyte project manager who didn't realize that he was supposed to double his estimate at the outset!

- *Guess the number I'm thinking of*—This is a game I learned in one of my first projects as a junior programmer. The user or senior manager has an "acceptable" figure for the schedule, budget, and/or other aspects of the negotiation, *but refuses to articulate it.* When the project manager offers his estimate of schedule and budget, the user/senior-manager simply shakes his head and says, "No." The implied message is, "That's too much. Guess again." The hapless project manager eventually (sometimes after half a dozen attempts!) comes up with an acceptable estimate, but because it's *his* estimate, the user/senior-manager is all the more determined to hold him accountable.

- *Double Dummy Spit*—"Dummy" is Australian slang for a baby's pacifier, and "spit the dummy" is an Australian phrase describing a baby so frustrated and angry that it spits out its pacifier. Thomsett uses this as a metaphor to describe the negotiating sessions when a senior manager erupts in a fit of rage when the project manager first makes his proposal for the death march project schedule and budget. The chastened manager scurries away, comes back with a revised estimate, and the manager erupts again—hence the "double dummy spit." The idea is to get the manager so cowed and terrified that he'll go along with anything in order to avoid yet another temper tantrum.

- *Spanish Inquisition*—This occurs when the project manager walks into a meeting of higher level managers, completely unaware that he is going to be asked to make an "instant estimate" for the death march project. Imagine a roomful of grouchy vice presidents staring at you while the CEO asks you in thunderous tone, "So, Smithers, when do you expect to get the Frozzle system done? I've told the whole management team that we'll have it online by March 13th of this year—you're not going to let me down, are you?" If you're brave enough to suggest that November 13th of *next* year would be a more realistic estimate, you'll have a dozen inquisitors questioning your intellect, your credentials, your loyalty, and perhaps even your religious faith.

- *Low bid*—With outsourcing a option in many organizations today, this game is becoming more and more common; it's also common in any situation where a software development organization is bidding against other competitors for the privilege of developing a system for a client organization. The game is obvious: The customer (or sometimes the development organization's marketing representative) tells the project manager that one of the other bidders has proposed a faster development schedule and/or a lower budget. This puts pressure on the project manager to not only match the competing bid (which may or may not be a real bid), but also to improve upon it in order to raise the chances of getting the contract. A variation on this game occurs when the client lets it be known that he's considering the option of not doing the project at all; a software development organization that's desperate to get the approval to initiate the project (perhaps because it will advance the career of the IS/IT vice president) will ensure that the project proposal is so attractive that it will be approved. Of course, this means that in many cases, one or more members of the IS/IT hierarchy *knows* that the project proposal is unrealistically optimistic and perhaps even a blatant lie. This in turn leads to the "gotcha" and "Chinese water torture" games described below.

- *Gotcha*—The "gotcha" game is sometimes played by the project manager as a way of getting revenge: Though he knows at the outset that the project proposal in unrealistic, he accepts it anyway, relying on the probability that by the time everyone is forced to face up to reality (e.g., a week before the deadline), it will be too late for the client to back out. But it's a dangerous game, because the client has to ask himself whether he wants to throw good money after bad; if the organization has a track record of previous projects running amok in this fashion, the client may decide to cancel the project and write off the expenses as a bad investment. But the chances are that the death march project *won't* be canceled right away because it's usually associated with business objectives, legal requirements, or political battles that are difficult to walk away from. But that doesn't prevent the customer from seeking revenge for having the game played on him, and the most obvious form of revenge is to fire the project manager. This is also a common political ploy for various higher level managers and marketing representatives (who may have been responsible for the death march project commitments in the first case) for escaping the problem of "guilt by association." Everyone can rationalize that the reason for the problem is the incompetence of the project manager; a new project manager is brought in, a more realistic set of revised project schedules and budgets may or may not be negotiated, and the project continues. Meanwhile, of course, nobody thinks to relax the pressure of overtime work on the technical staff members of the team.

- *Chinese Water Torture*—Rather than facing a high-risk, all-or-nothing showdown near the end of the project, another common game is to bring the bad news to the customer and/or higher management in small pieces. Imagine the scenario, for example, where the project manager's rational estimate for the project is 12 months; with forced overtime and lots of miracles, he thinks it might be possible to finish in six months, but management has imposed a four-month deadline upon the project. Reluctantly, the manager concedes and announces a series of "inch-pebble" deliverables for the project—for example, a new prototype version of the system will be delivered for customer review every week. The first deliverable turns out to be a day late, but the manager reasons that the delay represents 14-20% of the deadline for that deliverable (depending on whether the team is working a five-day week or a seven-day week); thus, he argues that the deadline for the final version of the system should also be pushed back by 14-20%. Management refuses to concede any slippage at this early point, but when the second inch-pebble is also a day late (meaning a cumulative delay of two days over a period of two weeks), the manager repeats his argument. Drip, drip, drip; it's like Chinese water torture—no one single piece of bad news is enough to kill you, but the cumulative effect can be fatal.

- *Smoke and mirrors*—Pity the poor project manager whose higher level IS/IT vice president has hired a metrics consultant with an estimating model that nobody understands. Software metrics are ultimately a form of statistics, and estimating models are based upon sophisticated mathematics. When put in the hands of the innocent, the naive, and/or the politically motivated, these tools can be used to "prove" the validity of almost any estimate. All of this is doubly dangerous if the metrics come from a vendor attempting to prove that the death march project will succeed because of the stupendous productivity of the vendor's CASE tools, visual programming language, or newfangled software-engineering methodology.

- *Hidden variables of maintainability/quality*—This is one of the more insidious games, and it can be played in a constructive or destructive fashion
  by knowledgeable project managers, higher level IS/IT managers, and/or
  customers. It's very simple: As a project manager, I can deliver an infinite
  amount of software to the customer in zero time *as long as it doesn't have
  to work and it doesn't have to be maintained.* Obviously, it would be foolish to propose a scenario this extreme, but the point is that quality (in the
  form of defects, portability, maintainability, etc.) is a project "dimension"
  that has to be taken into account when trade-offs are being considered
  among time, money, staffing, and other resources. Some customers are too
  naive to recognize this, and some of them have a very cold-blooded, short-
  term perspective: "I don't care if the system works two years from now,
  because I think the business opportunity will be gone—and in any case,
  I'll be gone. All I care about is that the system has to be available three
  months from now, and it has to work for 12 months after that." If the political pressure is strong enough, you may find IS/IT managers and the
  project manager adopting this attitude; it's far less common to see the
  technical staff members accepting it as a reasonable way of doing business. In the best of cases, this "game" represents the strategy of "good-
  enough" software that I described in my *Rise and Resurrection of the
  American Programmer;*[3] in the worst of cases, it's as dishonest and repre-
  hensible as several of the other political games described above.

# NEGOTIATING STRATEGIES

What should you do if you find yourself becoming involved in one of the political
games described above? Equally important, what should you do if you're an innocent
bystander—for example, a technical staff member of the project team—and you observe such games being played all around you as the project deadline, functionality,
and budget are being negotiated? Thomsett makes the interesting point that we all
learn these political games from our mentors, our managers, and the "elders" of the
political culture in our organizations; thus, even if we can't escape the games ourselves, perhaps we can refuse to teach them to our subordinates, in the hope that the
whole process of political games will die out after another generation of two.

It's a noble thought, but I'm not so optimistic. I sometimes think that political
behavior is genetic, firmly imprinted on our DNA pattern. But even if it's not this bad,
the reality is that political games of the nature described in this chapter are all around
us; none of this is unique to software projects, and all of us have been exposed to variations on these games throughout our lives. Even if it *was* unique to software projects,
there's enough mobility within the software profession that an organization is almost

certain to "infected" by highly political managers, vendors, and marketing representatives over a period of time. Political games something are we have to accept as an unavoidable phenomenon and cope with them as best we can.

One thing we *can* do—this also comes from Thomsett's excellent article—is avoid getting sucked into the trap of producing an "instant estimate" for a project. The Spanish Inquisition game is the worst form of this, but there are many lesser forms that take place in the planning and negotiation for death march projects. Whether it's innocent or malicious, the project manager will often be asked for an instantaneous "rough estimate" for the time or staffing required for some aspect of the project; once it's been blurted out in public, it often becomes a hard, unmovable requirement for the project. So, in any situation of this kind, the manager needs to respond with a statement such as "I'll need a day (or a week or a month—or even an hour!) to make some calculations before I can give you an estimate. I'll let you know by email." There are obvious political advantages to being prepared in advance, so that you've already done the necessary calculations before you get hit with the questions; but that's not always possible.

And it's not always possible to avoid the demand for an instant estimate. Suppose you're sitting in a marketing presentation, and the client turns to you and says, "Okay, Harriet, suppose we eliminate the interactive Web browser portion of the system and agree to do the whole thing on our inhouse network, with 10 of our people added to your project team. How long will it take you to get the job done?" All eyes turn to you, and you can see the marketing manager squirming; you probably know from all the discussions that have led up to this question that the politically acceptable answer is, "Three months—no problem!" Chances are that you cannot say, "Gee, I don't really know; we'll have to go back to the office and run that through our estimating model. And I'd also have to interview your ten people to see what their skills are..."

In a situation like this—and even in many of the situations where you *do* have some time to put together a formal estimate—it's crucial to state your estimates in terms of "confidence levels," or a "plus-or-minus" range. If you have absolutely no data with which to construct a detailed estimate, and if the death march project involves completely new technology and unknown people, then it might be prudent to say, "The project will probably take between three and six months," or "I think we can finish in six months, plus-or-minus 50%."

Of course, most project managers are aware of this technique, and they may or may not be using it already. Deciding how large or small the "plus-or-minus" range should be is part of the science of estimating, and I'll leave that to the textbooks listed at the end of this chapter. For death march projects, it's important to keep in mind the *politics* of stating confidence levels during the negotiating process. The most basic political reality, for example, is that anything you say about a plus-or-minus range will be ignored by everyone else that you're negotiating with.

Thus, if you're sitting in a planning session and you tell the customer and various other senior managers, "We should be able to get this project done in six months, plus or minus 25%," everyone will write down "six months" on their note pad.[4] No matter how many times you say it, they'll ignore it; and when your boss feeds the information back to you, you'll find that your deadline is six months. The only thing you can do is *never* drop the plus-or-minus qualifier in any verbal or written statements, promises, commitments, or estimates that you provide. It won't eliminate the problem, but it will provide a cover-your-ass excuse if the project ends up at the high end of your estimate.

One of the readers of the draft manuscript of this edition of *Death March* made an interesting comment along these lines:

> The problem I have with "estimate" is that I understand the word to mean, "best assessment knowing what is known at this moment and what can reasonably be predicted about the future." From experience, what I have seen happen is that once an estimate is published, it becomes a rock solid commitment representing the maximum amount of resources needed to accomplish the project phase or the entire project.
>
> Analysts, programmers, and other technicians understand that an estimate is an estimate. Maybe the project manager understands that too. However, somewhere in the "higher" levels of management, that understanding is transformed, usually into the word, "commitment." Sometimes, prior to project kick-off, top management understands "estimate" too. However, once the initial dollars are expended, an estimate usually becomes a "you bet your job if you do not keep to your commitment."[5]

Unfortunately, there's an uglier aspect of the political negotiation when you introduce the plus-or-minus qualifier into your estimate: You'll be accused of uncertainty, wishy-washiness, weakness, or even incompetence. This is particularly common in the "Marine Corps" style of death march projects discussed earlier in this book. What senior management really wants is a firm commitment—a *promise* that the project will be finished on a certain deadline, with a budget of a certain number of dollars, and a staff of a certain size. This gives them the enormous luxury of (a) no longer having to worry about the problem for the duration of the project and (b) having a convenient scapegoat to blame if the promise is broken. An estimate that takes the form of "X months plus or minus 50%, for $500,000 plus or minus 100%, and with 10 people, plus or minus 25" eliminates that luxury.

Jim McCarthy, in his excellent book, *Dynamics of Software Development* [5], suggests that the project manager needs to confront this head-on and persuade the customers and/or senior management that they need to share some of the burden of uncertainty that the entire project team will be living with on a day-to-day basis. Thus, the project manager effectively says to the customer or the senior management group, "Look, I *don't know* precisely when this project will finish—but since I'm the project manager, I'm far more likely than anyone else in the organization to figure it out as soon as it *can* be figured out. I promise you that once I know, I'll tell you right away."

Only a manager with a lot of self-confidence, *and* the ability to walk away from the assignment, has the *chutzpah* to say something like this in the politically charged atmosphere of a death march project. The time to say it is at the beginning of the project; after all, if the customer and senior management do not respect your ability as a project manager, and if they don't realize that you *do* have a better chance of knowing when the project will finish than anyone else, then why are they putting you in charge of the project in the first place? Are you being set up as a scapegoat? Are you going to be a "puppet manager," with all the decisions being made by other political manipulators in the organization? If so, now is the time to get out!

Similarly, if you're a lowly programmer on the project team and you see political games like this, it may be a strong indication that your project manager (a) doesn't have the confidence to believe in any estimate that he puts forth, (b) doesn't have the backbone to stand up for himself and for the project team, and/or (c) has gotten himself into a political situation where all the key decisions will be made by people who are not directly involved in the project. Again, this is a strong indication that the project is doomed; and before you get too deeply involved, it might be a better idea to seek greener pastures.

Having said this, I'm nevertheless well aware that it's extremely difficult for the project manager to persuade the various "players" to share the uncertainty of the project schedule, budget, and staffing decisions. A savvy customer will indeed do this; a sophisticated IS/IT organization will recognize all of this as an aspect of risk management, which needs to be carried out in a blameless political environment; and human beings who care about and respect one another will agree that it's unfair to make one member of a group carry the ulcer-generating pressure of a high-risk situation.

# WHAT TO DO WHEN NEGOTIATING FAILS

In the discussion above, I suggested that if the project manager can't persuade the customer or senior management to share some of the uncertainty associated with the schedule or budget of a death march project, he should seriously consider resigning from the assignment; the same goes for technical members of the project team. But this is only one aspect of a "failed" negotiating process; what should the manager do, for example, if he is 100% certain that the politically mandated deadline of six months cannot and will not be achieved? What should he do if he is 100% certain that the project must have a minimum of three people, but management will provide only two?

I've mentioned the option of resigning a few times already in this book, and I realize that it's not a practical option for some software professionals; indeed, it's more likely to be a problem for the project managers than the technicians, for the simple reason that project managers tend to be five to ten years older and are thus saddled with the impediments of mortgages, dependent family members, half-vested pension plans, and so on. They also tend to be more insecure about their chances of getting another job quickly, while the younger, unmarried project team members are typically much more confident that they can land another job within 24 hours.

It's important to realize here that I'm not recommending resignation as a form of punishment or revenge. It's simply the rational thing to do when faced with an impossible situation and implacable negotiating adversaries. Life will go on; there will be other projects; and there will be other jobs. As Sue Petersen remarked to me in a recent email message:[6]

> I've learned something from my kids, and I think it applies to work just as much as it does to home life...I *have* to protect myself, my energy level, my emotional and physical health, my quiet-time, and my work time. If I don't protect myself, I won't have anything left for them anyway.

But there's another issue associated with quitting that needs to be confronted here: the issue of loyalty and the "social contract" between the employer and employee. Up through the 1980s, many software professionals worked in large organizations whose corporate culture involved an assumption of a "job for life." While it was never as strict or as explicit as in Japanese companies, most of the programmers and software engineers at the major banks, insurance companies, government agencies, and computer companies (such as IBM and DEC) assumed that in the absence of war, famine, or plague, they would continue to rise through the organization until they finally retired at age 65 with a gold watch.

Small companies have never had this kind of culture, and many software professionals *have* worked for small companies, especially as computer technology has become so inexpensive that even a Mom-and-Pop grocery store can afford a PC and a Web server. And those of us who have worked for consulting firms, service bureaus, and various forms of entrepreneurial, high-tech startup companies have always known that there is no such thing as a lifetime social contract.

Software professionals in large companies have begun to learn this, too, because the era of downsizing, outsourcing, and re-engineering has caused major disruptions and unemployment in our field. This has been exacerbated by mergers and acquisitions in the computer field and also in highly competitive industries where information processing is a major part of the workforce. When Chemical Bank and Chase Manhattan Bank merged in the mid-1990s, for example, senior management had to deal with the problem of merging two entirely different hardware environments, systems environments, and IS/IT management hierarchy. And as I mentioned in Chapter 1, it's *exactly* this kind of situation that led to many of the death march projects that took place throughout the 1990s.

The problem in many of these large organizations is that while the employ*er* has definitely changed the social contract, the employ*ee* has not reacted accordingly. Many software engineers who have put in 10 or 20 years of loyal service still assume that (a) the company will take care of them, and (b) they should stand by the company, no matter how unpleasant it might be. And "unpleasant" is the operative term for most death march projects: it's not fun sacrificing all of your spare time, working to the point of exhaustion, and coping with stress and political tension. So why do we do it? Because we've signed on for life, and we feel that ethical people should honor their commitments.

However, if the employer has invalidated the social contract, then all bets are off; it's crucial to re-evaluate the relationship and see whether it's worth continuing at all. I certainly don't advocate unethical, immoral, or even amoral behavior—but I see nothing wrong with limiting my commitment to an employer to a period of a year or two, or for the extent of a single project. An employer who says to the death march project team members, "Get this system finished by December 31st or you're fired," is essentially articulating the same kind of "short-term" social contract.

The threat of being fired—which certainly does occur in death march project negotiations—is only one form of "hard-ball" negotiating; threats of being bypassed for a raise or promotion are also common. But if the social contract has been abandoned, and if you're dealing with a hard-ball negotiator in a death march project, then you have the right to play hard-ball, too. And one of the strongest bargaining chips in a negotiating session is your adversary's[7] recognition that you're ready and willing to walk away from the relationship if the results aren't mutually acceptable.

If senior management threatens to fire you if the death march project fails, or if you don't accept the unrealistic deadline they've imposed upon you (which may be two different ways of saying the same thing), then you should be equally cold-blooded in your demands. You may not get them to budge on the deadline, but you can probably be much more demanding than otherwise possible when it comes to staffing your project; I'll discuss this in more detail in the next chapter. And you can *definitely* be more cold-blooded when it comes to ignoring or breaking the administrative and bureaucratic rules and procedures that would other guarantee failure for the death march project.

A variation on this is the old adage of, "Act first, apologize later." It may be a waste of time to "negotiate" a reprieve from the various bureaucratic restrictions that you've decided will hamstring your project. It's certainly worth attempting to do so, because an edict from a high-level manager will usually give you sufficient authority to circumvent or ignore the minions of administrators, committees, and standards-enforcers who will swarm around the project. But if you get a wishy-washy answer—for example, "Well, we're not sure it's a good idea for your programmers to move off-site and have two PCs in their office; we'll check with the Building Services Committee and see what they think"—then stop wasting your time. Just go ahead and do it!

If you're clever, you can probably find a way to circumvent many of the bureaucratic obstacles in such a way that it will take six months for the bureaucracy to notice and to mount an offensive; by then, your project may have finished (or failed) anyway. And if the bureaucracy does mount an offensive, be prepared to play hard-ball: after all, your project is now well underway, and management probably can't afford the risk that you (and the entire project team) will walk out the door and force the project to be restarted. There are two points to keep in mind if you choose this approach:

- You have to be prepared to have your bluff called. If the Methodology Police visit your project and throw a tantrum because you're not using the company's official methodology, you may well get a furious phone call from your boss's boss's boss. You need to be prepared to say, "Mr./Ms. Big Shot, we've decided not to use the methodology because it will guarantee failure. If you feel strongly about this, my team and I are prepared to resign today—otherwise, I'd appreciate it if you would leave us alone and tell the Methodology Police to leave us alone, too. We have work to do." *This won't work unless the senior manager truly believes that you and your team* will *resign on the spot, if pressed.*
- You have to be prepared to deal with enemies who will hold a grudge even if your project succeeds. In the scenario above, you've challenged the authority of the Big Shot manager; he/she won't forget it. You've embarrassed the Methodology Police and made it more difficult to impose their methodology on other victims; they won't forgive you. Indeed, you may have burned so many bridges that at the end of the project, you (and perhaps the rest of the team, too) will be so unpopular that you'll have to quit.

If resignation and "hard-ball" negotiating are not options in your death march project, then what should you do if the negotiating process yields unsatisfactory results? Very simple: Redefine the nature of the project, as suggested in Figure 2.1 in Chapter 2. In the early stages of negotiation, you may have thought you were beginning a "mission-impossible" project: Given adequate resources and a talented staff, you might have been prepared to accomplish miracles. But if you're given inadequate resources and brain-dead programmers, then miracles are not going to occur.

Indeed, it's more likely that you're being pushed into a kamikaze project or a suicide project; only as a variation of the hard-ball negotiating process described above could we imagine that the outcome would be the "ugly" style of project described in Chapter 2. In any case, the key point here is that the project manager has to believe in the possibility of achieving the project goals (e.g., deadline, required functionality, etc.) and must be able to convince the team members of the viability of those goals without "conning" them. As John Boddie [9] points out in a superb book on managing "crunch-mode" software projects:

> The project leader who cares about his people will not try to sell them a bill of goods about the project. He will be honest about the level of effort it will require and its chances of success. Programmers aren't stupid. The experienced ones will have a keenly developed sense to tell them when they're being "fed a line." Most of them won't be a party to project games because they know they are the ones who will shoulder the burden when the crunch comes.

And if the project manager has determined that the death march project goals are *not* viable, but the project has to continue anyway, then it's crucial that the manager explain to the staff members that they are signing on for a suicide or kamikaze mission. Some will accept the mission anyway, and it's important for the manager to understand what their reasons are;[8] but others will resign.

There's an interesting aspect of ethics here. As noted earlier, I don't advocate unethical or immoral behavior of any kind, but I also believe that the negotiations surrounding a death march project almost always force the project manager to deal with the owner/customer and/or senior management as an adversary. The members of the project team, on the other hand, are like one's family. More than just treating the team members ethically and professionally, the manager should feel the responsibility of "taking care" of the team, to ensure that they don't become innocent victims in the political battles. I'm indebted to John Boddie [9] for tracking down a maxim from Napoleon that expresses this thought more eloquently than I could on my own:

> It follows that any commander in chief who undertakes to carry out a plan which he considers defective is at fault; he must put forth his reasons, insist on the plan being changed, and finally tender his resignation rather than be the instrument of his army's downfall.
>
> —Napoleon, *Military Maxims and Thoughts*

# NOTES

1. From: Doug Scott, 100072,1276
   To: Ed Yourdon, 71250,2322
   Topic: Death March Ch2 Queries
   Section: The Cutter Edge [14], Forum: CASE - DCI
   Date: Thu, Jul 11, 1996, 4:46:20 PM
   Ed,
   > I'm going to be suggesting in this next chapter that the project

>manager be sure to identify .....
>Are there any other significant constituencies that I've missed?
I think simply identifying them is a good first step, and then you
need to understand why they would want the project to succeed. Many
don't care, and could thus get in the way. Opponents would stick
out like a sore thumb.
But my biggest single obstacle in deathwatch projects has been my
own management. I came to the UK in 1972, and moved on to big
projects almost immediately. I don't think I learnt anything about
running projects since that date (I learnt a lot about politics,
but that's something else). You need to understand your own management's negotiating stance, and if they love to play roll over, you
have to keep them well away from the project.
>2. How important do you think it is for _all_ of the project team
>members to be aware of the existence of these constituencies and
>whether or not they can be viewed as a "friend" or "foe" of the
>death march project?
This has to be managed. In any project, having an external focus to
push against does help to solidify a team. But you mustn't allow
this to stop them helping you. If you need this, I'd say you need to
keep it to single individuals. Deathmarch projects, because of
their size and importance, will usually attract hostility from surrounding people anyway, so it won't be too difficult to create an
enemy - the trick will be to make sure that your potential helpers
aren't all enemies as well.
> *    mission impossible: if we succeed, we live happily ever after
Done that. I don't think I ever classified it as a deathmarch, in the
way I'd normally think of one. But I did develop an ulcer, so... <g>
> *    kamikaze: the project may succeed, but it will kill all of us
Dunno. The certain death is so demotivating, I'm not sure if people
would continue. They'd probably rationalise it into another type of
project.
> *    ugly: the project manager is prepared to sacrifice any
 >      and all of the team members in order to succeed.
Well, I think this comes with the territory. It's part of being a
death march.
> *    suicide: the project has no chance of success, and we're the
scapegoats
Yes, this seems to be one of the fears with death marches.
I don't think I can go along with your matrix, in this case. True
death marches have some characteristics - there is a (possibly
remote) possibility of success; it's so tightly time-boxed that
success within the timescales is difficult to imagine, and one of
the pastimes is to watch announced deadlines being slipped while
still being aware of the need for further slippage.
Personal satisfaction is never high on a death march, and the
chance of success is low - I guess that's what defines a death

march. Most death marches fall into your suicide category, I'm
afraid. If you had high personal satisfaction and high anticipation
of success (which I reckon are correlated anyway), that's not a
deathmarch.

As I say, I believe the true differentiator lies in the timescale,
rather than in personal feelings. If the timescale is impossible,
then you *know* you're on a deathmarch. The only question then is
whether you die expensively or slowly.

> How important do you think it is for the project manager to get a
> really good assessment of each team member's level of commitment?

If anyone asks me that question nowadays, I know to run a mile,
because that PM will turn the project into a death march. I've
never had trouble getting people committed, once I've set up an
environment where that commitment will pay results. But I have seen
many environments where overtime is regarded as more important than
what you're doing (a friend who's just joined Oracle is replete
with that attitude now), and I'm not at all impressed by their output.

> _negotiations_. I'll deal with that in Chapter 3

Let me know. when you need stories here. Many are so unbelievable
that it's not worth even telling (such as "I don't mind you refusing changes to the design even if it is a fixed price project - all
I have to do is ring your chairman, and he'll always tell you do
it.").

Doug (back on OS/2 and GCP)

**2.** From: John Boddie, 73757,3311
To: Ed Yourdon, 71250,2322
Topic: DM Ch2 done, Ch3 queries
Section: The Cutter Edge [14], Forum: CASE - DCI
Date: Fri, Jul 26, 1996, 8:39:15 PM
Ed,

re: if you know of any good negotiating strategies (other than
blackmail and torture, which I can't recommend in a book like this
<g>), let me know.

The only leverage that the manager has is to bring the risk of
failure out into the open and as publicly as possible start postu-
lating fallback positions.

Some useful questions during negotiations,

"If the system is ready on the fifth of September rather than on the
first, will we already have declared bankruptcy September second?"

"Is there an 80/20 rule here? If we deliver the critical 20 percent
that gives eighty percent of the value, do we need the twenty percent at initial roll-out?"

"Everybody wants things good, wants them fast, and wants them
cheap. Everyone knows that you can actually achieve any two of the
three. Which two do you want?"

The principle at work is to make those who are demanding the death

```
march look unreasonable if they are unwilling to consider more than
one possible outcome. Unless there is an acceptance of more than
one way to approach the problem, then there is no negotiation. All
the manager can say is, "We'll give it our best shot, but there are
no guarantees."
JB
```

3. *Rise and Resurrection of the American Programmer*, Edward Yourdon (Prentice Hall, 1996).

4. Actually, the politically astute people will take your worst-case estimate and add another "safety factor" before reporting it to their next higher level superior. Your estimate of six months, plus or minus 25%, thus becomes nine months or a year. Unfortunately, the politically naive, or the politically ambitious, will do just the opposite. Thus, the CEO may end up being told that your project will be done in four months or less.

5. Bob Speth email, July 16, 2003.

6.
```
From: Sue Petersen (WWL), 102354,1624
To: Ed Yourdon, 71250,2322
Topic: DM Ch2 done, Ch3 queries
Section: The Cutter Edge [14], Forum: CASE - DCI
Date: Fri, Jul 26, 1996, 6:55:26 PM
>>Another important question I want to discuss in this chapter:
what should the death march project manager do when, in his/her
sincere opinion, the negotiations have failed? At what point does
the manager resign, throw a tantrum, threaten to become the next
Unabomber, etc.? And when he/she reaches that stage, what responsi-
bility does he/she have to the project team, which may have already
begun working? <<
I've learned something from my kids, and I think it applies to work
just as much as it does to home life... I _have_ to protect myself,
my energy level, my emotional and physical health, my quiet-time,
and my work time. If I don't protect myself, I won't have anything
left for them anyway.
Sue P
```

7. Some readers will probably object to the customer's, or one's senior manager's, being described as an "adversary." But the very nature of a death march project implies that the owner/customer, and the various shareholders and stakeholders, are pushing the project manager into decisions that he would not make on his own.

8. It's possible, for example, that a disgruntled staff member may see the death march project as an excellent way of wreaking revenge upon the organization—and he may join the project team in order to make *certain* that the project fails.

# REFERENCES

1. Tarek Abdel-Hamid and Stuart Madnick, *Software Project Dynamics* (Prentice Hall, 1993).

2. Barry Boehm, *Software Engineering Economics*, Prentice Hall, 1981.

3. Barry Boehm, Bradford Clark, Ellis Horowitz, Chris Westland, Ray Madachy, and Richard Selby, "The COCOMO 2.0 Software Cost Estimation Model," *American Programmer*, July 1996.

4. Frederick Brooks, *The Mythical Man-Month* (20th anniversary edition), Addison-Wesley, 1995.

5. Jim McCarthy, *Dynamics of Systems Development* (Microsoft Press, 1995).

6. Robert E. Park, Wolfhart B. Goethert, and J. Todd Webb, *Software Cost and Schedule Estimating: A Process Improvement Initiative*. Technical Report CMU/SEI-94-SR-03, May 1994. Pittsburgh, PA: Software Engineering Institute.

7. Robert E. Park, *Checklists and Criteria for Evaluating the Cost and Schedule Estimating Capabilities of Software Organizations*. Technical Report CMU/SEI-95-SR-005, January 1995. Pittsburgh, PA: Software Engineering Institute.

8. Rob Thomsett, "Double Dummy Spit and Other Estimating Games," *American Programmer*, June 1996.

9. John Boddie, *Crunch Mode* (Prentice Hall/Yourdon Press, 1987).

# 4 People in Death March Projects

*Everything really interesting that happens in software projects eventually comes down to people.*

—James Bach

*A general is just as good or just as bad as the troops under his command make him.*

—Douglas MacArthur, Speech, August 16, 1962

Gerald Weinberg, author of the first book acknowledging that software developers are human beings,[1] likes to say that there are three problems with every project: people, people, and people. Aside from being a generally wise observation, it has enormous relevance for death march projects: If you have the wherewithal to emphasize *only one thing,* in order to improve the chances of success on a death march project, most project managers would agree that that one thing should revolve around "peopleware." That doesn't necessarily mean that a tightly knit team of superbly talented people will always be able to overcome a combination of mediocre processes, obsolete tools, uncooperative users, hostile stakeholders, an inadequate budget, and an outrageously aggressive schedule—but in a world of limited choices, I'd rather gamble on a talented team that can cope with all of these obstacles than hope that sophisticated programming tools and a detailed methodology will enable mediocre developers to overcome such obstacles.

So, if peopleware is the first and most important focus, what should we do? There's nothing magic about it; basically, it means insisting on the right to choose your own team. It means expecting the team to work some overtime hours, but remembering that they're on a marathon, and they should only be expected to sprint for the final 100 yards. It means rewarding them handsomely if the project succeeds, but not dangling extravagant awards in front of them all through the project, for it will distract them. It *definitely* means focusing on building a loyal, cohesive, cooperative team; it's important to have the necessary technical skills, but it's even more important to have complementary psychological constraints. Basically, that's all there is to peopleware in a death march project.

Unfortunately, there's more to it for many death march project managers, for they work in organizations that have a miserable peopleware culture even for normal projects. Though it might seem that such a culture would doom a death march project to certain failure, it sometimes turns out that just the opposite is true: as noted in Chapter 3, the project manager may have to accept an unreasonable schedule or budget, but can sometimes retaliate by being equally hard-nosed about various peopleware issues. Thus, the manager might insist on—and get away with—the right to hire the right people for the team, reward them properly, and provide them with them adequate working conditions.

And for precisely that reason, the death march project will be perceived as a threat to those who want to maintain the bureaucratic status quo. As noted in Chapter 3, the project manager may be able to circumvent the peopleware restrictions with an edict from senior management, but must be aware that in doing so, he or she earns the permanent enmity of the Office Police, the human resources department, and various administrators. However, if the death march project is a tremendous success, it may prove to be a catalyst to change the peopleware practices for subsequent "normal" projects.

In any case, my mission in this chapter is not to change the overall peopleware culture in an organization. Much has already been written about this, especially in such excellent books as *Peopleware*, by Tom DeMarco and Tim Lister [1]; I've provided a list of additional references at the end of this chapter. The basic question addressed by this chapter is: If you're already familiar with the "basics" of peopleware, what's different about a death march project?

# HIRING AND STAFFING ISSUES

The first thing that's different about a death march project is the emphasis on forming the right team. In my work with software organizations around the world, I've seen four common strategies for creating a death march team:

- Hire superstars and turn them loose
- Insist on a well-honed "mission impossible" team that has worked together before
- Choose mere mortals, but make sure they know what they're getting in for
- Take whoever you're given and convert them into a mission-impossible team

The first strategy is tempting because everyone assumes that the superstars are enormously productive and also clever enough to invent novel solutions to the death march requirements. However, it's also a risky strategy because the superstars typically have super-large egos and may not work well together. And it's impractical in most IT organizations because management isn't willing to pay the higher salaries demanded by the superstars. And even if you *could* afford them, chances are they wouldn't be willing to work on a death march project in your company—because they believe your company and your death march project are too boring. Instead, most of them are working at Microsoft, or their own startup company, or wherever they think the really exciting projects are taking place these days.

The second strategy is almost certainly the ideal one for most organizations because it doesn't require superstars; it's also the kind of project team glorified by the *Mission Impossible* TV series. However, if your organization is embarking upon its first death march project, then such a team doesn't exist. And if there were previous death march projects that turned out to be suicide, kamikaze, or ugly-style projects, then the teams are probably no longer intact. Thus, a strategy of keeping a *successful* death march project intact usually has to be planned in advance as a corporate strategy, on the assumption that death march projects will occur again in the future.

The third strategy is the most common in the organizations I visit, for obvious reasons. Most organizations have no superstars, and they have no survivors from previous death march projects. Hence, each new death march project is staffed anew. The team members are competent and perhaps better than the average developers in the organization, but they can't be expected to leap over tall buildings in a single bound. What's vital in this scenario is that the team members understand what they're signing up for; even though they're mere mortals, they will be called upon to perform extraordinary feats of software development.

The final strategy is one to be avoided at all costs. If the project turns out to be a dumping ground for personnel that no other project manager wants, then it's almost certainly a suicide project. Again, this has been glorified by Hollywood, especially in movies like the 1967 classic, *The Dirty Dozen*; the theme is that outcasts and misfits can be motivated by a tough, charismatic leader (Lee Marvin, in the Hollywood version) to perform miracles that nobody thought possible. Well, perhaps so; but Hollywood doesn't tell us about all of the misfit-staffed projects that fail. It seems to me that if you accept the assignment of managing (or participating in) a project of this kind, you've accepted the fate of suicide.

This brings up the central issue of staffing the death march project team: To what extent should the project manager insist on the right to make the staffing decisions? As noted above, most project managers have to accept the fact that they won't be given a *carte blanche* to hire the world's most talented superstars; and politics within the organization may make it impossible for the project manager to steal away the best people within the organization, because they're already involved in other critical projects or fiercely defended by other managers. Nevertheless, there is one aspect that I believe the manager should insist on, as an absolute right: the right to *veto* an attempt by other managers to stick an unacceptable person onto the team. To do otherwise is to add an unacceptable level of risk to a project that's probably already overburdened with other risks.

Obviously, this can lead to a variety of ugly political battles. The project manager is likely to hear soothing statements such as, "Don't worry, Charlie had some problems on previous projects, but he'll be fine on your project," or ego-boosting statements such as, "You're such a terrific manager that I'm sure you'll be able to turn

Charlie around and get some real productivity out of him," or various appeals to loyalty, bravery, and assorted Boy Scout virtues. My advice is to stand firm and insist on the right to reject anyone that you don't think will fit well into the team.

One of the criteria that should be used in such a decision is the likelihood of the proposed staff member's leaving before the project finishes. Obviously, most software developers won't tell you if they're planning to quit mid-way through the project; but some of them *will* tell you about anticipated personal priorities—marriage, divorce, a prolonged mountain-climbing expedition to the Himalayas, and so on—that could rule them out of consideration. In general, it's crucial to avoid losing people in the midst of a death march project; and it's highly desirable to avoid having to add new people in the middle of the project.

In Chapter 3, I discussed the options available to the project manager if negotiations fail: Quit, appeal to a higher authority, ignore the rules and make your own decisions, or redefine the project as a suicide mission. The possibility of ignoring the rules is usually more difficult, because adding extra personnel to the project team has payroll ramifications that are beyond the manager's control. However, it *is* sometimes possible to "borrow" people from another project or perhaps even to hire some temporary contractors.

It's also possible to isolate an unacceptable team member who has been put onto the project against the manager's wishes; the unacceptable team member can be given a harmless subproject to work on or sent away to research the mating habits of African *tsetse* flies until the project is finished. Doug Scott[2] described an even more elaborate version of this strategy in a recent email message to me:

> Death Marches often end up in the desperate situation where senior management will throw money at you—"You want another twenty people?". And I always accept. I put the bozos onto manning the coffee machine, changing fuses, and other essential work, while I hang on to the better ones. (Randomly, you will get a few good ones). Then you can assist the bozos to resign and keep pressing for more and more people to replace them. In one case, I cut to 20% of the original staffing level, and still maintained work output—but the quality of that output was excellent. That's no surprise to anybody, but it's by constantly demanding more resources and losing them that you can achieve it.

# LOYALTY, COMMITMENT, MOTIVATION, AND REWARDS

I discussed the issue of *commitment* to the death march project in Chapter 2; it's an essential element of the politics of such projects, but it's also a key element in the team dynamics that the project manager must try to maximize. Ideally (from the project manager's perspective), the team members will swear an oath of loyalty and dedication to the death march project above all else; for the young, unmarried techno-nerds, this is not as ridiculous as it might sound. However, it depends heavily on such things as the length of the project: total devotion may be feasible for a three- to six-month project, but probably not for a 36-month project.

It also depends heavily on the ability of the project manager to motivate the team members to *feel* loyal and committed. To some extent, this is a matter of charisma: Some managers generate such feelings of loyalty that their team members will follow them to the end of the earth, no matter how risky the project—and other managers are so uninspiring that their teams wouldn't exert any extra effort even if the project's objectives were to save mankind from an alien invasion.

Of course, one could argue that the project manager shouldn't allow anyone to join the team unless he or she *is* highly motivated. One could also argue that the issue is irrelevant, because most software developers are already motivated; as Tom DeMarco and Tim Lister argue in *Peopleware* [1],

> There is nothing more discouraging to any worker than the sense that his own motivation is inadequate and has to be 'supplemented' by that of the boss... You seldom need to take Draconian measures to keep your people working; most of them love their work.

But there are levels or degrees of motivation; we might expect a software developer to exhibit a certain degree of motivation for a normal project, but death march projects demand a higher degree of motivation to sustain the team members through months of exhausting work, political pressure, and technical difficulties. And the project manager faces the practical difficulty of not knowing just how motivated the team members are when the project begins. As Doug Scott[2] puts it:

> You're assuming that he knows who these people are when he gets them. I've usually had them assigned to me before I know how good/bad they are.

In many cases, the biggest factors in motivation/demotivation will revolve around the dynamics of the overall team; I'll discuss that in more detail below. But there are two specific issues that also have a significant impact on motivation, which are usually under the manager's direct control: rewards and overtime.

## Rewarding Project Team Members

Things would be difficult enough if we could solve the motivation problem by dangling large sums of money in front of all of the project team members (and the manager, too!). But Frederick Herzberg [2] suggests that money is not the answer:

> Money, benefits, comfort, and so on are "hygiene" factors—they create dissatisfaction if they're absent, but they don't make people feel good about their jobs and give them the needed internal generator. What does produce the generator are recognition of achievement, pride in doing a good job, more responsibility, advancement, and personal growth. The secret is job enrichment.

This may be an accurate assessment for normal projects, but money does play a factor in many death march projects. Indeed, it may be an overriding objective for the project as a whole: many software startup companies embark upon frantic death march projects, hoping that they will be able to develop a "killer app" for a new hardware gadget and sell millions of copies to an eager marketplace. If the project team members have stock options and profit-sharing plans, then financial rewards are obviously a very large part of the motivational structure of the project. Indeed, many Silicon Valley companies deliberately peg their salaries at 20-30% below the prevailing market rates, but provide ample stock options and/or profit-sharing plans to motivate the members of their technical staff. The strategy is not only to increase motivation, but also to reduce the fledgling company's cash outflow, since salaries are often the single biggest expenditure for a startup software company.

Of course, there *are* legitimate, exciting death march projects for which money is irrelevant. A software developer who is offered the once-in-a-lifetime chance to work on the equivalent of curing AIDS doesn't need money; he or she will cheerfully agree with Steve Jobs' comment about the Macintosh project that "The journey is the reward."

At the other extreme, I find death march projects taking place in moribund government agencies where the project is intrinsically boring, and where there is no hope of increased financial reward for *anyone* in the organization. Salaries are determined by one's civil-service grade level, and the salary structure is fixed by law; there are no bonuses, profit-sharing rewards, or stock options. In cases like this, it's obviously silly to even discuss financial rewards as a motivator: all it will do is frustrate the team.

But what about the organizations that have flexibility? If the death march project is important enough to the organization, then it's not beyond the realm of possibility to set aside a significant bonus pool to reward the team if it succeeds in delivering the project on time. The possibility of bonuses comes up in normal projects, too, but the monies involved are usually much more modest. It's nice to get a bonus check of $1,000 at the end of a normal project, but the tax authorities usually take a third for themselves, and the remainder is not enough to have a noticeable impact on the lifestyle of a typical middle-income software professional. But death march projects are different: a $10,000 bonus check might be enough to buy a new car (albeit a pretty modest one these days!) or finance a vacation to Bali. A $100,000 bonus check is enough to finance a child's Ivy League college education, or to buy a house (or at least the down payment on a house). And a $1,000,000 bonus check is enough to make retirement a serious possibility.

Assuming that such a bonus is possible, here are a few observations:

- Remember that a 20% salary increase means much more to a junior programmer earning $30,000 per year than it does to a senior programmer making $90,000 per year. At the higher salary, the marginal tax rate is usually much higher, often as high as 50%; thus, the programmer doesn't take home much more, the salary issue is more likely to be regarded as a hygiene factor. For the junior programmer, though, the tax rate is still reasonably low, and the extra 20% might be sufficient to cover the monthly payments on the programmer's first car, or to justify moving out of his/her parents' home to a first real apartment.

- Remember that the possibility of large sums of money can motivate people in a variety of ways. Management may assume that it will simply make everyone work harder, but it can also make individuals excessively critical and suspicious of other team members—for example, a team member will complain bitterly, "George was so selfish that he took Christmas Eve off, just to be with his stupid family, right when we were at a critical stage of testing. He's gonna screw us out of our bonus!"

- Remember that the size of the bonus doesn't have a direct, linear correlation with the productivity or number of hours worked by the project team. I've watched senior management in some organizations attempt to bribe the death march project team by offering to double the size of the bonus— usually because the project is behind schedule and management apparently believes that doubling the bonus will double the number of work hours by the project team. But if the team members are already working 18 hours per day, the laws of physics prevent even the most dedicated effort from doubling the work hours.[3]

- For the bonus to work as a motivator, the project team has to believe that it really exists and that senior management won't find a devious excuse to withhold it. Obviously, if the rewards are associated with success in the marketplace—for example, if the project succeeds, then the company can go public, unless the stock market collapses in the fashion that we witnessed during the dot-com collapse—then there are no guarantees. But if the reward is entirely at the discretion of senior management, and if the team believes that previous death march project teams had been unjustly cheated out of their reward, then the "promise" of a bonus will probably be a *negative* motivator. Similarly, if the project team members conclude that they have little control over the successful outcome of the project—for example, because, in addition to their software, the project depends on new hardware being developed by an outside vendor—then they may view the bonus being promised by management as a "random lottery" rather than as a motivating device.

- The team must also believe that the bonus will be distributed in an equitable fashion. That doesn't necessarily mean that every team member gets exactly the same share, but if the team believes that the project manager will get the lion's share of the reward, and that they'll end up with the crumbs, then the results are predictable. This needs to be discussed at the beginning of the project; it's unlikely that the team members will be pacified by statements from the manager such as, "Trust me, don't worry—I'll make sure everyone is taken care of in a fair manner."

For the projects that cannot or will not consider extravagant bonuses, it's important for the project manager to remember that there is a wide variety of nonfinancial rewards that can have an enormous impact on the motivation of the project staff. Again, this is an issue that we frequently see in "normal" projects, but it's more important here because everyone is being stretched to his or her limits. It's also important to remember that the pressure of the death march project team is felt by the spouse and/or family members of the death march staffers; as Doug Scott[2] puts it,

> The first priority is to take pressure off your staff, so the first recipient of the rewards should be to the partner and family of said staff—it's all very well in career/money terms, but it's the family who have to make the sacrifices. Bouquets of flowers are a start. Support the whole family—they're the ones doing it.

While a bouquet of flowers is a nice gesture, it's sometimes more meaningful to provide "practical" rewards to the family members—especially the spouse who is left juggling all of the household and child-care responsibilities while his/her "significant other" is working 'round the clock on the death march project. A thoughtful project manager might check to see whether the spouse needs a taxi service to pick up or drop off a child from school, or whether someone from the office could pick up some groceries on the way home to help the spouse who is stuck at home with sick children. And if the children are *really* sick and need medical attention, the project manager will move heaven and earth—and utterly destroy any bureaucratic obstacles—to ensure that the appropriate services are provided, in order to minimize anxiety on the part of the death march project member.[4]

Of course, the examples mentioned above *do* require money; but it's usually a very small amount of money, and it can usually be covered in the "miscellaneous" part of the project budget. Again, the corporate bureaucrats will probably whine and complain if they find out about it, for such expenditures usually don't conform to officially sanctioned procedures. The project manager who caves in to this kind of pressure is a spineless wimp; if necessary, the manager should pay for such expenses out of his own pocket, since he's usually making a much higher salary than the technical staff members. In any case, it's the manager's job to deal with the corporate bureaucracy here; the last thing we want is to have the technical staffers wasting their time and their emotional energy fighting with the accounting department about whether it was reasonable to order a pizza with two extra toppings, rather than the economy pizza, for a midnight dinner when the team is working late.

Modest rewards of this kind throughout the project will certainly help; but what about nonfinancial rewards of a more lasting nature when the project finishes? I'm not thinking of promotions or new career opportunities here, for those fall into the same category as overt financial rewards. Here are some examples of rewards that might not be quite as motivating as a million-dollar bonus check, but would nevertheless help ease the pain of a death march project:

- *An extended vacation*—If the project succeeds, give the team members a vacation of the same duration as the project. Most of us aren't quite sure what to do with a two-week vacation—but if we had a six-month *paid* vacation, it might motivate us to take that round-the-world sailing trip we've always dreamed of. An interesting test: Try this idea out on your manager and watch the reaction. If it's something like "What?!? Are you nuts? Six months vacation for a six-month death march project?!? We'll give you a couple days off, but don't push your luck!" it will give you a strong indication of management's implicit belief that software developers are nothing more than indentured servants. Such an attitude speaks volumes about the organization's concept of a social contract.

- *A paid sabbatical*—When the death march project is done, assign the team members to a six-month stint on "Project X." Question: what's X? Answer: *anything they want it to be*. Rather than immediately being assigned to another death march project (or equally bad, an utterly boring non-death march project), the team members can look forward to six months of learning about Web services, or researching the latest wireless computing technologies, or even returning to college to get their Master's degree. You'll have to be a little creative about the "official" name for X in order to confuse the bureaucrats; something like "the advanced nimbo-heuristic strategic-forecasting ubiquitous nano-system" might do the trick.

- *A fully equipped computing environment at home*—Even though PC hardware has gotten much cheaper and we all have something set up in our
home office, it's usually not the most up-to-date equipment; many of us
have a sluggish machine purchased a few years ago, while the rest of the
world has raced ahead to a new generation of machines with twice the
speed and four times the storage capacity. The interesting thing about
death march projects is that they often accumulate extra computer equipment because management is often prepared to throw extravagant sums of
money into the budget on the theory that advanced technology will save
the project. If there is leftover equipment at the end of the project, give it
to the team members as a bonus; if an outright gift breaks too many bureaucratic rules, then loan it to them.

## The Issue of Overtime

If bonuses and extended vacations are a motivator, then overtime during the project
would normally be considered a "demotivator." But it's almost inevitable on death
march projects; indeed, it's usually the *only* way that the project manager has any
hope of achieving the tight deadline for the project. And, as noted earlier, it often occurs without any explicit requests from the manager: young, fanatical, unmarried team
members who are excited by the challenge and the advanced technology associated
with the project will happily work 60, 80, or 100 hours per week.

Nevertheless, overtime has to be managed properly in order to avoid demotivating the team and endangering the success of the project. One way to manage overtime
is to ensure that senior management knows how much it costs; as consultant Dave
Kleist puts it,[5]

> Unless stock options for the company are distributed to team mem-
> bers as generously as to senior management, there are no forms of
> compensation for a deathmarch that would qualify as a reward (I'm
> using reward as a term with a positive tone). While the PM rarely has
> this control over compensation, what really should be done is imme-
> diate compensated overtime in the next paycheck. This gives some-
> thing back to the people sacrificing the most for the project, and
> punishes (through the budget) the people who need to learn the
> real cost of a project (senior mgmt, etc).
>
> If you're going to do a deathmarch, it's best to get paid by the mile.

Regardless of whether or not the team members are being compensated for their
overtime work, the worst mistake is not recording the overtime, on the theory that
since the team members aren't being paid for it, it's "free." While this may be an accurate perception on the part of the accounting department, overtime is *not* free from the
project manager's perspective. Even if we assumed that all team members could work

18-hour days forever, without ever becoming tired, it's crucial for the manager to keep track of how many "invisible" overtime hours are being contributed throughout the project; this is the only way the manager can accurately gauge the productivity of the team and the likelihood of reaching each mini-deadline throughout the project.

And as everyone knows, people *can't* work 18-hour days forever; and even if they try, they get tired. When they get tired, they get cranky and short-tempered; they also work less productively, and they make many more mistakes. All of this has a dramatic impact on the progress of the overall project, and the manager has to know when to relax the pressure and when to ask for more overtime.

This may not seem so important for a three- to six-month project, when a young, energetic project team can work "flat-out" from beginning to end. But on longer projects, careful management of overtime effort is crucial; the effects of long periods of heavy overtime are insidious, but nevertheless quite real. As Doug Scott[2] suggested to me in a recent email message:

> ...part of scheduling deliveries is to ensure that the overtime comes in bursts and is then allowed to diminish—you can't keep people working at 90% and over for very long.

And as John Boddie [3, page 124] points out, it's important that the manager recognize that each team member will have a different tolerance for overtime work:

> Individuals have different metabolisms. Some are night people, others work better in the early morning. Irrespective of type, nobody's health is going to be ruined by working ten-hour days. Once the project gets rolling, you should expect members to be putting in at least 60 hours per week. If they're not, check first to see if there's something in the way the project is organized that's frustrating them.

> The project leader must expect to put in as many hours as possible. This is done for two reasons. First, he must provide an example. You cannot expect people to work overtime if you're not doing it yourself. Overtime must be led. Second, he must be there to answer questions, cut through red tape, and fix problems that come up during odd hours.

One of the dangers that the project manager must watch for is excessive *voluntary* overtime on the part of enthusiastic young software engineers who don't know their own limits, and who don't appreciate the potential side-effects of working when they're exhausted. As suggested by Figure 4.1, net productivity might actually *increase* during the first 20 hours of overtime work, based on adrenaline, concentration, and so on. But sooner or later, everyone reaches a point of diminishing returns; and at some point, productivity begins to diminish because of increased errors and a lack of focus and concentration. Indeed, there comes a point where the team member becomes a "net negative producer," because the rework effort caused by mistakes and defects exceeds the positive contribution of new software developed. Thus, assuming that the scale in Figure 4.1 is accurate (which it may or may not be, for any individual software developer), the manager will probably want to encourage the developer to work as much as 60 hours per week; the period between 60 and 80 hours per week is where the manager should begin letting the developer set his or her own limits; and beyond 80–90 hours per week, the manager should insist that the developer go home and rest.

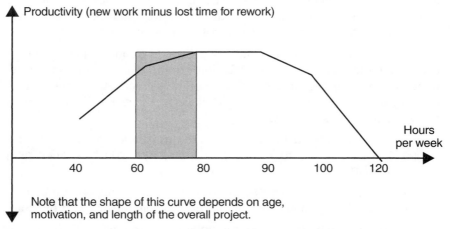

**Figure 4.1**   *Net Productivity Versus Hours Worked*

# THE IMPORTANCE OF COMMUNICATION

One of the important peopleware issues for death march projects is the nature and extent of communications between the project manager and the rest of the team. In my opinion, the ideal situation is one where the project manager has no secrets— everyone on the team knows everything about the project. This means that *everyone* on the team knows the *current* information about the project status, priorities, risks, constraints, politics, and so forth.

One reason for suggesting this is that it builds trust and loyalty among team members. If the team members are making extraordinary personal sacrifices on behalf of the project, it's usually very disillusioning to discover that the project manager has been withholding crucial information or has been playing political games behind the backs of the project team. And because death march projects tend to be intense and fast-moving, there's more of a chance than in normal projects that the team members *will* find out that information has been withheld or that political shenanigans are going on.

The obvious counter-argument to this philosophy is that the project manager should be buffering the team from distractions—especially the petty political games that surround the project on a day-to-day basis. In most cases, the team members will appreciate being spared all of the politics; but they also need to know that if they ask a direct question, their project manager won't obfuscate or lie to them. In most projects, normal or death march, there's a regular status meeting where questions of this kind can be raised; if the staff members are satisfied that they can find out what's going on whenever they need to, they'll be happy to concentrate 99% of their energy on their technical work.

Communication *between* team members is also crucial, especially in the unfortunate situation where the team members have not worked together before. It's crucial that intrateam communication be kept confidential (from outsiders) in order to encourage honest and frank exchanges of information. For most projects today, this strongly implies the need for electronic mail and various forms of collaboration tools along the lines of Lotus Notes. But in addition, the project manager should plan for weekly lunch, beer, or dinner sessions so that the staff members can interact with one another outside the normal office environment.

## TEAM-BUILDING ISSUES

Open, honest communications are an important ingredient in the process of building an effective team; choosing individuals who are compatible with one another is another key ingredient. As mentioned earlier, it's crucial that the project manager have the freedom to choose his or her team members, and it can be helpful to use techniques such as the Briggs-Meyers personality assessment tests to help anticipate how team members will interact with one another.

Yet another ingredient involves the concept of team *roles*. Many project managers focus on "technical" roles such as database designers, network specialists, user-interface experts, and so forth. But while these are all important, it's also important to think about the "psychological" roles that will be played by one or more team members. These roles are visible in "normal" software projects, too, but they are all the more crucial in death march projects. Rob Thomsett [4] has described the eight key project roles as follows:

- *Chairperson*—Controls the way in which a team moves forward toward the group objectives by making the best use of team resources; recognizes where the team's strengths and weaknesses lie and ensures that the best use is made of each team member's potential. As might be imagined, this person is often the official project leader; but in self-managing teams, it could be any one of the individuals.

- *Shaper*—Shapes the way in which team effort is applied; directs attention and seeks to impose some shape or pattern on group discussion and on the outcome of group activities. This individual may have the official title of "architect" or "lead designer," but the key point is that it's a "visionary" role. Especially in a death march project, it's crucial to have a single, clear focus on what the problem is and what the solution (design) should be.

- *Plant*—Advances new ideas and strategies with special attention to major issues and looks for possible new approaches to the problems with which the group is confronted. I like to think of this person as the "provocateur"—the person who introduces somewhat radical ideas and technologies into the group in order to help find innovative solutions to the technical problems confronting the death march team.

- *Monitor-Evaluator*—Analyzes problems in a practical manner and evaluates ideas and suggestions so that the team is better placed to make balanced decisions. In many cases, this person acts as the "skeptic" or "critic," thus balancing the optimistic proposals of the shaper and the plant. The monitor-evaluator is aware that new technologies don't always work, vendor promises about the features of new tools and languages are sometimes broken, and things in general don't always go as planned.

- *Company Worker*—Turns concepts and plans into practical working procedures; carries out agreed-upon plans systematically and efficiently. In other words, while the shaper is spouting grand technological visions, the plant is proposing radical new solutions, and the monitor-evaluator is looking for the flaws and shortcomings in those proposals, the company worker is the person who hunkers down in a corner and churns out tons of code. Clearly, a death march project needs to have at least a couple of these folks; but on their own, they may not bring the project to success because they don't have any grand visions of their own.

- *Team Worker*—Supports members in their strengths (e.g., building on suggestions), underpinning members in their shortcomings, improving communications between members, and generally fostering team spirit. In other words, this person is the "diplomat" of the team; he or she may be the project manager, but he or she could also be any one of the individuals on the team who happens to be a little more sensitive than the others about bruised egos and sensitive personalities. Again, this is often a crucial role in death march projects, because the team is often under a great deal of stress, and at least one or two of the team members is likely to begin behaving in an insensitive, "macho" fashion.

- *Resource Investigator*—Explores and reports on ideas, developments, and resources outside the group; creates external contacts that may be useful to the team and conducts any subsequent negotiations. I like to call this person the "scavenger," because he or she knows where to find spare a spare PC, an available conference room, an extra desk, or almost any other resource that the team needs. Such resources might or might not be available through official channels; but even if they can be procured in the "normal" fashion, it often requires filling out 17 forms in triplicate and then waiting six months for the bureaucracy to process everything. A death march project can't wait that long and can't afford to have all its progress brought to a halt because the vice president's administrative assistant jealously guards access to the organization's only available conference room. The team scavenger often has a network of friends and contacts throughout the organization from whom the critical resources can be begged, borrowed, or stolen; and the most important thing is that the scavenger *enjoys* this activity.

- *Completer*—Ensures that the team is protected as far as possible from mistakes of both commission and omission; actively searches for aspects of work which need a more than usual degree of attention; maintains a sense of urgency within the team. It's common to see this person taking on the dominant role during the testing activities at the end of the project life cycle, but it's just as important in the earlier stages, too. The team sometimes needs to be reminded—daily!—that it's not involved in a lifetime career, but rather a project with a hard deadline, with intermediate inch-pebbles that need to be accomplished in a timely fashion to avoid falling behind.

Unfortunately, even with all this effort, there's no guarantee that the project team will come together, or "jell," in a cohesive fashion. As Tom DeMarco and Tim Lister [1] put it in *Peopleware*:

> You can't make teams jell. You can hope they will jell; you can cross your fingers; you can act to improve the odds of jelling; but you can't make it happen. The process is much too fragile to be controlled.

If the jelling process is successful, there will usually be some visible signs. As DeMarco and Lister observe, successful teams typically have a strong sense of identity, a sense of eliteness, a feeling of joint ownership, and (at least on the "mission-impossible" style of death march projects) a feeling that they can do good work *and* have fun. On the other hand, while the organization may not be able to guarantee a successfully jelled team, it *can* cause what DeMarco and Lister refer to as "teamicide"—in other words, a conscious or unconscious decision to give up, and abandon all efforts to maintain a focused, cohesive team structure. The practices that typically lead to teamicide are these:

- Defensive management—Not trusting the team. Note that this is an area where the notion of a team "champion," discussed in Chapter 2, becomes essential.

- Bureaucracy—Too much paperwork. If the team has any sense, it will simply refuse to do the paperwork or will make vague promises to catch up with all of it after the project has finished.

- Physical separation of team members (e.g., in different buildings, different cities, different countries). Email, videoconferencing, and Web-based collaboration tools can obviously reduce this problem substantially, but physical proximity is essential to maintain the team spirit so essential to the success of a death march project.

- Fragmentation of people's time—Especially in situations where the team members devote part of their time to the official death march project, but another part of their time to maintaining an old legacy system, or serving on the committee for the company Christmas party.

- Quality reduction of the product—While the team members may be prepared to accept a certain level of quality reduction in order to deliver "good-enough" software on time, there is usually a threshold below which they refuse to go. The quality issue may involve defects (bugs), missing functionality, primitive user interface, or shoddy documentation,

- Phony deadlines—That is, deadlines so aggressive that the team has absolutely no faith in its ability to meet them. This form of teamicide usually transforms a mission-impossible team into a suicide team.

- Clique control—Splitting up teams when the project finishes. As noted earlier in this book, some teams find that the project they're working on is intrinsically boring, and the users to whom they deliver their software are ungrateful louts; so the satisfaction to be derived from the project comes from the pleasure of working with a certain group of people. Indeed, the satisfaction may be so great that the team members look forward to the prospect of continuing to work together on future projects. But ironically, the team spirit that made the team succeed is often regarded as a political threat to management; hence the common practice of breaking the team apart upon the completion of the project. This is turn is such a demoralizing prospect that the team may disintegrate even before the project deadline.

A final point about team jelling: Even when it happens, it doesn't happen on the first day of the project. As Robert Binder [5] observes, a typical team goes through a four-stage evolutionary process, which also applies to the vision-building process of developing a shared understanding of the application problem and the general structure of the solution:

- *Forming*: Team members define goals, roles, and direction of the team
- *Storming*: The team sets rules and decision-making processes, often renegotiates (argues) over team roles and responsibilities.
- *Norming*: Procedures, standards, and criteria are agreed upon.
- *Performing*: The team begins to function as a system.

In the ideal case, a project team may have gone through most of the "forming" and "storming" stages before the project even begins because the team members have worked together on previous projects. However, every project is different; and every project team usually includes one or two new people, which is bound to cause a certain amount of forming and storming. But whether the overall process takes a day or a week or a month, it has to occur; if at all possible, the project manager will try to get the team members assigned to the project well before the official "kick-off" date of the project, in order to be at the "performing" stage when the project officially begins.

It's also important to remember that even when a team has jelled, it can fall apart because of the pressure of the death march project. Dale Emery[6] recommends that the project manager keep a watchful eye on the team dynamics:

> Pay attention to the relationships within the team, and put some effort into maintaining people's ability to work together over time. A death march project creates tremendous pressure that can amplify small disturbances into major conflicts. Periodic check-ins to "take the temperature" of the group can help you and the team deal with relationship and communication problems while they are still small.

In the worst case, though, the team might never get past the first two stages; or to put it another way, the team may commit teamicide because of the various problems listed earlier. And by the time the project manager (or some level of management above the project manager) notices that teamicide has occurred, it's probably too late to form a new team. *C'est la vie.*

# WORKPLACE CONDITIONS FOR A DEATH MARCH PROJECT

The issue of decent offices—versus Dilbert-style cubicles—has been debated for so many years in the software development field that it seems pointless to bring it up again. Tom DeMarco and Tim Lister [1], whose work has already been cited numerous times in this chapter, have discussed the benefits of decent office working conditions at length in their *Peopleware* opus; software developers who say their workplace is acceptably quiet, for example, are one-third more likely to deliver zero-defect work than those who work in noisy office environments with uncontrollable interruptions. And in a survey of some 600 software developers, DeMarco and Lister were able to make a persuasive argument that those working in reasonable office conditions—with the ability to divert phone calls, silence the phone, close the door, and prevent needless interruptions—were approximately 2.6 times more productive than those working in the usual office environment.

Though DeMarco and Lister published their work in 1987, it doesn't seem to have done much to the workplace conditions for more software developers—*except in software-product companies.* The working conditions at companies such as Microsoft and many of the software product companies are civilized indeed: private offices with doors that close, access to kitchens stocked with soda, juice, and other beverages; and a "permanent" phone number that follows the programmer in the event that he or she is reassigned to a different office.

As for the software developers who work in banks, insurance companies, government agencies, manufacturing organizations, and the hundreds of other companies for whom software is still generally regarded as an "overhead" expense: Offices tend to be replaced with cubicles and the ability to concentrate on one's intellectual efforts ranges from poor to nonexistent. Stale Muzak wafts through the air, phones ring incessantly, dogs bark, people yell, and there is no way to prevent anyone from the mailroom messenger to the CEO from butting his or her head into your office to interrupt you. As DeMarco and Lister put it,

> Police-mentality planners design workplaces the way they would design prisons: optimized for containment at minimal cost. We have unthinkingly yielded to them on the subject of workplace design, yet for most organizations with productivity problems, there is no more fruitful area for improvement than the workplace.
>
> As long as workers are crowded into noisy, sterile, disruptive space, it's not worth improving anything *but* the workplace.

Unfortunately, my complaining about the situation isn't likely to have any more of an effect on the industry than DeMarco and Lister's far more detailed and eloquent discussion. But remember that we're talking about death march projects here: Different rules apply, and I believe that the project manager should adopt the philosophical position that *no* rules apply.

If you're a death march project manager with a nearly impossible deadline, then the message that decent office conditions can lead to a 2.6-fold improvement in productivity should be enough to motivate you to break *lots* of rules. Whatever you accomplish probably won't be permanent: As soon as the project is over, the Furniture Police will swoop in and re-assign everyone to the same miserable cubicles occupied by the rest of the staff. But if the death march project lasts only six months, and if you're clever, you might be able to provide decent working conditions without the Furniture Police even figuring out what's going on.

Here are some possibilities:

- *Frontal attack*—If you have a project champion and/or project owner desperate to get the project finished, explain to him or her just how important it is to put your project team into an effective environment. If the project champion is a high-level manager, it should be relatively easy to arrange a temporary transfer of the project team.

- *The "skunk works" mystique*—Most senior managers have heard of the notion of a "skunk works"; thus, rather than asking to locate your project team in the executive suite, where each office has its own private bathroom, ask for permission to relocate the team to an abandoned warehouse.

- *Squatter's rights*—Commandeer empty office space that has been sitting unoccupied while the Furniture Police try to figure out how many hundreds of people they can cram into it. Possession is 90 percent of the battle; while the bureaucracy complains, debates, and sends angry memos back and forth, you might even be able to finish your project and disappear back into the anonymous cubicles again.

- *Telecommute*—Tell everyone to work at home and arrange to have your weekly status meetings at the local McDonald's (at 9 a.m., the place is likely to be empty). It may take weeks for anyone to notice that the project team has disappeared. As an additional diversion, you can put scarecrow-style dummies at the desks normally occupied by the project team; management will have a hard time distinguishing them from the other zombies in the office.

- *Switch to the graveyard shift*—This is more extreme, but can be effective if much of the project work can be carried out without interacting with the user community. It's unpleasant asking everyone to change his or her work schedule to the midnight-to-eight shift, but it's virtually guaranteed to eliminate the normal interruptions. A strategy like this is sure to evoke the wrath of bureaucrats throughout the organization, but the wonderful thing is that the bureaucrats aren't in the office in the middle of the night! They'll send angry memos and email messages; the best strategy is to ignore them and pretend that you never received them. If that doesn't work, then simply refuse to change your schedule; unless they turn off the lights or change the locks on the office door, there's not much they can do within the duration of a typical death march project.

- *Barricades and buffers*—If your team is in a typical "open office" environment and the strategies discussed above aren't feasible, then do whatever you can to ensure that the project team members are located in contiguous cubicles. Then take whatever further steps are necessary to barricade that set of cubicles from access by the rest of the office herd. Disable the inter-com and the loudspeaker that blares noise from the ceiling (and be pre-pared to do so weekly, as the janitorial service will probably do their best to repair it). Unplug the phones or, as DeMarco/Lister recommend, stuff cotton into the ringer portion of the hand-set. If you can take over an entire floor or a whole building, so much the better. Erect a pirate flag atop the building, as Steve Jobs did with the Macintosh project team at Apple; in-stall a guard to shoo away unwanted visitors.

Some of these actions will provoke a more violent response from the corporate bureaucracy than others; the team and its manager will have to decide which strategy is most effective. But I want to emphasize that I'm serious about *all* of these strate-gies, despite the obvious fact that they violate the "rules" that one finds in almost ev-ery large company. Confronting the bureaucracy in this fashion is not for the timid; but by the same token, death march projects are not for the timid. If the death march project manager isn't willing to stand up and fight for decent working conditions, then why should the project team be willing to make extraordinary sacrifices on behalf of the organization and the project manager?[7, 8]

## SUMMARY

Talented people, cohesive teams, and decent working conditions are not enough to guarantee success in a death march project; but the absence of these elements is al-most enough to guarantee the project's failure. As we'll see in the next two chapters, good software *processes* and good technology are also important ingredients for suc-cess; but the most important ingredient of all is the people. As Ronald Reagan put it:

> Surround yourself with the best people you can find, delegate
> authority, and don't interfere.
>
> —Ronald Reagan, from *Reagan's Reign of Error*,
> "Mission Impossible" (ed. by Mark Green and Gail MacColl, 1987)

## NOTES

1. Surely you know what this book is: *The Psychology of Computer Programming*, first published in 1971, shortly after the invention of electricity and long before the Inter-net was anything more than a twinkle in anyone's eye. A "silver anniversary" edition was published by Dorset House in 1998.

**2.** From: Doug Scott, 100072,1276
To: Ed Yourdon, 71250,2322
Topic: Ch3 done, Ch4 queries
Section: The Cutter Edge [14], Forum: CASE - DCI
Date: Mon, Jul 29, 1996, 3:52:07 PM
Ed,
> 1. How crucial is it for the death march project manager to have
> the freedom to choose his/her project team members?
It's another aspect of death march projects that the PM usually has
no (or not enough) choice in the people. Having said that, it would
be a dream project indeed if you had all the people you wanted -
there just aren't enough good people to go around.
> should the project manager resign on the spot?
You're assuming that he knows who these people are when he gets
them. I've usually had them assigned to me before I know how good/
bad they are.
There is a counter-measure to this, which I have used successfully.
Death Marches often end up in the desperate situation where senior
management will throw money at you - "You want another twenty people?". And I always accept. I put the bozos onto manning the coffee
machine, changing fuses, and other essential work, while I hang on
to the better ones. (Randomly, you will get a few good ones). Then
you can assist the bozos to resign and keep pressing for more and
more people to replace them. In one case, I cut to 20% of the original staffing level, and still maintained work output - but the
quality of that output was excellent. That's no surprise to any-
body, but it's by constantly demanding more resources and losing
them that you can achieve it.
> 2. How should the project manager handle the issue of rewards?
The first priority is to take pressure of your staff, so the first
recipient of the rewards should be to the partner and family of
said staff - it's all very well in career/money terms, but it's the
family who have to make the sacrifices. Bouquets of flowers are a
start. Support the whole family - they're the ones doing it.
> 3. What about overtime?
In a death march, it's unavoidable, as you suggest. But part of
scheduling deliveries is to ensure that the overtime comes in
bursts and is then allowed to diminish - you can't keep people
working at 90% and over for very long. I've never been in an organisation which paid overtime, and I really don't like it - it smacks
of rewarding those who aren't doing well enough. Better to reward
those still standing at the end with bonuses - and that's counted
in months' salaries, not a pie and a pint at the local pub.
> what are the most important things for the manager to do in a
> death march project, vis-a-vis peopleware and teamwork?
Be there. Listen. Represent their views back to senior management,
and ensure that the trivia is dealt with quickly and efficiently.

```
Get the coffee, if that's all he can effectively do. Contribute.
> what are the most important things they should do for themselves,
> and for their fellow team-mates, during the project?
The same. Help each other, so that the work gets done in the quick-
est possible time. You might even get home early.
I note that I'm worrying a lot about married folk, but that's
because the spouses are often ignored in death marches, and I've
seen many a marriage (including my own) go west because of a death
march. It needn't be so, if managed well. Single folk have more
freedom to choose, and less reason to feel trapped.
Doug
```

3.  You might object that this is common sense, and no manager could be so stupid; this
    suggests that you haven't been reading enough *Dilbert* cartoons and that you've never
    heard of Will Roger's observation that "Common sense isn't common."

4.  During the height of the dot-com boom, many high-flying Silicon Valley companies
    took advantage of so-called "concierge" companies, which provided services for pick-
    ing up dry cleaning and groceries, shopping for birthday cards and anniversary presents,
    and other personal errands. Alas, the concierge companies were themselves dot-com
    operations, so the vast majority of them collapsed along with all the other dot-coms!

5.  ```
    From: Dave Kleist, 70730,1613
    To: Ed Yourdon, 71250,2322
    Topic: Ch3 done, Ch4 queries
    Section: The Cutter Edge [14], Forum: CASE - DCI
    Date: Tue, Jul 30, 1996, 9:55:08 PM
    Ed,
    >> 2. How should the project manager handle the issue of rewards? <<
    >> 3. What about overtime? While rational people might argue that
    overtime is not a good idea for "normal" projects, it's pretty hard
    to avoid in a death march project. How much should be expected? <<
    How much can be afforded? Unless stock options for the company are
    distributed to team members as generously to senior management, there
    are no forms of compensation for a deathmarch that would qualify as a
    reward (I'm using reward as a term with a positive tone). While the
    PM rarely has this control over compensation, what really should be
    done is immediate compensated overtime in the next paycheck. This
    gives something back to the people sacrificing the most for the
    project, and punishes (through the budget) the people who need to
    learn the real cost of a project (senior mgmt, etc).
    If you're going to do a deathmarch, it's best to get paid by the
    mile.
    - Dave
    ```

6.  ```
    From: Dale Emery (SL), 72704,1550
    To: Ed Yourdon, 71250,2322
    Topic: Ch3 done, Ch4 queries
    Section: The Cutter Edge [14], Forum: CASE - DCI
    Date: Wed, Jul 31, 1996, 5:21:01 PM
    ```

Ed,
>> 1. How crucial is it for the death march project manager to have
the freedom to choose his/her project team members? No one doubts
that it's important, but _how_ important? If senior management
says, "Sorry, but the only available people for this project are
Neurotic Ned, Moron Mary, and Zombie Zack," should the project manager resign on the spot? <<
Freedom to choose project team members is about as crucial as your
freedom to decide any other parameter of the project. Even if you
can't choose the schedule, you can still be honest about how that
schedule will affect other parameters. Even if you can choose the
project team members, you can still be honest about how their capabilities will affect other parameters.
>> 4. Aside from the issue of managing overtime, what are the most
important things for the manager to do in a death march project,
vis-a-vis peopleware and teamwork? <<
Always remember that the people working for you on the project are
exactly as important as you and your manager, and exactly as important as the project's customers. If you allow this balance to tilt,
and start treating the people on the team as if their needs are not
important to you, they'll very quickly get the hint. Then, guess
what happens to the commitment you wrote about earlier.
Pay attention to the relationships within the team, and put some
effort into maintaining people's ability to work together over
time. A death march project creates tremendous pressure that can
amplify small disturbances into major conflicts. Periodic check-ins
to "take the temperature" of the group can help you and the team
deal with relationship and communication problems while they are
still small.
>> 5. Same question from the perspective of the team members: what
are the most important things they should do for themselves, and
for their fellow team-mates, during the project? <<
Stay in touch with what you are giving up and what you are gaining
by working on the project. Check now and then to make sure the balance is in your favor. If it isn't, do something to get it back in
your favor. The key is to stay aware of what you need and what
you're willing to do to get it.
Remember that you are here by choice. Work on improving your alternatives to continuing on the death march project. It is marvelous
what having choices can do for your attitude.
Dale

7. On the other hand, one of the problem of tactics that are guaranteed to annoy the
bureaucracy is that key people outside the team may become reluctant to help you. As
Paul Neuhardt explained in a recent email message to me:

When it became obvious that we were lost in the desert, I kept things going for a
time with the old "We'll get things going again soon" speech. Before long, any

moron could see this project wasn't going anywhere, so I looked for a new approach. I tried "Hey, let's do it our way and to heck with management." This worked for awhile, but some of the key people we needed outside of the team were so scared of management that they wouldn't help us until we got the green light from the executive suite. Next was, "There's a management shakeup in the works. If we outlive the current managers, we can get back on track." Yeah, right. The faces changed but the song remained the same.

**8.** From: Paul Neuhardt, 71673,454
To: Ed Yourdon, 71250,2322
Topic: Ch3 done, Ch4 queries
Section: The Cutter Edge [14], Forum: CASE - DCI
Date: Mon, Jul 29, 1996, 10:56:27 PM
Ed,
I will confess here and publicly: I was a failure as a death march manager. At least, I think I was. The reason I say that is that eventually I lost the ability to keep my team motivated.
My experiences as manager of death marches are both what I described earlier as "Lost Patrol" projects. They might not have been death marches if we ever had a fixed target to shoot for, but with the goal changing daily we thrashed along forever with expectations from senior management high and our ability to succeed becoming increasingly low. I had built a team of people who genuinely believed in the project. The wanted to learn new technologies, broaden themselves and improve the state of the systems at the company. And, while bonuses for completing a project weren't going to be handed out, there were promotions, raises and prestige to be had, all of which motivated my team.
When it became obvious that we were lost in the desert, I kept things going for a time with the old "We'll get things going again soon" speech. Before long, any moron could see this project wasn't going anywhere, so I looked for a new approach. I tried "Hey, let's do it our way and to heck with management." This worked for awhile, but some of the key people we needed outside of the team were so scared of management that they wouldn't help us until we got the green light from the executive suite. Next was, "There's a management shakeup in the works. If we outlive the current managers, we can get back on track." Yeah, right. The faces changed but the song remained the same.
By this time I was probably the most disgruntled person on the project. I had not only been sent into the desert to die, but I had convinced several people I liked and respected to come with me. I was not only mad, I was guilty. Needles to say, when all you want to do is throw one rip-snorter of tantrum ending in the words "Take this job and shove it" it is pretty close to impossible to motivate people to keep marching. I know I couldn't find what it took inside of me. I found another job, apologized to the team for taking them into Hell with me, and left. In this at least I managed to lead by

example. Of the 10 people on my team one year ago, only one still works for that company.

Not that this is what you asked for, but I feel better for having gotten to say it. And no, I'm not paying you $150/hr (or whatever it is that shrinks get these days). I will, however, buy you a drink next time you are in Boston. Look me up.

# REFERENCES

1. Tom DeMarco and Tim Lister, *Peopleware*, Dorset House Publishing, second edition, 1997.

2. Frederick Herzberg, "One More Time: How Do You Motivate Employees?" *Harvard Business Review,* Sept.–Oct. 1987.

3. John Boddie, *Crunch Mode*, Prentice Hall/Yourdon Press, 1987.

4. Rob Thomsett, "Effective Project Teams: A Dilemma, a Model, a Solution," *American Programmer*, July–August 1990.

5. Peter R. Scholtes, Brian L. Joiner, and Barbara Streibel, *The Team Handbook*, (Oriel, Inc., 1996).

6. Rich Cohen and Warren Keuffel, "Pull Together," *Software Magazine*, Aug. 1991.

7. Larry Constantine, *Constantine on Peopleware*, Englewood Cliffs, NJ: Prentice Hall, 1995. ISBN: 0-13-331976-8.

8. Larry Constantine, *The Peopleware Papers,* Englewood Cliffs, NJ: Prentice Hall, 2001. ISBN: 0-13-060123-3

8. J. Daniel Couger and Robert A. Zawacki, *Motivating and Managing Computer Personnel,* New York: John Wiley & Sons, 1980. ISBN: 0-471084-85-9.

9. B. Curtis, W.E. Hefley, and S. Miller, *People Capability Maturity Model*, Draft version 0.3, Pittsburgh, PA: Software Engineering Institute, April 1995.

10. Tom DeMarco and Timothy Lister, "Programmer Productivity and the Effects of the Workplace," *Proceedings of the 8th ICSE,* Washington, DC: IEEE Press, 1985.

12. Tom DeMarco, *Slack: Getting Past Burnout, Busywork, and the Myth of Total Efficiency.* Broadway Books, 2001. ISBN: 0-76-790768-X.

11. J. Richard Hackman (ed.), *Groups That Work (and Those That Don't): Creating Conditions for Effective Teamwork,* San Francisco, CA: Jossey-Bass, 1990. ISBN: 1-555421-87-3.

12. Watts Humphrey, *Managing for Innovation: Leading Technical People,* New York: McGraw-Hill, 1987. ISBN: 0-135503-02-07.

13. Magid Igbaria and Jeffrey H. Greenhaus, "Determinants of MIS Employees' Turnover Intentions," *Communications of the ACM*, February 1992.

14. J.R. Katzenbach, and D.K. Smith, *The Wisdom of Teams,* Boston, MA: Harvard University Press, 1993. ISBN: 0-8754843067-0.

15. Guy Kawasaki, *The Macintosh Way: The Art of Guerrilla Management,* Glenview, IL: Scott Foresman and Company, 1989. ISBN 0-06-097338-2.

16. J.P. Klubnik, *Rewarding and Recognizing Employees,* Chicago, IL: Irwin Publishers, 1995.

17. Otto Kroeger and Janet M. Thuesen, *Type Talk: The 16 Personalities That Determine How We Live, Love, and Work,* New York: Bantam Doubleday, 1988. ISBN: 0-440-50704-9.

18. Susan A. Mohrman, Susan G. Cohen, and Allan M. Mohrman, Jr., *Designing Team-Based Organizations,* San Francisco, CA: Jossey-Bass, 1995.

19. Peter Senge. *The Fifth Discipline: The Art and Practice of the Learning Organization,* New York: Doubleday, 1990. ISBN: 0-385260-94-6.

20. S.B. Sheppard, B. Curtis, P. Milliman, and T. Love, "Modern Coding Practices and Programmer Performance," *IEEE Computer*, December 1979.

21. Paul Strassmann, "Internet: A Way for Outsourcing Infomercenaries?" *American Programmer*, August 1995.

22. Auren Uris, *88 Mistakes Interviewers Make and How to Avoid Them,* New York: American Management Association, 1988.

25. Rob Thomsett, *Radical Project Management,* Englewood Cliffs, NJ: Prentice Hall/Yourdon Press, 2002. ISBN: 0-13-009486-2.

23. J.D. Valett and F.E. McGarry, "A Summary of Software Measurement Experiences in the Software Engineering Laboratory," *Journal of Systems and Software*, Vol. 9, No. 2, 1989, pp. 137–148.

24. Susan Webber, "Performance Management: A New Approach to Software Engineering Management," *American Programmer*, July–August 1990.

25. Gerald Weinberg, *The Psychology of Computer Programming,* New York: Van Nostrand Reinhold, 1971. ISBN: 0-442-29264-3.

28. Gerald M. Weinberg, *Understanding the Professional Programmer*, New York: Dorset House, 1988. ISBN: 0-932633-09-9.

29. Mike West, "Empowerment: Five Meditations on the Soul of Software Development," *American Programmer*, July–August 1990.

30. Ken Whitaker, *Managing Software Maniacs,* New York: John Wiley & Sons, 1994. ISBN: 0-471-00997-0.

# 5  Death March Processes

*Methodology gives those with no ideas something to do.*

—Mason Cooley, *City Aphorisms,* Eleventh Selection

*Traditional scientific method has always been at the very best 20-20 hindsight. It's good for seeing where you've been. It's good for testing the truth of what you think you know, but it can't tell you what you ought to do.*

—Robert M. Pirsig, *Zen and the Art of Motorcycle Maintenance*
Part 3, Chapter 24 (1974)

If you remember only one word from this chapter—or for that matter, the entire book you are now reading—it should be *triage.* You might have assumed, from the title of this chapter, that I would be concentrating on familiar methodologies such as structured analysis, or formal process disciplines such as the SEI Capability Maturity Model (CMM), or various iterative/prototyping approaches generically referred to as "rapid application development" (RAD) and "eXtreme Programming" (XP). These are all important and relevant ideas, but the most important idea of all is this: *you don't have enough time in a death march project to do everything the users are asking for.* If you build your processes and methods around that sobering fact, you have a chance of succeeding; if you begin the project with the notion that coding can't commence until all the structured analysis data flow diagrams have been approved by the user, you'll definitely fail.

This doesn't mean that we should ignore all of the other process-related ideas and strategies. I'll cover them later in this chapter, but as you'll see, my general opinion is that they should be introduced as part of a *strategic* corporate decision, rather than foisted upon a death project team as a desperate tactical ploy to avoid what would otherwise be a failure. And the concept of triage applies here, too: If pressed, a death march project team will abandon what it feels is unhelpful or unessential (such as detailed business-process descriptions in a structured analysis model) and devote its resources to whatever it feels is most helpful. Similarly, a project manager who has only a few moments to read this chapter should read the most important thing, and skip the rest if necessary; I've organized the discussion in this chapter with that in mind.

## THE CONCEPT OF TRIAGE

The word "triage" comes from the Old French *trier,* which means "to sort." The *American Heritage Dictionary* (3rd edition) defines it as follows:

**tri·age** (trê-äzh´, trê´äzh") noun

1.  A process for sorting injured people into groups based on their need for or likely benefit from immediate medical treatment. Triage is used on the battlefield, at disaster sites, and in hospital emergency rooms when limited medical resources must be allocated.

2.  A system used to allocate a scarce commodity, such as food, only to those capable of deriving the greatest benefit from it.

Most of us are familiar with the medical connotation of triage, but the second dictionary definition is more relevant for our discussion of death march projects: allocating a scarce commodity (the scarcest of which is usually *time*) in such a way as to derive the greatest benefit from it. Or, as Stephen Covey puts it in *First Things First*, "the main thing is to make sure that the main thing *is* the main thing." (Covey's book focuses heavily on how best to manage one's time, which we'll discuss in more detail in Chapter 8).

Most prototyping and RAD/XP strategies are compatible with triage, and a few even mention the concept explicitly. But the emphasis in most RAD approaches is simply to get something—anything!—working quickly so that it can be demonstrated to the user in order to (a) demonstrate that tangible progress has been made, and (b) solicit feedback on the functionality of the system and (mostly) on the user interface. That's all very useful, but if the project team has devoted its resources to building initial prototypes with "sexy" but nonetheless nonessential features, then the team *and* the user are wasting their time.

The reason for this is because of the subtle but insidious assumption made by most software engineering methodologies—whether they are based on the classical "waterfall" life cycle, or the more recent "spiral" and prototyping methodologies. The assumption is, "Somehow, we'll get it *all* done by the time the deadline arrives." Perhaps this is because many of us grew up in households where we were told by our parents that we had to finish *everything* on our plates before we could leave the dinner table; in any case, the unspoken motto of many project teams is, "We will leave no requirement unfulfilled."

A noble motto indeed, but almost always unachievable in a death march project. As I mentioned in Chapter 1, most death march projects have "official" requirements that exceed the team's resources—specifically people-resources and time-resources—by 50–100 percent. The response by the naive death march project team is to hope that by working double overtime, the deficit can somehow be overcome; the response by the cynical "suicide mission" team is to assume that the project will be 50–100 percent behind schedule, just like every other project. But even the cynical team is usually wrong, for they still assume that sooner or later (usually *much* later!) they'll eventually implement all of the functionality requested by the user.

The key point about death march projects is that not only will some requirements remain unfulfilled when the official deadline arrives, but some of them *will never be implemented.* Assuming that the familiar "80-20" rule holds true, the project team might be able to deliver 80 percent of the "benefit" of the system by implementing 20 percent of the requirements—*if* they implement the right 20 percent. And since the user is often desperate to put the system into operation far earlier than the project team thinks reasonable, the user might take that 20 percent, begin using, and never bother asking for the remaining 80 percent of the system's functionality.

This is extreme and simplistic, of course, but in virtually all of the death march projects that I've been involved with, it made enormous good sense to separate the system requirements, triage-style, into "must-do," "should-do," and "could-do." The meaning of these three terms is obvious, and the fact that there are only three prevents the irrelevant squabbles as to whether a specific requirement should be categorized as a "priority-6" or "priority-7" requirement. Having performed such a triage, the obvious project strategy is to focus on the "must-do" requirements first; if there is time left over, then focus on the "should-do" requirements; and if a miracle occurs, then work on the "could-do" requirements.

Failure to follow such a strategy *from the beginning of the project* usually leads to an ugly crisis toward the end of the project; in addition to the nasty politics, it also produces what my colleague Dean Leffingwell refers to as "wasted inventory." To understand why, consider what happens at the beginning of a typical death march project: Nobody is willing to admit that the schedule is unrealistic, least of all the key users and senior management! The project manager and the team members may have a bad feeling in the pit of their stomach that they've embarked upon a suicide mission, but if they're optimistic they may believe that it will be a "mission impossible" project where a miracle saves them later on. The key point here is that the deadline is far enough away—typically six months or a year—that nobody has to face up to the reality that the objectives are impossible.

Indeed, the political pressures and the team's naiveté may even prevent a reassessment mid-way through the project. Ironically, the problem is often compounded if the project team members have been following some form of RAD/prototyping approach, for they've probably demonstrated one or more prototype versions of the system to the user, which can prolong the illusion that everything will be done on time. But by now, the project team members are probably beginning to realize that they're in over their heads; and if it's the manager's first death march project, he often has the naive belief that senior management and the user will eventually come to their senses.

Alas, things don't usually work out that way. An "ugly crisis" finally occurs when the user and/or senior management finally has to face the undeniable reality that despite the demands and despite the sincere promises from the project manager, the system is not going to be delivered on time. This often occurs a month before the deadline, sometimes a week, sometimes the day before the official deadline! Depending on how the political battles have been proceeding up to this point and on how exhausted and frustrated the project manager has become, there are several possible outcomes. What often happens is that senior management concludes that the entire problem is the fault of the project manager; that hapless individual is summarily fired (if he hasn't quit already!) and a new project manager is brought in with blunt instructions to "Clean this mess up and get the system delivered."

The replacement manager may be a battle-scarred veteran from within the organization or perhaps a consultant from the outside. And sometimes the new manager *does* find that his predecessor made a number of basic management mistakes (e.g., no schedule at all, or no work breakdown schedule); sometimes, the new manager's 20-20 hindsight concludes that the original manager was basically doing the right things, but couldn't avoid becoming the sacrificial scapegoat when senior management finally had to accept the fact that its original demands were impossible to achieve.

Whatever the assessment, one thing is almost certain: The replacement project manager has to address the fact that the complete set of project requirements cannot be finished in time for the original deadline—if that weren't the case, the original project manager probably wouldn't have been fired in the first place. So what does the replacement manager do? The two most obvious options are

- Renegotiate the deadline
- Renegotiate the requirements for the system

The first option might be acceptable, but it's unlikely in a death march project: After all, the reason the users were asking for an unreasonable schedule in the first place is that they desperately need the system to cope with some business demand. And since the negotiation being carried out by the replacement project manager is taking place at a point in time relatively close to the original deadline, there's a good chance that the user community has already begun making plans of its own to put the new system into operation. The last thing they want to hear is that it's going to be delayed another six to 12 months.

Thus, the most common—and successful—negotiating ploy involves a triage of the original requirements. Note that the replacement project manager is negotiating from a position of strength: it's not his fault that the project is in such a mess, and there's an unspoken awareness that management and the users were pretty stupid to have gotten themselves into this situation in the first place. The new project manager may even base his acceptance of the assignment on a successful outcome of the nego- tiations—for example, with a statement like, "If you want me to take over this disas- trous project, then you're going to have to accept the fact that we can deliver only a small percentage of the original functionality in time for your deadline. That's the sit- uation; take it or leave it."

So far, all of this is fairly straightforward—even though it's discouraging, as a consultant, to see it happening over and over again. But this is where my colleague, Dean Leffingwell, asks the question, "What about the inventory?" That is, what about all of the work-in-progress created by the project team *before* the "ugly crisis" oc- curred and the new project manager took over? Chances are that the project team had written a lot of code and maybe some test cases; they might have had some documen- tation, and some design models, and some structured analysis models. What happens to all of that "inventory" of partially completed work? The sobering answer: Most of it gets thrown away.

This might seem like an unnecessarily pessimistic statement. After all, why not simply put all of that partly finished work aside, and return to it later on? In the best of all worlds, this is exactly what happens; but it presumes the existence of a good set of tools and processes for version control, configuration management, source code con- trol, and so on—all of which are often abandoned in the heat of battle, when the team is concentrating on producing as much output as possible.

But the real reason why all of this partially completed work ends up being wast- ed inventory is that *no one will ever have time to come back to it.* Assuming that the project team (now under the control of a new manager, whom it may or may not re- spect) is able to deliver the "bare minimum" of critical functionality, it's usually so exhausted that half the staff quits. And the users are so disgusted with the project that they never bother asking for the rest of the unfinished functionality; or conversely, they're so satisfied with the minimal functionality that they never bother asking for the rest of the system. Even if they do, and even if the original team is still intact, there's a good chance that so many architectural changes were made in the attempt to deliver a "bare-bones" system that the half-finished pieces of work (which relate to noncritical requirements) can no longer be used.

Note that none of this discussion has anything to do with structured analysis or the SEI-CMM or any of the other "textbook" forms of methodologies and software processes. It's just common sense; but it's *critical* common sense in a death march project. For it to work, *all* of the shareholders and stakeholders have to agree as to which requirements fall into the "must-do" category, which ones are "should-do," and which ones are "could-do" requirements. Obviously, if the project owner categorically insists that *all* of the requirements are "must-do" items and that nothing falls into the other two categories, this whole discussion is a waste of time.[1] And if the various shareholders and stakeholders cannot reach a consensus about the triage items, then the project team will be paralyzed, attempting to do everything for everybody when they lack the resources to do so.

Unfortunately, the "ultimate reality" is that most organizations lack the discipline, experience, or political strength to deal with these issues at the beginning of the project. Nothing that I've described in the preceding paragraphs is "rocket science," and even the most technologically illiterate manager or business user can understand the issues; indeed, they would apply just as well to *any* kind of project that has to cope with limited resources and inadequate time. But even though everyone understands the issues intellectually, the political battles surrounding death march projects make it almost impossible to reach a consensus on a reasonable triage. It's only when the "ugly crisis" occurs that the various parties finally agree on something that they *should* have agreed upon when the project began.

The exception to this gloomy prognosis is the organization that has adopted death march projects as a way of life. Obviously, users and senior managers are not stupid, and they usually do learn from their experiences—even if it takes three or four disasters for the lessons to sink in. As mentioned above, the original death march project manager is usually a victim of the inability to perform an early triage, but the survivors gradually figure out what it's all about.

# THE IMPORTANCE OF REQUIREMENTS MANAGEMENT

The discussion above suggests that death march projects need to focus on a new aspect of the system development life cycle: *requirements*. Why do I say "new"? After all, every project has requirements and it's not as if software developers are completely unaware of the concept.

But traditional software engineering methodologies—including the various "structured" and "object-oriented" methodologies that several of my colleagues and I have developed over the past 20 years—have concentrated on *modeling* the requirements, usually with graphical techniques such as data flow diagrams or entity-relationship diagrams. What I'm talking about in this chapter is *managing* the requirements during the hectic days of a death march project.

These two concepts—modeling and managing—are not contradictory or incompatible. You can devote time and energy to both of them; if a death march project team finds that it's helpful to draw object-oriented analysis models to form a better understanding of the requirements of their system, I have no objection. My only caveat is that the team should do what *it* thinks important and helpful, not what the Methodology Police think is the "proper" way to do things.[2]

But my experience has been that the majority of death march projects do *not* use formal modeling techniques such as Structure Analysis/Structured Design (SA/SD) or Object Oriented Analysis/Design (OOA/OOD). Sometimes it's because they think these methodologies are too cumbersome and bureaucratic; sometimes it's because they think the CASE tools that support them are too clumsy; and often it's because they don't see an automated means of translating their analysis models into working code which, they realize, is the *only* thing the user cares about.[3]

Indeed, in the extreme case, the project team won't create *any* documents of the user requirements; their defense (which every project manager has heard by now!) is that it takes too long and is too susceptible to change, and besides, the users don't really know what they want anyway. Thus, the team typically relies on prototyping tools and methods, not only to produce the all-important visible evidence of progress throughout the death march schedule, but also to elicit the true requirements of the system.

From the "triage" perspective of this chapter's first section, there's one major problem with this: it doesn't give us an organized way to *manage* the requirements. At any moment in time, how can we tell which requirements are "must-do," which ones are "should-do," and which ones are "could-do"? It's interesting to note that the SA/SD and OOA/OOD methodologies don't focus on this either; one could document the prioritization decisions by color-coding the bubbles in a data-flow diagram, but that's not what the diagram was originally intended for. SA/SD and OOA/OOD are intended more for *understanding* the requirements and *explaining* the requirements than for managing them in a dynamic fashion.

It's the *dynamic* element of requirements management that usually causes the difficulties. If we could get all of the shareholders and stakeholders to agree on the triage priorities at the beginning of the project, and if those priorities never changed throughout the duration of the project .... well, if you believe *that*, then surely you believe that elephants can fly. What happens in *real* death march projects is usually a combination of the following dilemmas:

- The shareholders and stakeholders can't agree completely on the triage priorities. Of course, if they are in total disagreement, the project is paralyzed; but it's not uncommon to see 80 percent of the requirements prioritized, and then the project commences while the politicians continue to squabble about the remaining 20 percent. High-priority requirements sometimes emerge at the last moment from this squabbling; it drives the project team nuts, but that doesn't prevent it from happening.

- Circumstances change *within* the team as the project continues. For example, the project manager arrives in the office one morning and discovers that his two best programmers, Matilda and Ezekiel, have decided to form a reggae band and have just left for Nashville to seek a recording contract.

These things aren't supposed to happen, but they do. The manager's first three questions are, "What 'must-do' requirements were those two scoundrels working on, and what was the status of those requirements, and to whom can I re-assign them?"

- Circumstances change *outside* the project team. Budgets are expanded or reduced, depending on the company's financial fortunes. Deadlines are moved up or moved back (though hardly ever back!) as the marketing department becomes aware of changes in the competitive situation in the marketplace. Government regulations change, technology changes (not always for the better!), suppliers come and go, *ad nauseam*. Each of these external events is likely to have some impact on the triage decisions.

- There is often a "moment of truth" when the users, senior management, and project team members have to admit that they won't finish the system in time. Of course, if they have done a good job of triage prioritization at the beginning of the project, this crisis might not occur at all; but what if the team has to confess that it can't even finish all of the "must-do" requirements in time for the deadline? As noted earlier, the original project manager is usually beheaded and a replacement is brought in; and if the new manager can extend the deadline, then the triage decisions may not have to be changed. But it's also common at this point to see a hard-nosed re-evaluation of those early triage decisions. With the deadline looming only a few weeks away, the users might be forced to admit that some requirements they had earlier described as *absolutely* essential are not so essential after all.

I could continue with these scenarios, but you get the point: Managing the priority of requirements is a critical part of the "process" of death march projects. Now, this would be a straightforward activity if a death march project only had a dozen requirements; we could scribble them on a paper napkin and simply review them whenever necessary. But most projects have hundreds of requirements, and many have thousands; the Boeing 777 aircraft (which could be regarded as a bunch of software with wings) is rumored to have had 300,000 requirements. Not only that, the requirements usually can't be treated as independent, standalone items; some requirements are dependent on other requirements, and some requirements spawn (or are further described by) subrequirements.

This implies the need for methods, processes, and tools for representing the relationships between requirements, and for managing large quantities of relationships. And in this area, familiar techniques such as structured analysis and object-oriented analysis *do* help; unfortunately, those techniques have traditionally ignored the *attributes* of a requirement, such as priority, cost, risk, schedule, owner, and the developer to whom it has been assigned. As a result, the project teams that have been aware of the need for managing their requirements have used home-grown tools based on spreadsheets, word processors, or jury-rigged 4GL databases to provide some degree of automation support.

Fortunately, a new breed of software tools is emerging to provide a more comprehensive and sophisticated degree of support; among the tools now available are Requisite Pro (from Rational Software, now part of IBM), DOORS (from Zycad Corp.), and RTM (from Marconi Systems). Since this chapter is concerned with processes rather than tools, I won't go into the details of these three products; but since tools *affect* processes, it's important that you know they exist.[4]

There is one aspect of the process-tool combination that deserves special mention here. As noted earlier, many death march project teams abandon formal SA/SD or OOA/OOD because they feel it's too bureaucratic and time-consuming. Interestingly, the shareholders and stakeholders feel the same way. Given their choice, they prefer not to be forced to learn how to read data flow diagrams; indeed, the higher level echelons of managers and end-users complain that they don't understand all of those "technical" diagrams. They also have little patience for wading through hundreds of pages of diagrams and meticulous details about data element definitions or process specifications. With enough time and patience, the project team can overcome the resistance and persuade the end-users that the elaborate models are useful indeed—but in death march projects, there is very little time and very little patience.

What the users *can* understand is their own native language—for example, English is used for most North American projects. And what they *are* willing to read is a terse document of 10–20 pages that summarizes the requirements for the system. The requirements may be referred to as "features" in such a document, and the overall document may be known as a "Product Requirements Document" (PRD) or "high-level specification" or some other convenient phrase. But the key point is that it's English, it's terse, and it's to the point; it shouldn't contain a lot of marketing "fluff," and it shouldn't have obscure terminology or notation that makes key users stop and ask, "What on earth does *this* mean?" Ideally, each paragraph, or even each individual sentence, should be directly related to a requirement that both users and project team members can use as a starting point for their subsequent work.

The interesting thing about this is that we already have a familiar tool for creating such requirements documents; it's called a "word processor." Indeed, it's interesting that the initial version of such documents often emerges from the user's world— for example, in the form of a memo from the marketing VP to the CEO about the need for a sexy new Widget product with features X, Y, and Z to compete against the Whizbang product from Blatzco Inc.—even before the IS/IT department hears about it. At this early stage, the users view the word processor as *their* tool, and they view the marketing memo as *their* document; as a result, they're usually far more willing to participate in subsequent discussions about triage prioritization if the same tools and documents can continue to be used. Thus, we're beginning to see a shift towards *document-centric* requirements management, where the tools used by the IS/IT specialists (e.g., Requisite, DOORS, or RTM) are tightly integrated with the word-processing tools and documents that the users understand.[5]

One last point about all of this: It's essential that *all* of the shareholders and stakeholders be involved in the process of creating the initial requirements document and carrying out the triage prioritization. This is true for all projects, of course, but the time-pressure and political squabbles associated with death march projects often tempt the project manager into thinking, "Well, we'll just forge ahead without that idiot Melvin in marketing; all he'll do is disagree with everything, anyway..." The problem is that Melvin often turns out to have some significant political clout, and if he feels he's being ignored (and that the project manager thinks he's an idiot!), he'll probably find a way to sabotage the project.

In theory, everyone understands and agrees with this point—but in practice, it's amazing to see how many requirements sneak into death march projects. Additional requirements, modifications to existing requirements, and not-so-subtle suggestions to ignore certain requirements—all of these will come in "over the transom" to the project team, in the form of conversations, email messages, and one-on-one meetings with the project manager. Many of these suggestions will be prefaced by such smooth words as, "Sorry I didn't think about bringing this up in our meeting last week, but..." or "I wish we had time to run this new requirement by the formal steering group, but..."

Whether the project manager has a formal steering group—in other words, a group that represents the shareholders and stakeholders, reviews the progress of the project, and makes the definitive decisions about triage priorities—is something I won't comment on; this depends on each organization's style of managing and running projects. But what *is* essential for the survival of the death march project is that the modifications to the original requirements "baseline" be documented and made publicly visible for all of the shareholders and stakeholders to see. If the VP of finance wants to slip a new high-priority requirement into the project, that's fine; but the project manager should ensure that the VP of marketing and the CEO can see that it's there.

# SEI, ISO-9000 AND FORMAL VERSUS INFORMAL PROCESSES

Some project managers might read the preceding section of this chapter and complain, "Wow! That sounds *much* more formal than anything we've ever done!" Having encountered such a reaction in some consulting engagements, I'm often stymied. On the one hand, I believe that the documentation, prioritization, and management of requirements are essential (regardless of what tools or techniques are used to accomplish the task). On the other hand, I worry that if an entirely new, alien process is introduced to a project team that already has more than it can handle, the new concept—for example, requirements management—may turn out to be the straw that breaks the camel's back.

Indeed, I don't have a good answer for this dilemma other than hoping that perhaps the project team will be able to manage *one* new idea among its collection of tools and processes. But I worry even more when I see teams embarking upon a death march project with the decision (or more commonly, the edict foisted upon them by the Methodology Police) that they *must* embrace a formal process approach such as the SEI-CMM or ISO-9000. Formal processes are great if you know what you're doing and if you've used the processes before. But the reality is that such formal processes typically *haven't* been used at all in the organization; the death march project is the pilot project for structured analysis or ISO-9000.

What insanity! It really *is* the straw that breaks the camel's back; after all, the typical death march project is trying to do something that's never been done before, and (despite my warnings in Chapter 4) the team often consists of people who have never worked together before. As if that wasn't enough, now they have to learn how use an unfamiliar methodology or process, one which they're not sure they believe in the first place, and one which they're convinced will slow them down. Why is it that the Methodology Police are so surprised to see resistance in circumstances like these? Consultant Doug Scott gave me an example of this situation in a recent email message[6] to me:

> On one project I know, they needed a diagrammer for the ERDs, so they bought Excellerator. Having found that it supported SSADM (which must be the methodologist's methodology) adopted it without any training or induction for the staff. Then they found that the pace of the project slowed significantly (in fact, it nearly halted) while everyone was busy reading manuals and learning software tools and deciding what they should do next (and re-doing what they had done earlier in the "wrong" sequence). For death march watchers, an almost ideal scenario. Oh, and the project manager was sacked half way through the project, but that's normal.

And as Paul Maskens argued in another email message:[7]

> A death march project is not the time for staff to learn a new (or their first) methodology. OTOH it would contribute greatly to the chances of project death if they *did* learn a new methodology at the same time.

To succeed, the death march project team needs to agree on which processes will be formalized—perhaps source code control and change management, and (hopefully) requirements management—and which processes will be carried out on a completely *ad hoc* basis (e.g., user-interface design). There's no point mandating a particular software process if it's not going to be followed; the Methodology Police force is wasting its time if it tries to do so, and it will cause the project team to waste *its* time, which is far more valuable (the Methodology Police have nothing useful to do anyway other than running around the IS/IT department harassing hapless project teams!).

This means that the death march project manager must impose the processes that he or she feels essential, in a dictatorial fashion—for example, "Anyone who modifies our source code without going through the change-management process will be fired summarily!" Or the project team members must *sincerely* agree to adopt the process because they believe that it will be cost-effective. This is more likely to occur if the project team members have worked together before, so that they share a common experience with various software development processes; it's less likely to occur if one team member stands up and says, "I deeply believe that structured analysis is critical to the success of our project" when the other team members have no idea what he's talking about. Another corollary of this principle: It's usually a disaster to introduce a new, unfamiliar process into a death march project, even if the team collectively believes that it will help. The learning curve, and the inevitable confusion and bickering over the details of the process, will usually outweigh its benefits.

This means that such formal approaches as SEI-CMM, ISO-9000, or the introduction of new analysis/design methodologies should be done somewhere outside the death march projects. The sensible thing to do is introduce these processes as part of a long-term corporate strategy, to experiment first with a pilot project (which should *not* be a death march project), and then support it with appropriate training. As Sharon Marsh Roberts put it in a recent email message[8] to me:

> Cowpokes don't need the manure to be cleaned from the pasture. Programmers don't need to have the "methodology" gurus clean up the deliverables.

> But if someone wants to have a formal software process, then the folks doing the programming should be protected from that extra effort.

If all of these things have been done, and if all other development projects are already operating at level-3 on the SEI-CMM scale, *then* it becomes interesting to ask whether such processes should also be used on a death march project. As Watts Humphrey once remarked in a conference speech about the SEI-CMM, "If a process can't be used in a crisis, it shouldn't be used at all."

I'm not sure that many would agree with Humphrey's assertion, particularly if the death march project is viewed as a once-in-a-lifetime exception to the norm. If indeed this is the case, then perhaps it does make sense to abandon the formal processes and let the death march team use whatever *ad hoc* techniques they feel appropriate. But remember my assertion in Chapter 1: Death march projects are becoming the norm, not the exception. If this is the case, then the official corporate processes should be amended as necessary to make them suitable for a death march project. Then, and only then, does Humphrey's statement make sense.

In the meantime, if you *do* feel compelled to make a death march project team practice some form of process improvement, my recommendation is to look at Watts Humphrey's Personal Software Process (PSP). I summarized its characteristics in my *Rise and Resurrection of the American Programmer*, but you should really read Humphrey's *A Discipline of Software Engineering* [4]. Fair warning, though: It's 789 pages long.

# GOOD-ENOUGH SOFTWARE

The triage prioritization discussed above can go a long way toward making a death march project "rational" in its behavior. For success, it's not required to implement *all* of the requirements; it's "good enough" if we can implement the "must-do" requirements and a reasonable number of the "should-do" requirements.

But there's another aspect of software development that causes difficulty in death march projects: the implicit demand for *absolute* quality. This is usually expressed in terms of defects (bugs), but it may also be expressed in terms of portability, platform independence, flexibility, maintainability, and a few dozen other "ilities." It's hard enough to achieve these objectives in normal projects; it's almost impossible to do so in death march projects. Instead, the project team has to decide—and if at all possible, get concurrence from the shareholders and stakeholders—what's *good enough*.

The reason this is so important is that the achievement of absolute "ilities" consumes project resources—especially time. If you want to develop a certifiably bug-free program, complete with a mathematical proof of correctness, it's going to take time; it may also require a higher level of talent than the project team can provide. It's also going to consume some of the energy of one or more people on the project team, which means that those people won't be available to work on other requirements. In short, achieving such "ilities" as reliability, portability, and maintainability requires a trade-off, and it has to be taken into account as part of the triage prioritization discussed above.

Death march project teams have to confront this unpleasant reality because the alternative is usually "perfect" software that isn't finished when the all-important deadline arrives. It's better if the team is aware of the pragmatics of good-enough software at the beginning of the project, but my experience has been that many traditional software developers accept the notion of good-enough software development only when their backs are against the wall—for example, when they're facing the "ugly crisis" discussed earlier, a month or two before the deadline.

Up to that point, they'll complain, "How would you like it if we used your 'good-enough' approach for the software in a nuclear reactor or an air traffic control system?" The answer, of course, is that I wouldn't like it at all; and if someone proposed a death march project for those kinds of high-reliability applications, I would stop flying on airplanes and I would move as far away as possible from nuclear power plants. But we don't usually see death march projects of this kind; it's more likely to be the payroll system for the nuclear power facility, or the airline reservation system used by the airline. Payroll systems and airline reservation systems aren't supposed to fail, either, but the immediate consequences of a failure aren't as serious.

In any case, *perfect* reliability, maintainability, and portability are not necessary, practical, or even desirable in most death march projects. Indeed, perfection isn't possible even in normal projects—it's just that we can afford to set our standards much higher because we usually have fewer constraints on time, budget, or personnel resources. For death march projects, though, what the users *really* want is a system that's cheap enough, fast enough, feature-rich enough, stable enough, and available soon enough. That's their definition of "good enough."

Why do we fail to achieve "good-enough" software? It's usually because of a combination of the following reasons:

- We have a tendency to define quality *only* in terms of defects without thinking about other aspects of quality which include, from the user's perspective, the "quality" associated with having the system ready for use on a certain date.

- We assume that fewer defects = better quality, and we assume that "mo' better" quality is *always* preferred by the user—even though there are circumstances where the user would be willing to trade off some defects in return for an earlier delivery, or a product that runs on a wider variety of hardware/software platforms, and so forth.

- We tend to define quality (defect) objectives *once*, at the beginning of the project and keep them fixed, even though circumstances change dynamically throughout the project.

- We've been told for such a long time that *processes* are crucial that we often forget that processes are "neutral"—a fool with a "process-tool" is still a fool. You don't get quality by blindly following the details of structured analysis *or* the recommendations of SEI-CMM.

- We pursue quality with a *fixed* process that we define once, at the beginning of the project (or, even worse, for all projects in the whole company)

- We underestimate the nonlinear trade-offs between such key parameters as staff size, schedule, budget, and defects—all of which are key issues for death march projects.

- We ignore the dynamics of the processes: time-delays, feedback loops, and so on. Heavy overtime by the project team this week may appear to increase productivity and advance the progress of the overall project; but it can lead to more bugs next week (something the end-user and senior management may not be aware of), which will lower next week's productivity (in terms of productive output) and perhaps set the project even further behind.

- We ignore the "soft factors" associated with the process such as morale, adequacy of office space, and so forth.

How do we achieve "good-enough" software? As James Bach[5] points out, it requires several things:

- *A utilitarian strategy*—The art of qualitatively analyzing and maximizing net positive consequences in an ambiguous situation—encompassing ideas from systems thinking, risk management, economics, decision theory, game theory, control theory, and fuzzy logic.

- *An evolutionary strategy*—Not only with regard to the project life cycle, but also an evolutionary view of our people, processes, and resources.

- *Heroic teams*—Not the Mighty Morphin Genius Programmers but ordinary, skillful people collaborating effectively.

- *Dynamic infrastructure*—The antithesis of bureaucracy and power politics. Upper management pays attention to projects, pays attention to the market, identifies and resolves conflicts between projects, allows the project to "win" when there are conflicts between projects and organizational bureaucracy.

- *Dynamic processes*—Processes that support work in an evolving, collaborative environment. Dynamic processes are ones you can always question because every dynamic process is part of an identifiable metaprocess.

A reader who reviewed the draft manuscript of this edition of *Death March* made a very perceptive observation about the "good-enough" concept at a very special point in time: the "end-game," at the end of the project. Writing about an "ugly" death march project that he had observed from a safe distance, Michael Church wrote:

> There was pressure on the project managers to declare it done even though they must have known it wasn't ready, put it into operation, and never mind that the customers would start calling in with complaints about what doesn't work properly (yet). (It could be that they were naive enough to think it was going to work, but I am giving them the benefit of the doubt.) If they are lucky, the system will live

and limp along until enough bugs get corrected (in extended development or maintenance mode), or performance issues are addressed, to make the project into a real success (hopefully sooner rather than later). But there are other (nastier) scenarios.

A state of affairs such as this is more likely to occur with a death-march project than with a more "normal" project.[9]

This emphasizes even more strongly why the end-user community has to participate in the negotiations and discussions about what constitutes "good enough." It is a decision that will not only affect the initial decision to conclude that the development effort is "finished" (so the vendor can be paid, the exhausted programmers can take a vacation, and senior management can declare a success), but also the ongoing, productive use of the system over a period of several years.

# BEST PRACTICES AND WORST PRACTICES

On more than one occasion in this book, I've warned about the dangers of allowing the Methodology Police to impose a set of rigid methodologies or software processes upon a death march project team. The same advice holds for external consultants, gurus, witch doctors, faith healers, snake-oil salesmen, and textbooks—even *this* textbook; if I've recommended something that doesn't make sense and that the project team can't carry out with enthusiasm and sincerity, then ignore it!

But this is particularly true of methodologies and software processes. Rather than following a set of practices that somebody else has recommended—or even worse, a set of practices imposed in a top-down fashion by managers and methodology committees who usually don't know what they're talking about—it's far better to follow a set of practices that the team itself regards as "best" for the circumstances. That's the essence of the "best practices" approach that has been gaining popularity in the past couple of years: a grass-roots approach to identifying, documenting, and evangelizing software development organizations that *real developers* have found successful.

Unfortunately, death march project teams often don't have much to go on because theirs is often regarded as the first such project within the organization. Or even if it isn't the first one, it's still regarded as an exception, so nobody has bothered cataloging the techniques that worked and the techniques that didn't. Even worse, the death march projects tend to have a high mortality rate (otherwise, they wouldn't be called "death march" in the first place!). Thus, the people who would be most likely to provide useful advice for the next such project have quit, been fired, committed suicide, suffered a nervous breakdown, or withdrawn into a shell of cynicism.

If you are indeed embarking upon the first death march project the organization has seen, then it's likely that the best you can do is document whatever practices and processes have worked in your project for the benefit of the next death march that follows. One way of doing this is by conducting a "project audit" at the end of the project, but this rarely occurs, and the results are usually so boring that nobody bothers reading it. The reasons are obvious: As mentioned earlier, the project team is so exhausted, frustrated, and frazzled at the end of the project that the notion of documenting its experiences is likely to be met with hoots of scorn; furthermore, many of the most valuable contributors have long since disappeared by the end of the project.

Thus, what you should consider as an alternative is a series of "mini-audits" throughout the project. If you have mini-milestones (sometimes known as "inch-pebbles") such as delivering a new version of a prototype to the user, then schedule a half-day mini-audit immediately after the inch-pebble. What practices worked well and what was a disaster? What should be emphasized more heavily for the next milestone and what should be abandoned? The point here is that this kind of self-reflection is useful for the project team itself; the fact that it will also be helpful to future death march project teams is icing on the cake. Also, the team is usually in better spirits during these intermediate inch-pebble meetings and their comments are likely to be fresher, more candid, and less cynical.

For the organizations that have no best-practices material available, I'll recommend a few sources. I covered the topic in one chapter of my *Rise and Resurrection of the American Programmer*; you should also look at the World Wide Web site maintained by consultant Christine Comaford at http://www.christine.com for another collection of best-practices material. Perhaps the most ambitious project underway today is the Airlie Council's efforts within the U.S. Defense Department; you can find this information on the Web at http://spmn.com.

I've listed below the "principal best practices" that the Airlie Council has recommended. Remember my earlier advice *not* to adopt this kind of information as a "stone tablet" containing "commandments" that must be followed. But it could be a useful starting point for your own collection of best-practices ideas.

- *Formal risk management*—This is a concept I'll discuss later in this chapter.
- *Agreement on interfaces*—Hardware interfaces, software interfaces, and interfaces between your system and other external systems.
- *Peer reviews*—Or inspections, walkthroughs, reviews, and so forth. These are commonly understood but often rejected by death march projects, for they feel the effort will slow them down. Intellectually, most of us agree that peer reviews are beneficial, but given the kind of pressure we see in death march projects, there's a tendency for everyone to hunker down and churn out his or her own work without bothering to have it reviewed by the other team members.

- *Metric-based scheduling and management*—This says that we should base our schedules and estimates on metrics derived from previous projects. But as noted earlier, there may not have been any previous death march projects, and if there were any, it's unlikely that anyone bothered recording any useful metrics (other than a body-count of human casualties). But if there are any metrics available from "normal" projects, these can be used to calibrate the estimates being produced in the death march project—if only to see how hysterically optimistic those estimates really are!

- *Binary quality gates at the inch-pebble level*—In other words, rather than having milestones every three months, during which the project team reports that it is 97 percent done with all coding, there should be weekly or even *daily* inch-pebbles with "binary" indications of progress. One means of accomplishing this is the "daily build" strategy discussed later in this book.

- *Project-wide visibility of project plan and progress versus plan*—This is consistent with my recommendations in earlier chapters. Things are tough enough in a death march project without having the manager hide the status from the rest of the team.

- *Defect tracking against quality targets*—One of the ideas here is that defects identified, tracked, and resolved *early* in the development process cannot only give an indication of the defect levels in the final delivered system, but can also eliminate defects when they are relatively inexpensive, rather than waiting until the system-testing stage of the project.

- *Configuration management*—Whether this is called version control, source-code management, or some other term, it's usually regarded as an essential practice in most high-pressure projects.

- *People-aware management accountability*—Alas, this is something that most death march projects *don't* pay enough attention to; as mentioned earlier, many death march projects are set up as suicide missions or kamikaze-style projects.

One of the most important contributions of the Airlie Council is the notion of *worst practices*; this is particularly applicable to death march projects, where it's often more important to avoid disasters than it is to find the best possible way to do things. The Airlie Council's list is summarized below:

- *Don't expect schedule compression of >10% compared to the statistical norm for similar projects.* Of course, if you really believed this one, you wouldn't even start a death march project!

- *Don't justify new technology by the need for schedule compression*— You've got enough problems in a death march project without debugging new tools and technology by using beta versions of software from your friendly tool vendor. I'll discuss this in more detail in Chapter 10.

- *Don't force customer-specific implementation solutions on the project—* This is useful advice for *any* project.

- *Don't advocate the use of silver bullet approaches—*This is something worth remembering when your management proposes (right after it has been visited by a persuasive vendor!) that your project can be "saved" by some new-fangled tool or development methodology.

- *Don't miss an opportunity to move items that are under external control off the critical path—*If your project team can't control it, then having it on the critical path makes it all the more risky. This applies to things such as vendor tools, hardware boxes, software packages, and other components from external vendors; but it also applies to both tangible deliverables and political decisions made by various shareholders and stakeholders surrounding the project.

- *Don't expect to achieve an accurate view of project health from a formal review attended by a large number of unprepared, active reviewers—*The project team doesn't have to worry about this, for it already *knows* that such review sessions are political rituals. The advice is aimed more at the senior managers who watch the death march project from a safe distance, trying to find out whether it's in trouble.

- *Don't expect to recover from a schedule slip of >10 percent without a >10 percent reduction in software functionality to be delivered—*This is crucial advice for a death march team because there's a good chance that the schedule *will* slip by more than 10 percent during the course of the project. Indeed, even a 10-percent slippage is dangerous in a death march project, for the team is probably already working so much overtime that they don't have the additional capacity to work 10 percent *more* hours in each day. But the main point of this suggestion from the Airlie Council is to remind the project manager that people-time and software-functionality are not exchangeable in a linear fashion.

During the past year, I've posed two questions to several hundred software managers in seminar audiences around the world: "If a colleague of yours was about to embark upon a death march project, what is the *one thing* that you would advise him/her to do in order to succeed? And what is the one thing you would advise him/her *not* to do?" I've been intrigued to see that *nobody* has *ever* identified tools or technology as the "one most important thing," nor has anyone mentioned formal methods or techniques such as structured analysis or object-oriented design. A few people have recommended peopleware strategies (e.g., "hire good people," and "make sure that the team is really committed to succeed"), but most of the recommendations have centered on the issue of negotiations, scope management (which is handled well by the triage concept discussed earlier), and risk management (which I'll discuss below).

One last concept from the Airlie Council might be useful for death march projects, though it's likely to be used more by the managers *outside* the project than the manager or team members *inside* the project. It's called the "breathalyzer test": What questions would you ask a death march project team to quickly determine whether it was so out of touch with reality that it should be shut down? These are also the sort of questions that consultants often ask when they are asked by senior management to review the status of a project. I've been in that position myself, and I can usually tell the project is in trouble when I see the glazed eyes of the project manager, who looks like a deer caught in the headlights of an onrushing car.

Sometimes questions such as "Do you know who your customer is? Do you know who you're supposed to deliver this stuff to?" lead to an embarrassed silence, while everyone on the project team looks blankly at one another and then stares at the floor. If you need some more breathalyzer-test questions, here's the list from the Airlie Council:

- Do you have a current, credible activity network supported by a work breakdown structure (WBS)?
- Do you have a current, credible schedule and budget?
- Do you know what software you are responsible for delivering?
- Can you list the top ten project risks?
- Do you know your schedule compression percentage?
- What is the estimated size of your software deliverable? How was it derived?
- Do you know the percentage of external interfaces that are not under your control?
- Does your staff have sufficient expertise in the project domain?
- Have you identified adequate staff to allocate to the scheduled tasks at the scheduled time?

As mentioned earlier, the reason the breathalyzer test is administered is that someone in the organization—usually *not* the project manager, but someone much higher in the management ranks—has a "gut feeling" that the project is in trouble. For their own political survival, the project manager and the entire team should ask the same questions of one another periodically. And the project manager should be on the lookout for other signs that the project is in trouble even when things look okay on the official PERT chart:

- Key project team members are quitting—This may occur for a number of reasons, but it's important to get a sense of whether team members are losing faith in their ability to finish the project. If key members begin quitting, others may follow.

- The "inverse Dilbert correlation factor"—The more Dilbert cartoons pasted on office doors and bulletin boards, the less well off the project is.

- Excessive gallows humor—If the project team begins wearing black shirts to the office, or piping funeral dirges through the Muzak system, you're in trouble.

- New names for the project, for example, "Project Titanic"—Another form of gallows humor, but usually a more serious indication that the project team has lost faith, lost respect, and lost any real interest in whether the project will ever succeed.

- An ominous silence from end-users and senior management, who used to ask on a daily basis how the project was coming along—By the time you recognize this, it may be too late to recover, but you should have at least a few days to update your resume.

- Thrashing: lots of activity but no sign of forward progress—Avoiding this is what the "inch-pebble" idea and the "daily build" strategy are all about.

# DEATH MARCH MEETS XP

One of the most popular and intriguing of the "process"-related ideas to emerge in the late 1990s and early 2000s is XP. The fact that a project team is using XP does not necessarily mean that the project meets all of the criteria and characteristics of a death march project, as discussed in this book; nor is there a 100% overlap of strategies and techniques between XP and the techniques discussed in this book. On the other hand, I believe there is a great deal of commonality—after all, the very word "extreme" in XP implies that the project has aggressive goals that transcend the abilities of normal people working in a normal fashion.

On the other hand, a very strong theme running through most XP books, articles, training courses, and presentations is that of a *partnership* between the developers and the stakeholders who help articulate the system requirements, exercise the prototypes, and ultimately decide whether the emerging system-prototypes can eventually be put into productive use. This is indeed a highly desirable scenario, and it's the kind of situation that one would expect to see in the "mission impossible" type of death march shown in the top-right quadrant of Figure 2.1.

Unfortunately, many death march projects fall into the other three quadrants of Figure 2.1—in other words, ugly projects, suicide projects, or kamikaze missions. In particular, death march projects are often hostile encounters between aggressive outsourcing vendors (otherwise known as "system integrators," "software houses," "consulting firms," and so forth), and defensive clients who are not quite sure whether they are being serenaded, seduced, or raped. In such a political environment, many of the eminently commendable principles of XP have little or no chance of being implemented;[10] instead, some of the more aggressive ideas in this book must be followed.

Nevertheless, I see no reason why a death march project manager should avoid making opportunistic use of some key XP concepts to the extent that they make sense in his or her project. Among these concepts are the following:

- Plan for "versions" or "releases" on short, two-week cycles; as the XP advocates like to say, "Ship early, ship often."

  ♦ The functionality associated with each new version/release is based on "conversations" with users.

  ♦ If necessary, the functionality can be documented in a rigorous, detailed fashion—for example, using OO methodologies such as UML. However, if the overall schedule is aggressive, and if there is a significant amount of functionality that has to be delivered within a short, two-week time-frame, then this kind of documentation will be one of the first things to be jettisoned in the "triage" approach discussed earlier in this chapter.

  ♦ In each new release, the team should commit to delivering the same amount of functionality that it was able to produce in its previous release. There is a natural tendency to become increasingly aggressive—"If we delivered 500 function points in the last release, let's commit to delivering 600 in this release!"—but this kind of over-commitment is bound to lead to disaster sooner or later.

- If the death march project is going to last for more than, say, six months, then a schedule should be based on a sustainable 40-hour week. Not only is this humane and civilized, but it's also intelligent: it's okay to sprint for a 100-yard dash, but if your project is a marathon, then you have run at a sustainable pace in order to avoid burning out after the first few miles.

- Don't design for anticipated "future" needs, but instead make the best possible design for today.

  ♦ This is a profound change from the "old" paradigm in which it was assumed that requirements-based errors were extremely important and that it was thus cost-effective to invest as much time and effort as necessary (either by writing detailed specifications, or by building intricate prototypes) to obtain "correct" requirements from users.

♦ The new paradigm, emphasized heavily by XP, is that since it's usually impossible to obtain correct requirements no matter how hard you try, it doesn't pay to invest more than enough effort to merely achieve a "good-enough" understanding of the requirements. The primary reason this paradigm "works" is that today's developers have much more powerful development tools than were available 10–20 years ago, which facilitates faster, cheaper, and easier modifications—indeed, entire rewriting of portions of a system.

• The time, effort, and resources that were previously invested in oh-so-careful requirements analysis should now be invested in "continuous re-factoring"—in other words, constantly re-organizing, re-architecting, and rearranging the objects, modules, or other components of the emerging systems. Such an approach works best in a tool-supported, object-oriented development approach.

• "Pair programming" is an important theme of the XP movement: Two software engineers work together on each discrete development effort. Not only does this provide valuable "insurance" if one of the developers gets run over by the proverbial beer truck in the middle of the project, but it typically turns out to be faster and more cost-effective to have two pairs of eyes peering at code as it is being written at breakneck speed.

• Collective ownership of code means that anyone on the project team can change the code written by any other member of the team. This doesn't make any sense unless the project team has an automated change-control tool such as PVCS or Microsoft SourceSafe, but such tools are widely used and readily available today (including open-source products for those whose budgets are limited). As a practical matter, it makes sense to encourage a "community property" environment if a death march (or XP) team is working round-the-clock: Stopping the entire team's progress because nobody can find Sally's code to fix a critical bug just doesn't make sense. But as one can imagine, implementing such a policy can create major political battles if the team is not accustomed to such behavior and if it hasn't been persuaded that it's a good idea.

• Programmers write test cases *before* writing code on the theory that if you don't know how you'll test the code to ensure that it's working correctly, you ought not to be writing the code in the first place. Again, the political ramifications are likely to be significant for a team that has never been exposed to such radical (but nevertheless common-sense and hard-to-refute) policies. A corollary of this guideline is that all such test cases are saved and incorporated into an ever-growing library of test cases for subsequent regression testing.

# CONCLUSION

It's all too easy to go overboard with many of the ideas that I've discussed in this chapter and thus fall into the deadly trap of mind-numbing, time-wasting bureaucracy. But as Stephen Nesbitt reminded me in an email message[11] that arrived just as I had reached the end of this chapter without a clever way of bringing things to an end:

> ...the absence of standards and methodology can also turn a project into a Death March. On my last project for example, the unrealistic delivery schedule was used as an excuse to avoid the following:
>
> 1) Checking source code into the configuration management system resulting in project source code spread across 3 different computer systems at 2 geographic locations. As a consequence a significant amount of time was wasted trying:
>
> a) to build the software.
>
> b) to determine who had what version.
>
> c) to determine why the software worked on one system and not another.
>
> 2) Registering features/defects into the configuration management system. This effectively crippled QA because it was impossible to easily determine what was in work and could be ignored, what was completed and could be tested, and what was pending so that appropriate test plans could be designed.
>
> 3) Recording basic requirements, design decisions and assumptions, milestones *within* the development of project modules, and appropriate unit tests. The consequence here was to drastically impede communications within the project team not only on current project status but also basic decisions made at the beginning of the project.
>
> Inevitably development response was that these process activities represented "overhead" and thus, by definition, were *useless* activities. Technical management generally concurred and, when the drop dead date loomed, process and methodology were given the heave ho.

Please don't interpret this chapter as an excuse not to have any processes, methods, or techniques at all; indeed, that will kill a death march project, too! The trick is to find the ones that matter, the ones that work, the ones that the team will follow naturally and unconsciously. This last point is crucial: The team members will be under a lot of stress and pressure and will have to do a lot of things by instinct. If they are overburdened with new, unfamiliar processes so complex that they have to stop every five minutes and consult a textbook to figure out what to do, then all is lost. So keep it simple—and if the team can remember only one word, remember what it is: *triage.*

# NOTES

1. Indeed, I would suggest that the project manager and his or her team members use this as a litmus test at the beginning of the project. If the user, the project owner, the senior managers, shareholders and stakeholders all refuse to accept the notion of this kind of hard-nosed *triage* prioritization, then the most rational thing to do is resign from the project before things get any worse!

2. This is a preview of a more elaborate discussion of "best practices" that you'll find later in this chapter.

3. By contrast, in a "normal" project, the SA/OOA models are often perceived as a useful product in their own right. The users and business policy-makers will huddle around the data-flow diagrams and mutter to one another, "So *that's* what our business is all about! Maybe we should do a re-engineering project and change all of that before we build a new software system!"

4. Veteran software engineers will recall the old adage from Abraham Maslow, "If your only tool is a hammer, then all the problems facing you look like nails."

5. I have to confess that this is a disguised marketing pitch, since it's one of the key features of the Requisite product, and I'm a stockholder and Board member of Requisite, Inc. In my role as an objective author, I heartily encourage you to investigate all three requirements management products mentioned here.

6. From: Doug Scott, 100072,1276
   To: Ed Yourdon, 71250,2322
   Topic: Ch4 done, Ch5 queries
   Section: The Cutter Edge [14], Forum: CASE - DCI
   Date: Tue, Aug 13, 1996, 4:41:31 PM
   > 1. How important is it to use traditional methodologies like SA/
   SD
   > or OOA/OOD in a death march project?
   I'd have thought that they can contribute to the deathmarch more
   effectively than most. On one project I know, they needed a dia-
   grammer for the ERDs, so they bought Excellerator. Having found
   that it supported SSADM (which must be the methodologist's methodology) adopted it without any training or induction for the staff.
   Then they found that the pace of the project slowed significantly
   (in fact, it nearly halted) while everyone was busy reading manuals
   and learning software tools and deciding what they should do next
   (and re-doing what they had done earlier in the "wrong" sequence).

For deathmarch watchers, an almost ideal scenario. Oh, and the
project manager was sacked half way through the project, but that's
normal.

> How important is it to teach those methodologies (whichever one
> you think is best) to the team before the project begins?

Well, I guess you can gather from the above that I believe in
training for ANYTHING before applying it. The fact that you're
adopting a technique which will fundamentally decide the way you
work, record all your requirements, and govern the nature of the
generated code, you'd think that a slight amount of training would
be beneficial, wouldn't you? A lot of training would be better, of
course. But when you're on a deathmarch, you don't have time for
that.

A little sideline quote that I received from a Systems Manager the
other day: I said I wanted to spend the first nine months of the
project getting the design right, and he responded by saying "You
can't do that - you've got to deliver the Name and Address file in
twelve months." (!) It's not a deathmarch. It's not a deathmarch.
It's not a deathmarch. Yet.

> 3. How important is the SEI-CMM or ISO-9000 or any other "formal"
> software process approach within the context of a death march
> project team?

Not at all, I'd say. I don't know SEI-CMM, apart from what I've
seen here, but ISO-9000 is self-certified, so it doesn't pose a
problem here at all. If it does, you hire a specialist whose job is
to cook the books.

> 4. Almost all death march projects follow a RAD or prototyping
> approach

Well, what's worse is that suddenly when people realise that the
deadline's going to slip, RAD suddenly rears its ugly head. Obviously, RAD is all about tightly constrained environments, whereas
the deathmarch is plagued by vague or exaggerated requirements. I
can't see how an attempt to RAD a deathmarch can succeed, unless
you turn it into producing a "navigable model" or some such prototype so as to get the management off your back.

> 5. If you could only get the project team to focus on ONE process
> approach, what would it be?

For me, it's all working in small teams, tightly focussed, and each
one delivering *something*, so there's an end in sight. Checking
each others' work is the other aspect I'd introduce. Not necessarily walkthroughs (although that's a more formal part of it), but
simply ensuring that someone else who is knowledgable can help with
any task. Share the workload, the problems, and the vision.

> 6. If there was one kind of process approach that you would
> strongly advise the death march project to AVOID

Large user groups (such as a Model Office) who have control of the
design. If the number of users involved is too great, the business

will give you only those it can spare, and they will continually
argue amongst themselves because they don't know. We've had to pull
a project to a dead halt while we pulled in some senior users to go
through all the requirements and sort out the wheat from the chaff.
Meanwhile 60 implementors twiddled their thumbs for a couple of
weeks.

> 7. How important is all of this process stuff, in comparison to
> the issues of peopleware

People, people, and people - the three most important things you
need on any project. Get the best and keep them, and lose the rest.
You can work with a team one-third the size of what you think if
they're good, and if they're that good, they'll adopt a common,
useful process. So process is important, but good people come
first, and when they're that good, they'll adopt good practices
which aren't a drag on the project.

Tools/technology come ahead of processes, I believe, and it's the
one thing the managers can do for their staff that can help significantly.

Doug

**7.** From: Paul Maskens (UK), 104074,3277
To: Ed Yourdon, 71250,2322
Topic: Ch4 done, Ch5 queries
Section: The Cutter Edge [14], Forum: CASE - DCI
Date: Thu, Aug 15, 1996, 5:33:12 AM

>> 2. What if the death march project team has never used such
methodologies before? How important is it to teach those methodologies (whichever one you think is best) to the team before the
project begins? <<

Is there any time at all "before the project begins"?

A death march project is not the time for staff to learn a new (or
their first) methodology. OTOH it would contribute greatly to the
chances of project death if they DID learn a new methodology at the
same time.

Paul

**8.** From: S. Marsh Roberts [ICCA], 70007,4251
To: Ed Yourdon, 71250,2322
Topic: Ch4 done, Ch5 queries
Section: The Cutter Edge [14], Forum: CASE - DCI
Date: Wed, Aug 14, 1996, 7:58:31 AM

>> 1. How important is it to use traditional methodologies like SA/
SD or OOA/OOD in a death march project?<<

It can't hurt to have clear ways of communicating with the users
and clear deliverables to them.

>>2. What if the death march project team has never used such meth-
odologies before? How important is it to teach those methodologies
(whichever one you think is best) to the team before the project
begins?<<

It depends on whether members of the team have the experience that the team as a whole lacks. I'd say that the core members need to "know their stuff" for the most part.

>>3. How important is the SEI-CMM or ISO-9000 or any other "formal" software process approach within the context of a death march project team? Is it better to follow an "ad hoc" approach, and just assume that the pressures of a death march will force everyone to operate as a "cowboy" programmer? ("cowperson" would probably be more politically correct, but it sounds too clumsy <g>)<<

Cowpokes don't need the manure to be cleaned from the pasture. Programmers don't need to have the "methodology" gurus clean up the deliverables.

But if someone wants to have a formal software process, then the folks doing the programming should be protected from that extra effort.

>>4. Almost all death march projects follow a RAD or prototyping approach to systems development (or spiral, or scrum, or iterative, or various other related ideas) instead of the old-fashioned waterfall approach. That point hardly seems worth emphasizing—but are there any special caveats or exceptions or details about RAD/prototyping/etc., that you would be sure that a death march project manager understood?<<

Understand this: the feedback that you got from the user is critical. They don't care how you meet their requirements, and if they have seen "early miracles" of pretty screens and promised functionality, don't ever let them down.

>>5. If you could only get the project team to focus on ONE process approach, what would it be? Walkthroughs? Change management (aka version control, configuration management, etc.)? Formal analysis/design methodologies? Something else?<<

Walkthoughs or reviews with the key (or a few key) user(s)? I really think that one of the more major problems of systems projects is that there is a cycle of delivery and failure to satisfy.

>>6. If there was one kind of process approach that you would strongly advise the death march project to AVOID (because it takes too much time, is too risky, or whatever), what would it be?<<

Anything that is extremely complex and technical and theoretical is wasted on a death march. Nobody can see further than the next deliverable.

>>7. How important is all of this process stuff, in comparison to the issues of peopleware (which I discussed in Chapter 4), and tools/technology (which I'll get to in Chapter 6)? <<

The tools are useful, but they should only illustrate and enable. The process is a means of getting to the human side of the effort. The peopleware is the most important.

Sharon

**9.** Michael Church email, July 16, 2003.

**10.** The situation is exacerbated by the fact that XP has typically *not* been used in any previous projects within the organization. Thus, even if the overall political climate was reasonably open and friendly, there would probably be some resistance to XP ideas such as "pair programming."

**11.** From: "Stephen Nesbitt", INTERNET:Snesbitt@gomontana.com
To: Edward Yourdon, 71250,2322
Date: Thu, Aug 15, 1996, 2:18 AM
RE: Death March & Methodology Police
Ed:

Three weeks ago I was 35 year old [xxx] systems engineer providing quality assurance services on an ugly Death March project here in Bozeman, MT. I'm still 35 but I resigned my position because, after 18 months, the stress, despair and lack of job satisfaction were simply too much to take. With no dependents I could afford to simply walk away even if it is financially uncomfortable.

As such, I am finding your draft chapters for Death March particularly relevant as I try to understand what happened over the last 18 months, and as I start the process of looking for an employer where Death Marches are not the norm (or at least not ugly or suicidal ones!)

In reading Chapter 2 you made a number of references to the "methodology police" as one of the factors which can turn a project into a Death March - the implication being that methodology and standards can cripple an already marginal project. I think this is absolutely true.

I am bothered, however, that the converse was not mention P that the

absence of standards and methodology can also turn a project into a Death March.

On my last project for example, the unrealistic delivery schedule was used as an excuse to avoid the following:

1) Checking source code into the configuration management system resulting in project source code spread across 3 different computer systems at 2 geographic locations. As a consequence a significant amount of time was wasted trying:
a) to build the software.
b) to determine who had what version.
c) to determine why the software worked on one system and not another.

2) Registering features/defects into the configuration management system.

This effectively crippled QA because it was impossible to easily determine what was in work and could be ignored, what was completed and could be tested, and what was pending so that appropriate test plans could be designed.

3) Recording basic requirements, design decisions and assumptions,

milestones _within_ the development of project modules, and appropriate unit tests. The consequence here was to drastically impede communications within the project team not only on current project status but also basic decisions made at the beginning of the project. Inevitably development response was that these process activities represented "overhead" and thus, by definition, were _useless_ activities. Technical management generally concurred and, when the drop dead date loomed, process and methodology were given the heave ho. The results were significant:

1) One system was finally put into production 1 year after delivery. That additional year was spent correcting significant design and implementation flaws which, in addition to requiring massive amounts of engineering resources, also resulted in millions of dollars of fines.

2) One system was put in production with three brand new, never tested systems. The result was the need to dedicate engineering resources for a period of one month to provide continuous around the clock supervision. It also led to the general perception by the customer that the system was not working - a perception that has not yet been changed.

3) One system was put in and totally failed leading to:

a) $20 million dollars in fines on a $35 million contract.

b) Loss of another multimillion dollar contract.

c) Removal of the system by the customer.

Perhaps a little methodology would not have made any difference. On the other hand, how could it have made things worse?

I hope that the final form of Death March will address this very issue - recognizing that absence of _appropriate_ methodologies can transform a project into a Death March just as completely as the overzealous application of _inappropriate_ processes, methodologies and standards. As a battle weary infantry man, I also hope that the final book will provide insight into recognizing the appropriate from the inappropriate.

Thanks for your time, and I apologize for the length of my post. Enjoy your summer along Flathead Lake.

-steve

Distribution:

 Edward Yourdon 71250,2322

# REFERENCES

1. Alan M. Davis, *Software Requirements: Objects, Functions, and States,* Englewood Cliffs, NJ: Prentice Hall, 1993.

2. Mark C. Paul, Charles V. Weber, Bill Curtis, Mary Beth Chrissis et al, *The Capability Maturity Model: Guidelines for Improving the Software Process,* Reading, MA: Addison-Wesley, 1995.

3. Watts Humphrey, *A Discipline of Software Engineering,* Reading, MA: Addison-Wesley, 1995.

4. James Bach, "The Challenge of 'Good Enough' Software," *American Programmer,* October 1995.

5. Jim McCarthy, *Dynamics of Software Projects*, Microsoft Press, 1995.

6. G. Pascal Zachary, *Show-Stopper!* New York: Free Press, 1994.

# 6 The Dynamics of Processes

*...System dynamics is a method for studying the world around us. Unlike other scientists, who study the world by breaking it up into smaller and smaller pieces, system dynamicists look at things as a whole. The central concept to system dynamics is understanding how all the objects in a system interact with one another. A system can be anything from a steam engine, to a bank account, to a basketball team. The objects and people in a system interact through "feedback" loops, where a change in one variable affects other variables over time, which in turn affects the original variable, and so on.*

—from the MIT System Dynamics in Education Project, *http://sysdyn.clexchange.org*
(revised and adapted from Chapter 4 of
*Rise and Resurrection of the American Programmer*)

In many death march projects, the most serious problems are not so much *technical* as they are political, social, cultural, and people-oriented. And while there are a number of peopleware-oriented approaches that can improve things considerably—recruiting better people, motivating them more effectively, and organizing them into productive teams—the problem is that all of this works within an organizational context. And the organizational "system for building systems" is so complex that we often don't understand how it works. Indeed, quite often it *doesn't* work: The project team is paralyzed because of the subtle and unexpected consequences of management decisions and policies.

This has occurred despite the noble efforts of many IT organizations to formalize and improve their software processes with techniques ranging from RAD to XP to disciplined SEI-CMM initiates. As we'll see in this chapter, many of these improvement efforts fail because they fail to acknowledge the *dynamics* of the process (especially the time-delays and the feedback loops) and because they ignore the "soft" processes that play a major role in the real-world behavior of software projects. Hence, there has been a great deal of interest in the past few years in the concept of modeling and simulating the dynamics of such processes; we'll discuss the simulation concepts in Chapter 11, but in this chapter we'll look at some fundamental concepts that may help the death march project manager make more informed decisions.

System dynamics is a concept that has been around for several decades; much of the work carried out in the U.S. in this area can be traced back to the pioneering efforts of Jay Forrester [2] at MIT in the early 1960s. But much has obviously changed since then; we now have desktop computers that facilitate instantaneous interactive model simulation rather than batch systems with one-week turnaround; we have visual modeling languages rather than FORTRAN-like languages such as DYNAMO, which were difficult for end-users to grasp; and we've applied the general concepts of system dynamics to somewhat smaller, more specific problems than the "global model" project that Professor Forrester and his colleagues at the Club of Rome undertook in the 1960s.

One example of a smaller, more specific problem area is that of software processes. Beginning with the pioneering effort of Tarek Abdel-Hamid [1] at MIT in the early 1990s, researchers and process-improvement mavens have been experimenting with the use of system dynamics to achieve a deeper understanding of how the software process *really works* in an organization, in order to have a better chance of improving it. To the extent that these insights can help a project manager understand how things *really work* in the high-pressure crucible of a death march project, they can significantly improve the odds of success.

# MODELS OF SOFTWARE DEVELOPMENT PROCESSES

Most of us interpret the word "model," in the context of discussions about software project management, in terms of graphical abstractions of software—for example, UML diagrams, structure charts, entity-relationship diagrams, and so forth. And in the context of software "processes" and business re-engineering, it's quite common to see models in the form of "work-flow" diagrams or flowcharts.

But that's not how most real-world software managers organize their day-to-day activities. When was the last time a project manager said to everyone on his or her team, "Okay, team, let's gather around the conference table to look at our work-flow models to see what we should be doing today!"? Indeed, managers *do* use such models to plan and discuss overall strategy; but they use a variety of alternative forms of models to cope with problems and to make the day-to-day operational decisions of running a project. Of these alternative forms, the two most important to discuss are *mental models* and *spreadsheet models*.

## Mental Models

A mental model is just what the term implies: a model that one carries around in one's head for dealing with a problem or situation. Such a model may be based on experience or intuition, or on folklore and myth; it may be influenced by politics and a wide spectrum of human emotions. But the key characteristic of a mental model is that it hasn't been written down; and in many cases, it hasn't been articulated in any form and simply represents the "private practice" of software managers as they go about their jobs.

The "official" portions of an organization's software process typically *have* been written down (whether anyone reads them, understands them, or has any intention of following them is an entirely different matter!). Thus, the official model of the software process might say, "First we determine the requirements of our software product, and until those requirements have been accepted by the testing department, anyone attempting to write code or perform detailed design will be executed at sunrise—because we want the testing department to be developing testing procedures in parallel with the implementation work, and they can't do that if they don't know what requirements they're supposed to test for." All of this involves some issues that are important and perhaps controversial; and one can imagine constructive discussions taking place where the activities describe above are modeled in terms of data-flow diagrams or some other mechanism.

But what about the *mental* model that pops up in a manager's head when his or her programmers arrive in his office one morning, halfway through the project, and glumly announce, "Surprise! We have no idea how this happened, but when we woke up this morning, we figured out that we're six months behind schedule!"? The immediate mental model used by the inexperienced project manager concludes with the action plan: "Hire more people right away!" Why? Because the mental model says something like this: "We need to have more work done within a fixed amount of time because we can't delay the project deadline. More people will do more work, therefore the way to get all the required work done is to hire more people."

Of course, many veteran project managers have an entirely different model. They quote, both from their textbook reading of Fred Brooks' *The Mythical Man-Month,* and from their own personal experience, Brooks' Law: *Adding more people to a late software project just makes it later.* Same situation; different mental model. And so the reaction of many project managers—*especially* in death march projects—is based on another mental model: *We have an infinite amount of unpaid overtime available.* If the project is behind schedule, ask the team to "volunteer" for some overtime until the project is back on schedule. If the project schedule is undeniably optimistic from the very beginning, then announce a policy of mandatory overtime from the very beginning of the project—and make sure everyone understands that promotions, raises, bonuses, stock options, and other rewards depend on enthusiastic compliance with the policy.

Here's a third mental model that has been consciously and deliberately used on some of the death march projects I've observed: if you're behind schedule half-way through the project, cut the project team in half. Darwinian principles will ensure that only the fittest will survive the cut, and those survivors will hunker down and start coding furiously; they won't have any time to attend meetings, write memos, or other time-wasting activities. If you're still behind schedule six months later, cut the project team in half again.

And if you think that one is controversial, consider the mental model from a tough-as-nails project manager who has overseen a number of high-pressure development projects for Wall Street financial services firms.[1] It goes like this: *All* projects are behind schedule—it's just a question of when you discover that fact, and how the project team will respond to the discovery. So you might as well plan for it: Create an *extreme* "artificial" crisis in the early days of the project and observe what happens. Predictably, some people will quit because they can't stand the pressure; some will ignore the crisis and continue to work 9-to-5 schedules; some will respond to the pressure in a variety of neurotic or anti-social ways (nervous breakdowns, breaking into tears, bringing a gun into the office, etc.). And some—who often turn out to be the quiet, unassuming members of the project team—will rise up and become heroes, taking charge of the situation and dealing with the crisis.

The Wall Street manager likens the process to a shakedown cruise of a battleship. The artificial crisis allows him to "calibrate" the project team, so he knows how it will respond when the *real* crisis occurs, which it inevitably will. Having accomplished the calibration, he declares the crisis "solved," relaxes the pressure, and continues on with the project.

The point here isn't whether you agree or disagree with *any* of these mental models for dealing with a deadline crisis; the real point is that there are probably a dozen variations of these mental models in your own organization, and you've never discussed them with your colleagues or fellow project managers. Obviously, all of these models can be discussed in a normal conversation; but you can imagine how heated the debates will become when discussing the "artificial crisis" model. Instinctively, we all know that the actions suggested by these models have consequences; our instinctive reaction is to shout, "Yeah, but if you do *X* then *Y* will happen... and in turn, that will make *Z* happen..." How can we communicate our ideas about these issues without degenerating into shouting matches? As we'll see later in this chapter, there are now some very powerful *visual* modeling techniques that make rational discussions of these mental models much easier—*and if they do nothing else, they emphasize the fact that arbitrary management decisions are likely to cause a complex "ripple effect" of consequences.*

There is also an issue of "organizational learning" involved here: Let's assume, for the purposes of discussion, that all of the mental models illustrated above are actually being used within your IT organization. It's reasonable to imagine that some of the mental models work very well and that others are a disaster. It's also quite possible that a crude, primitive mental model has been refined over the years by (successful) veteran project managers to the point where it's now fairly subtle and sophisticated. How do we pass on this knowledge to fledgling project managers who are about to undertake their first "real" project?[2] Wouldn't it be nice to have a mechanism for discussing and illustrating the key mental models, so that experience could be passed on? How else are we *really* going to accomplish "process improvement" in an IT organization?

There's something else to notice about the examples used above: They would almost never be incorporated in the "official" software process model of the organization, for they deal primarily with "social" issues. As Tarek Abdel-Hamid [3] points out:

> *Many studies have indicated that managers often deal with the problems they encounter in terms of mental models that do not necessarily include all the elements or aspects of the problematic situation.*

> *Technically trained managers, in particular, tend to underestimate the influences of their internal social systems. The result is often dysfunctional behavior.*

While the "official" components of a software process model—for example, the choice of a waterfall model versus a prototyping or iterative model—are obviously important, the "soft" issues are just as important. Indeed, they're often *more* important precisely because we don't talk about them. So, if we're going to improve our software processes, we need to have a mechanism for discussing and illustrating, and learning about the "soft" components of the overall software process model.

## Spreadsheet Models

What else do project managers use for guiding their projects besides the "mental models" formed by experience, intuition, or superstition? Obviously, many managers use the PERT charts or Gantt charts provided by today's convenient PC-based project management packages. Indeed, if you walk into a project manager's office, you're likely to find several people huddled around a PERT chart showing the "critical path" for the project; such diagrams do provide a useful and important visualization of key aspects of the project.

It's also quite common to see project managers hunched over their desks, staring intently at rows and columns of a spreadsheet; it wouldn't be too much of an exaggeration to suggest that Microsoft Excel is the most commonly used project management tools in IT organizations. Consider, for example, the spreadsheet shown in Figure 6.1 below, which shows some planning figures for a hypothetical software development organization. Such a model provides useful information, and most managers would argue that they provide some degree of "insight" into the process (or project, or organization) they are studying. And as everyone knows, a number or formula can be changed in any of the spreadsheet cells, and all of the other cells will be updated appropriately.

Nevertheless, there is a fundamental problem with Figure 6.1: It's *visually static*, in the sense that it hasn't changed between the time you first looked at it a moment ago and the time you've looked at it again just now. While the columns of the spreadsheet clearly imply that the behavior of a software organization *over time* is being modeled, we don't *see* the dynamics in any visual sense. Among other things, we don't see the behavior—which might or might not turn out to be interesting—*between* the "snapshots" represented by the columns for fiscal quarter 1, 2, and so on. And if we're dealing with a "pattern" that takes more than eight fiscal quarters to become apparent, we won't see it at all on the spreadsheet.[3]

| FISCAL QUARTER | 1 | 2 | 3 | 4 | 5 | 6 | 7 | 8 |
|---|---|---|---|---|---|---|---|---|
| CASE Tools ($000) | $75 | $75 | $75 | $75 | $75 | $75 | $75 | $75 |
| CASE Training ($000) | $50 | $50 | $40 | $30 | $20 | $20 | $10 | $5 |
| Flextime | Y | Y | Y | Y | Y | .Y | Y | Y |
| Raises (%/yr) | 0.05 | 0.05 | 0.05 | 0.05 | 0.05 | 0.05 | 0.05 | 0.05 |
| Office space | $650 | $650 | $650 | $650 | $650 | $650 | $650 | $650 |
| Participation | 0.7 | 0.7 | 0.7 | 0.7 | 0.7 | 0.7 | 0.7 | 0.7 |
| Capital budget | $17.5 | $17.5 | $17.5 | $17.5 | $17.5 | $17.5 | $17.5 | $17.5 |
| Operating budget | $9.8 | $9.6 | $9.4 | $9.0 | $8.6 | $8.0 | $7.4 | $6.7 |
| Backlog (systems) | 147 | 144 | 141 | 136 | 132 | 126 | 121 | 115 |
| Rookies-headcount | 45 | 43 | 41 | 39 | 37 | 35 | 34 | 33 |
| Veterans-headcount | 152 | 154 | 156 | 158 | 160 | 161 | 162 | 163 |
| Develop. rate | 15.19 | 14.58 | 14.14 | 13.72 | 14.31 | 14.91 | 16.01 | 17.15 |
| Turnover | 3 | 4 | 5 | 6 | 5 | 4 | 4 | 3 |

**Figure 6.1**  *A typical spreadsheet model for project planning*

There's another interesting problem with spreadsheets: Because they're often associated with financial planning activities, we tend to include only the "tangible" things that the "bean-counters" in our organizations want to measure—for example, people, money, workstations, lines of code, and so on. As a result, there's a subtle bias against measuring the "soft" factors in a project—for example, morale, motivation, perceived quality, and accumulated knowledge about a software development methodology.

To illustrate how important this can be, imagine the behavior of a project manager as he watches his team attempt to use a new software methodology—for example, object-oriented design—on a mission-critical project with a tight deadline. The manager's fundamental question is, "Will my project team accumulate enough knowledge, *quickly enough*, about this new technology in order to reap enough benefits from the technology to obtain enough of a productivity improvement to finish the project earlier than would have been possible with the conventional technology we were using previously?" If it appears that the team is struggling with the new technology and failing to accumulate knowledge quickly enough, then the new technology can be abandoned before the project is doomed.

"Accumulated knowledge" is a good example of a "soft" factor; while experienced educators might have some more-or-less quantitative metrics in this area, most software project managers would argue that it's not something they can express in inches, gallons, or pounds per square inch. Consequently, many will argue that no attempt should be made to measure it at all, and they ultimately eliminate it as a "real" phenomenon in their planning. But though they may lack some acceptable quantitative metrics, they can tell you whether the project team has a "lot" or a "little" of accumulated knowledge, and they can tell you whether it's increasing or decreasing. That's enough to form the basis for a rough but useful measurement approach. And it's important: Failing to measure it is equivalent to arguing that it doesn't exist—and yet most managers will agree that the presence or absence of accumulated knowledge *does* matter.

Precisely because such a phenomenon *is* "soft" in nature, we have to treat any associated metrics about it with some healthy caution; it's usually not appropriate to measure such things to three decimal places. But we can use the soft metrics to look for major trends and order-of-magnitude differences in behavior. A very practical question that the project manager might want to ask about the above scenario, for example, is "What would happen to my budget and my schedule if I sent my project team members to some intensive training classes, and as a result they accumulated knowledge about the object-oriented methodologies twice as quickly?"

## Static Versus Dynamic Models

In the discussion above, I referred to Figure 6.1 as a "visually static" model, but there's a far more important aspect of "static" versus "dynamic" that needs to be discussed. Virtually all of the interesting, nontrivial processes that we're likely to study will have a number of important but subtle interactions between the components of the process, and those interactions change over time. The situation above involving "accumulated knowledge" is one example: It changes on a day-to-day basis, and the manager has to continually re-assess it in order to make the best possible decision.

Also important is the nature of the interactions *between* various components in a process. As my colleague Tom DeMarco once observed in a moment of deep metaphysical insight, "Everything is deeply intertwingled." If we change one component of a system, it's likely to have an impact somewhere else—and the interactions involve time-delays and feedback loops. These interactions may have been incorporated into a spreadsheet model such as the one shown in Figure 6.1, but they're not visible to the casual observer. The interactions are equivalent to relationships between cells in the spreadsheet, and those relationships are expressed by appropriate mathematical formulae embedded in the spreadsheet cells. If we use a spreadsheet package and "click" on a cell, then we can see the formula it contains; but if we look at the spreadsheet as a whole, none of the cell-to-cell relationships are visible.

The combination of several interacting components can cause an interesting "ripple effect" in a software organization. Consider the first two items in Figure 6.1, in which a hypothetical software development organization is investing heavily in CASE tools, but spending progressively less money each quarter on associated training. If the

CASE tools impose a formal, rigid methodology for which the staff has not accumulated much knowledge, it wouldn't be surprising to see the development productivity *decline* for the first few time periods; indeed, this is indicated near the bottom of Figure 6.1. But in many organizations, when there is a combination of declining productivity and frustration with the inability to use new CASE tools, morale plummets. Morale, being a soft factor, wasn't included in Figure 6.1, but it certainly does exist. And when morale goes down, employee turnover goes up—more people are likely to quit.

Here's where things start to get interesting. If people in a software development organization quit, who are the first ones out the door? *The people with the highest productivity!* After all, they're the ones who can get the best job offers and they're also the ones likely to be most frustrated by the situation in their current environment. As a result of their departure, the *average* productivity in the organization falls further, which drives down morale... which raises the turnover rate... which pushes more of the remaining highly productive people out the door... and the vicious cycle continues until the organization is left with nothing but zombies who look like cast extras from *Night of the Living Dead*.

If this example sounds too contrived,[4] consider a more mundane example involving project estimating. When estimating a software project, almost all managers add a "safety" factor (otherwise known as a "contingency factor," or a "fudge factor," or various other colorful terms); and they often do this without considering the dynamics involved. But as Abdel-Hamid and Madnick [6] point out, a different safety factor creates a different project. If a project team learns that its manager has published an official project schedule with a safety factor of *zero*, its members immediately modify their behavior by eliminating what they consider "nonessential" work; depending on the nature of the project, this may include documentation, testing, quality assurance, attendance at weekly staff meetings, answering electronic mail, or taking time off to watch their children participate in school events. Conversely, a project schedule with an enormous safety factor leads to "Parkinson's Law": The work expands to fill the available time.

A few of the IT organizations that have reached level 3, 4, or 5 on the SEI process maturity scale have begun to realize that these issues of "process dynamics" are indeed important. Even if we leave out the soft factors for the moment, the impact of feedback loops and time-delays in the process can have an enormous impact on the success of the software process. To use a simple example, consider the impact of defects that are injected into the analysis phase of a classical waterfall software process, but which are not detected until the programming or testing phase. In a formal, rigorous software process, this means that we must "cycle" back to the analysis activity again to fix the defect—and then push the corrected analysis-product forward through design and coding until it reaches the testing step again. Of course, it's possible that the defect-correction activity was faulty, and our testing process may uncover yet another defect... which means that *several* cycles may be necessary before a satisfactory result can "exit" from the testing phase. All of this has a significant impact on the overall "cycle time" of the process, which our software development organizations are striving to improve.

# VISUAL MODELS

If the dynamics of a software process are important, how can we study them? As suggested above, spreadsheets are inadequate, for they don't illustrate the interdependencies and feedback loops between components of a process. Instead, visual models are usually better for illustrating the "holistic" nature of a process; such models invite discussions, comments, and "yes...but..." arguments.

The argument for visual models should not come as a shock to most software professionals, for we have long used visual modeling techniques to illustrate the technical components of the systems we build for our customers. And since a software process could be regarded as the "system for building systems," it makes good sense to use familiar modeling tools such as data-flow diagrams, entity-relationship diagrams, object-oriented diagrams, and so on as the basis for modeling a software process.

There's only one problem: All of these familiar graphical notations are *visually static*. With few exceptions, the notations were invented prior to the introduction of modern CASE tools—and as a result, we're accustomed to drawing the pictures on a piece of paper or displaying them on a passive CASE display. When you display a data-flow diagram on a typical CASE tool, it doesn't "move"—it doesn't show the dynamics of the underlying process for which it serves as a model. To do that would require *animation*, which most CASE vendors have never considered.

As a result, the software organizations that are trying to achieve a deeper understanding of their software processes are turning to simulation tools that provide simple but powerful mechanisms for representing the dynamics of a system. One such product is iThink,[5] which uses a notation somewhat like data-flow diagrams to represent a system; a small example is shown in Figure 6.2 below.

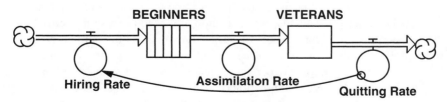

**Figure 6.2**  *A typical iThink model*

Obviously, these diagrams are visually static, too, when you see them in a printed book like this. But when displayed on a computer screen, the model-builder has the ability to animate the diagrams by instructing iThink to run a simulation of the process. In addition to an animation of the diagram in Figure 6.2, both software packages can produce the usual array of charts and graphs to describe the behavior of key process variables over time.

The syntax of iThink and similar tools would fill a book of its own, and the details of building system dynamics models is also a subject unto itself. But while some of the real-world modeling projects have turned out to be enormously ambitious and complicated, it takes relatively little work to become sufficiently familiar with this kind of technology to begin building useful models of the software process. A small example is provided below.

# AN EXAMPLE: TAREK ABDEL-HAMID'S SOFTWARE PROCESS MODEL

Perhaps the most famous example of a system dynamics model of the software development process has been created by Professor Tarek Abdel-Hamid and published in textbook form by Abdel-Hamid and Madnick [1]. It represents the project management activities in a medium-sized software development project, using conventional development tools and a classic waterfall development process. While it doesn't accurately represent many of today's projects that use rapid prototyping, visual development tools, libraries of re-usable components, etc., it nevertheless provides a very important starting point for an organization that wants to better understand the interactions between different components of its software development process.

The model contains components that describe human resource management within a project, as well as software production, testing, quality assurance project control, and project planning. For a full description of the model, including its implementation in a simulation language known as DYNAMO, consult Abdel-Hamid and Madnick [1]. For the purposes of illustration, I'll describe portions of the human resource component of the model.

From the project manager's perspective, the members of the team can be categorized as beginners or veterans; Abdel-Hamid and Madnick use the term "rookies" and "pros," as shown in Figure 6.3 below.[6] The "dynamics" of the human resource management process involve the hiring of new people, as required, the "assimilation" of rookies into pros as they become experienced, and the eventual departure of pros as they quit or die of old age. In the visual notation of iThink, the "clouds" represent the "boundary" of the model; we don't know or care where the rookies come from, nor do we care where the pros disappear to when they leave the project. Project team members "flow" through the "pipelines" represented by the double-headed arrows, and they remain for periods of time in the "reservoirs" represented by the rectangular boxes in Figure 6.3.

The "bubbles" attached to the pipelines are "flow regulators," much like a spigot on a water faucet; they control the rate at which items move through the pipelines.

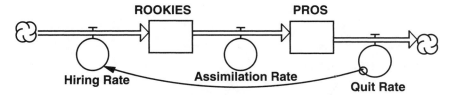

**Figure 6.3**  Abdel-Hamid and Madnick's human resource model, Part 1

One advantage of *any* visual model is that it gives us something to talk about. For example, when considering the model in Figure 6.3, a number of things occur to us:

- We could question the basic assumption implied by Figure 6.3 that all newly hired people are rookies; why not allow for the possibility of hiring experienced "pros"? Abdel-Hamid and Madnick address this issue explicitly by arguing that *all* new members in a project team are rookies, even if they have worked in the software field for 25 years. While the newcomers to the project team may be experts in hardware and software technologies, they typically don't know the nuances of the project itself—for example, the buzzwords and acronyms, the politics and personalities, and the details of whatever technical work took place before they arrived. However, someone with 25 years of experience will probably assimilate himself or herself into the project team much more rapidly than someone who just graduated from college last week; thus, as we'll see below, the "assimilation" regulator in Figure 6.3 is *not* a constant.

- What about the assumption that rookies don't quit? Figure 6.3 clearly implies that rookies either remain rookies forever (if they're trapped within the rookies reservoir) or they eventually flow through the pipeline and are promoted to the status of pros; the model clearly shows that only pros disappear into the clouds. Obviously, this might not be a realistic assumption in some organizations, and the model might have to be adjusted to make it more realistic.

It's important to note that the second issue is one that can be discussed and debated without any consideration of the dynamics—in other words, a traditional dataflow diagram, as well as the visually static representation of Figure 6.3, is adequate for ensuring that all of the decision-makers in our organization have the same "shared mental model" of the process of software people entering and leaving the organization.

But the reality of human resource management is actually more complex than shown in Figure 6.3; one level of elaboration is shown in Figure 6.4 below:

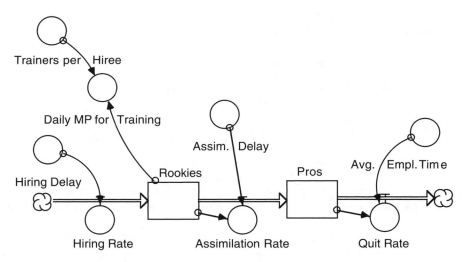

**Figure 6.4** *Abdel-Hamid and Madnick's human resource model, Part 2*

This version of the model shows three "converters" that influence the behavior of the regulators on the pipelines. In a real-world environment, we could imagine that an appropriate means of describing the assimilation rate and the quitting rate might be a "normal distribution"—that is, a certain percentage of the pros quit almost immediately after entering the pros reservoir and a certain percentage remain in the reservoir until they die of old age. If we're willing to accept the notion of a normal distribution, then the parameter that we'll probably want to "play with" is the "average empl. time" that represents the "mean" quitting rate.

But the "hiring delay" bubble in Figure 6.4 represents something entirely different: a time-delay. Without a description of how it actually works in iThink, think about the reality of what happens in most organizations when the project manager calls the human resources department and says, "I need two more programmers for my project." The answer is typically something like, "Okay, fine, that will take three months." Meanwhile, the project has to continue muddling along, and the project manager must continue worrying about the chances he'll meet his deadline.

One of the "system dynamics" questions that becomes relevant in such a discussion—especially when faced with aggressive deadlines in a death march project—is, "How would the behavior of the entire project change if the hiring delay imposed by the human resources department was only one month instead of three months? What would happen if it were reduced to *zero*?"

Two bubbles in the top left portion of Figure 6.3 describe another aspect of newly hired people: They need to be trained. When combined with other portions of the overall Abdel-Hamid/Madnick model, we begin to see one aspect of Brooks' Law, which argues that adding more people to a late software project just makes it later: the addition of new people consumes some of the resources of existing staff members, for training purposes.

Figure 6.5 shows a further elaboration of the human resource component of a software-process model: Now we take into account the possibility that staff members may be *transferred* from a project team to some other part of the organization. One might argue that from the project manager's perspective, a "transfer" is no different from quitting; after all, the net result is that the staff member disappears into the clouds. But there *is* a difference, and it's indicated by the flow-regulators labeled as "transfer delay" on the pipelines emanating from the rookies and pros reservoirs. This corresponds to the real-world experience of many managers: When an employee quits, he or she disappears from the team immediately; but if someone tries to "steal" your team members by transferring them out of your team to a different project, you can usually delay the transfer for several weeks or months to ensure that your work-in-progress is finished.

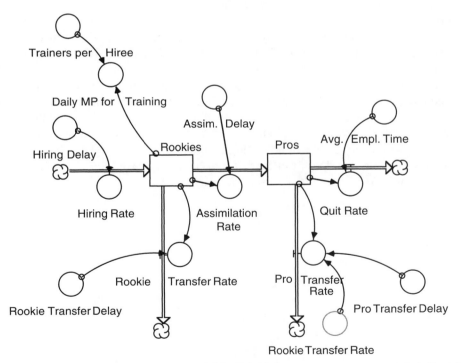

**Figure 6.5**  *Abdel-Hamid and Madnick's human resource model, Part 3*

Finally, Figure 6.6 shows the complete human resource component of the Abdel-Hamid/Madnick model. The additional components shown in Figure 6.6 address the truly fundamental question that the project manager has to cope with on a day-to-day basis: *How many* new people should I hire onto my project team? This involves a calculation in a different part of the model (one that is not shown here) to determine the "work force level needed," based on the productivity of the existing staff members, how close the project is to the deadline, and various other factors that affect the manager's "willingness" to augment the team. However, the "needed" work force may be limited by various constraints; in the top right corner of Figure 6.6 is a bubble labeled "ceiling on new hires" which involves some calculations about the number of new hirees that can be accommodated by "full time equivalent" (FTE) members of the team.

Note also that the "work force gap" bubble serves as an *input* to the "rookie transfer rate" and "pro transfer rate" bubbles in Figure 6.6. This reflects the fact that the project manager might determine that he has a surplus of project team members (perhaps because the team was more productive than expected, or because there were fewer defects to correct, etc.), and that he wants to initiate a transfer in order to trim the size of the team.

A common reaction to the model shown in Figure 6.6 is, "Well this is all very interesting, but it's *very* complicated. And I don't see what it has to do with the use of object-oriented technology and the latest programming tools that I'm using to increase productivity in my team." True—but it *does* provide more insight into the dynamics of team members arriving and leaving the project team, which can often have just as large an impact on project success as the choice of programming languages.[7] And though Figure 6.6 looks a bit complicated at first, the visual notation is straightforward enough to make it digestible after a little study. Finally, keep in mind the consequences of the "head-in-the-sand" reaction to all of this: If the project manager decides that the process illustrated in Figure 6.6 is so complicated that he doesn't want to think about it, that doesn't mean that it disappears. *These issues exist in real-world projects, whether we want to acknowledge them or not.*

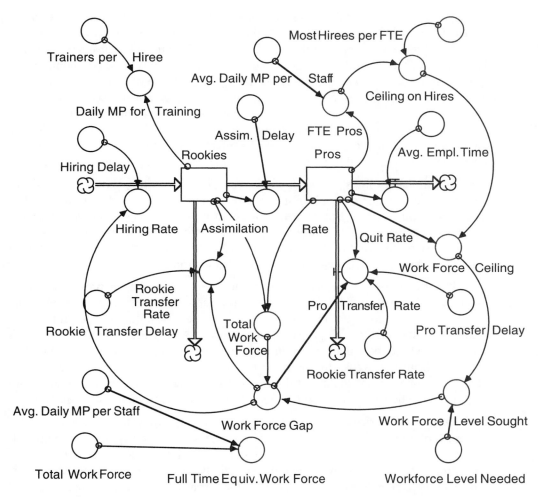

**Figure 6.6** Abdel-Hamid and Madnick's human resource model, Part 4

# SUMMARY AND CONCLUSIONS

In an ideal world, the manager of a death march project would have the time, the money, the patience, and the technical resources to create a systems dynamics model of the key elements of his or her project—in other words, something as detailed and sophisticated as Figure 6.6, but representing the entire project rather than just the human-resource "sub-system" discussed in the previous section.

The primary reason for constructing such a model is to use it as the basis of "what-if" experiments, *especially* to look for "nonlinear" behavioral aspects of the overall project. In some cases, for example, it might turn out that a substantial increase in a particular "parameter" (such as the number of new rookies hired per month) has a negligible impact on a key parameter such as "expected date of completion." In other cases, a seemingly modest change in a seemingly minor parameter (such as the "quitting rate" for veterans in Figure 6.6 above) can have an enormous impact *which nobody anticipates in advance.* The reason for the "nonobvious" consequences is that we humans have a difficult time calculating the quantitative impact of multiple variables interacting with one another in the context of time-delays and feedback loops.

Unfortunately, most of us don't live in an ideal world—and *very* few death march project managers are given the time or resources to create the kind of models discussed in this chapter. But even the most hard-pressed manager has *some* time and *some* resources—even if it's only a single person who spends only a single hour or two identifying the kind of time-delays and feedback loops that are likely to have a significant systems dynamics-related impact on the project.

If nothing else, the visual notations illustrated in this chapter provide a convenient, effective manner for everyone to achieve a so-called "shared mental model" about key assumptions that may determine the success or failure of the project. For example, if the death march project manager says, "A critical success factor for this project is going to be reducing the 'turnaround time' for stakeholder approval on key decisions from two weeks to one day," it would be nice for everyone—and in this case, "everyone" means higher level managers and other key project stakeholders—to see where and how that "project parameter" will affect the "dynamics" of the project.

From my experience as a management consultant, I know that everyone is in far too much of a hurry to stop and think about such issues at the beginning of a project. Sadly, the impact of nonlinear system dynamics sometimes becomes evident only after a project failure—and even then, the system dynamics are often ignored or overlooked completely while everyone looks for the "straw that broke the camel's back." It may be politically satisfying to look for a scapegoat, a single decision or a single mistake that appears to have caused the downfall of the entire project; but even a rudimentary systems-dynamics postmortem will usually demonstrate that there were *numerous* interdependencies, combined with subtle feedback loops and time-delays.

By the time such a postmortem takes place, though, the project has collapsed, the project manager has been fired, the project team members and end-users have moved on to greener pastures, and the lawyers and auditors have been called in to assess blame and responsibility.

One can only hope that the project manager will learn a lesson from all of this—and *next* time, perhaps find the relatively small amount of time and resources needed to perform a modest system dynamics review of the key elements of the project.

# NOTES

1. These were characterized as "ugly" projects in Chapter 2: The project will succeed, but there will be a lot of blood on the floor when it finally ends.

2. As my colleague Tim Lister likes to say, the training we provide for new project managers usually consists of two words: "Good luck!"

3. Obviously, we could add more columns to the spreadsheet, but we rapidly run out of room within the constraints of most printed sheets of paper. We could rotate the paper by 90 degrees and let the columns march down the page, but it's a clumsy solution.

4. It *is* realistic, by the way—I've seen it on consulting visits to several large *Fortune* 500 organizations and government agencies. To make matters worse, management often exacerbates the problem by putting more and more pressure on the ever-shrinking staff, insisting that they work long hours of overtime, and so on.

5. Available from High Performance Systems, Inc.; see www.hps-inc.com for more details.

6. It's typically useful to make such a distinction because the rookies can be presumed to have a different productivity and a different cost (salary, benefits, etc.) from the pros.

7. Remember also that I've shown only a small portion of the Abdel-Hamid/Madnick model here; other subsystems *do* deal with the actual "production" of software, where the project manager can experiment with different assumptions about the productivity impact of the latest whiz-bang CASE tools and programming languages. And other portions of the model also deal with additional "soft" human issues—for example, what happens if the project manager discovers that he's behind schedule and decides to compensate by asking the project team to work overtime?

# REFERENCES

1. Tarek Abdel-Hamid and Stuart E. Madnick, *Software Project Dynamics: An Integrated Approach,* Englewood Cliffs, NJ: Prentice Hall, 1991.

2. Jay Forrester, *Industrial Dynamics,* Cambridge, MA: MIT Press, 1961.

3. Tarek Abdel-Hamid, "Organizational Learning: the Key to Software Management Innovation," *American Programmer,* June 1991.

4. G.P. Richardson and G.L. Pugh, III, *Introduction to Systems Dynamics Modeling with Dynamo*, Cambridge, MA: MIT Press, 1981.

5. Tarek Abdel-Hamid and Stuart E. Madnick, "Impact of Schedule Estimation on Software Project Behavior," *IEEE Software,* May, 1986.

6. Tarek Abdel-Hamid and S. E. Madnick, "Lessons Learned from Modeling the Dynamics of Software Project Management," *Communications of the ACM,* December, 1989.

7. Peter M. Senge, *The Fifth Discipline: The Art and Practice of the Learning Organization,* New York: Doubleday, 1994.

8. Tarek Abdel-Hamid, "Thinking in Circles," *American Programmer*, May 1993.

9. Brad Smith, Nghia Nguyen, and Richard Vidale, "Death of a Software Manager: How to Avoid Career Suicide though Dynamic Software Process Modeling," *American Programmer,* May 1993.

10. Karim J. Chichakly, "The Bifocal Vantage Point: Managing Software Projects from a Systems Thinking Perspective," *American Programmer*, May 1993.

11. Ernst W. Diehl, "The Analytical Lens: Strategy-Support Software to Enhance Executive Dialog and Debate," *American Programmer*, May 1993.

12. Chi Y. Lin, "Walking on Battlefields: Tools for Strategic Software Management," *American Programmer*, May 1993.

13. Kenneth G. Cooper and Thomas W. Mullen, "Swords and Plowshares: The Rework Cycles of Defense and Commercial Software Development Projects," *American Programmer*, May 1993.

14. Rembert Aranda, Thomas Fiddaman, and Rogelio Oliva, "Quality Microworlds: Modeling the Impact of Quality Initiatives over the Software Product Life Cycle," *American Programmer*, May 1993.

15. Tony Variale, Bob Rosetta, Mike Steffen, Howard Rubin, and Ed Yourdon, "Modeling the Maintenance Process," *American Programmer*, March 1994.

# 7 Critical-Chain Scheduling and the Theory of Constraints

*The greatest obstacle to discovery is not ignorance—it is the illusion of knowledge.*

—Daniel Boorstin (Librarian of Congress),
*Washington Post,* Jan. 29, 1984

## INTRODUCTION

An implicit premise of this book, at least for the last several chapters, is that a death march project represents dysfunctional behavior on the part of the customer, end-user, stakeholders, or entire organization—which the project manager has to cope with, survive, and hopefully overcome in a successful fashion. After all, what kind of rational, intelligent, ethical, fair-minded person would ask a project manager to accomplish something in half the amount of time that would normally be scheduled or with half the budget or half the number of software engineers?

But here's a radical thought: What if the "twice-as-fast" schedule actually represents *normal* behavior for an IT project, and it's been the dysfunctional behavior of the organization that prevented that kind of accelerated schedule from ever taking place? Instead of desperately looking for strategies to enable a project to take place twice as fast as "normal," what if we decided that our objective was to remove the dysfunctional obstacles that traditionally doomed our projects to take *twice as long* as they should have?

Such a thought is *so* radical that many project managers will reject it immediately and insist that we return to the "real world" for some "practical" strategies on succeeding with death march projects. But if you're willing to "suspend your disbelief" for a moment and explore the radical thought in more detail, you would probably ask four questions:

- What are some examples of "dysfunctional" behavior within organizations that routinely lead to IT projects (as well as many other "production" projects outside the world of IT) which take twice as long as they should?

- How can we get senior management and stakeholders to understand and agree that such behaviors really are dysfunctional—and more important, how can we transform the entire organizational culture into a more "rational" set of behaviors?

- If the organization were to exhibit rational behavior, what kind of strategy would yield the best results for scheduling tasks and activities in a software development project?
- How can we operationalize such a strategy in order to provide specific, tangible procedures, guidelines, and checklists for project managers to use on a day-to-day basis?

A collection of fascinating answers to these questions—generally referred to as the "theory of constraints" and "critical-chain scheduling"—has developed over the past twenty years, largely through the passionate and eloquent advocacy of Dr. Eliyahu Goldratt [2, 4]. Indeed, the ideas have been so widely praised and endorsed, and have achieved such impressive results, that one wonders why they have not become the "mainstream" of project management. One plausible answer is that many organizations *are* dysfunctional and it's very difficult to change deeply entrenched dysfunctional behavior in the absence of a skilled "therapist," and in the absence of a crisis that threatens the organization's very survival.

A full treatment of critical-chain scheduling, and the theory of constraints, would fill an entire book; indeed, several excellent books have already been published and are listed at the end of this chapter [2, 4]. My objective here is to provide an introduction to and overview of the concepts, along with a few practical nuggets of advice that a death march project manager can put to good use. Beyond that, I enthusiastically recommend one or more of the books listed at the end of the chapter—perhaps they will convince you that your organization *is* dysfunctional, and that you should do something about it!

# WHAT ORGANIZATIONAL BEHAVIORS ARE DYSFUNCTIONAL?

In the years since the publication of the first edition of *Death March*, the American public has been exposed to story after story of dysfunctional corporate behavior caused by greed, arrogance, hubris, and a total absence of ethical behavior. But that is not the subject of this chapter: Our objective here is not to explain what caused the debacle at Enron or Worldcom, but merely to focus on the dysfunctional behavior associated with schedules, estimates, and the day-to-day attempts throughout a project to achieve the deadlines and budgets that have been imposed. Perhaps in the most extreme case, this can escalate into behavior worthy of indictments, arrests, and lawsuits; but in most cases, it merely leads to project overruns, disgruntled customers, and demoralized workers.

Much of this dysfunctional behavior can be understood by using the "system dynamics" concepts discussed in the previous chapter. Indeed, the organizational "system for building systems" is far more complex, with many more "cause-and-effect" feedback loops and time-delays than most managers realize. And as emphasized in Chapter 6, the organizational system includes a number of "soft" factors such as morale that are simply not on the "radar screen" of the typical mid-level or senior manager.

For example, imagine what happens if some event—for example, an unpopular management decision to eliminate end-of-year bonuses—causes employee morale in the IT organization to decline. One of the many possible consequences of *decreased* morale is *increased* turnover—perhaps not immediately, but over the next several months, it's likely that additional people will look for jobs elsewhere. But who are the IT people most likely to leave? Typically, the people with the highest productivity, and the greatest skills; after all, they are the ones most likely to be able to find opportunities elsewhere, even if there is a recession. But if high-productivity individuals leave, what does that do to the average productivity in the organization? And if average productivity drops, perhaps causing schedule delays and cancelled projects, what does that do to employee morale? What began as a single event, with a single (perhaps predictable) response has now turned into a "vicious circle" that can easily spiral out of control, until the IT organization is populated only by misfits and malcontents who simply cannot find a job anywhere else.

Of course, this example has nothing to do with scheduling and project management *per se*; but it *does* involve compensation and employee rewards. In general, organizations reward and punish, measure and monitor their employees on a *local* basis, even though they are (or should be) interested in achieving *global* results. From a system-dynamics perspective, this can lead to a number of dysfunctional scenarios, none of which were intended by well-meaning managers or loyal employees.

For example, the organization *should* say to a project manager, "All we care about is that the entire project is finished on time; we don't care how you organize the tasks and activities within the project. If the project succeeds, we'll provide an aggregate bonus for the entire team." But in almost every organization, the dominant organizational culture insists that the project manager partition the project into small tasks and activities; and the culture makes it abundantly clear to the individual workers that they are expected to finish each of their individual tasks on time. Indeed, it often turns out that a worker who has a perfect record of delivering his own tasks on time will be rewarded regardless of whether the project succeeds; and the worker who delivers some of his tasks behind schedule will be punished, even though the project succeeded.

Of course, it's possible that none of this has been documented; it's even possible that mid-level and senior-level managers will adamantly deny that such a culture exists. But to the workers, actions speak louder than words; as they see which actions lead to which results, they adjust their behavior accordingly. And while they may feel too embarrassed to admit it openly, the reality is that if they have to choose between the project's success and their own success, self-interest will generally prevail.

What does this mean from a practical perspective? It means a worker will provide a "worst-case" estimate for his own tasks in order to minimize the chances of being late. In some cases, he'll be very vocal about his strategy and his manager may even agree with the strategy; but in other cases, he'll do his best to hide the "buffer" that he has built into his estimate, for he worries that his manager will remove it as unnecessary padding. And while this may seem reasonable, even rational (after all, we've all been doing it that way ever since we entered the work force!), consider what happens *when the "worst case" doesn't happen.*

In a "normal" scenario, none of the worst-case contingencies are needed: no instances of Murphy's Law occur, no unforeseen problems or crises occur, and the task is finished *before* the deadline. But how many workers—whether they be programmers, database designers, or assembly-line factory workers—will tell their boss they've finished ahead of schedule? The worker can think of a thousand reasons to keep the early completion quiet, not the least of which is fear of punishment from the boss[1] ("Aha! So you really *did* pad your schedule! Next time, I'll cut your estimate in half!"). Indeed, we've developed a familiar "law" to describe one aspect of this phenomenon: Parkinson's Law, which says that work expands to fill the available time. All of this is so familiar that you may not even consider it dysfunctional; but when we compare it to the behavior we might expect in a "rational" world, in two later sections of this chapter, the difference will seem like night and day.

Before we move forward to a discussion of "rational" worlds, though, consider another dysfunctional reaction to the scenario just described. If all of the workers provide worst-case estimates of all of their tasks and then carefully "pace" themselves so as to achieve nothing better than those worst-case estimates, the aggregate sum of all such estimates is likely to lead to a project-completion date far later than is acceptable. And when the project manager (or the project stakeholders to whom he reports) realize this, their reaction is predictable: They'll arbitrarily cut the schedule by whatever percentage is required in order to meet the predetermined deadline. And that cut, first imposed at the "global" level, will then ripple down to the individual tasks; thus, each worker will be told, "Yes, I know you said your 'conservative' estimate for this task was 10 days, but we have to cut 20% off the schedule in order to meet the deadline that we've promised. So, even though I know it's not really fair, I can only give you eight days to finish that task."

Let's assume, for the purpose of this discussion, that the worker's original estimate of 10 days was carefully calculated so that he could legitimately say to his manager, "There's a 99% chance that I'll have this task finished by the end of 10 days, and only a one percent chance that I'll be late!" That's fine, but it's highly unlikely that the worker would have bothered, during his initial estimating process, to figure out what the probability of success would be for an eight-day schedule. And when the eight-day schedule is arbitrarily imposed upon him, it's also unlikely that he'll bother going back to recalculate the probability of success. After all, why bother? As far as the worker is concerned, the probability no longer matters, because he feels he no longer has any opportunity to negotiate or bargain—he's been given the unilateral decree that eight days is now the deadline, so he shrugs his shoulders and starts working.

The result is that the availability of that worker's time on the eighth day, ninth day, and 10th day is now impossible to judge accurately. The manager may *think* that the worker will finish on the eighth day (because he thinks, "I have decreed that it will be so, and therefore it *will* be so"), but he has no rational basis for such a thought; and the worker has abdicated all sense of responsibility and judgment about when he'll finish. As a result of this dysfunctional turn of events, both worker and manager are operating in the dark.

Here's another example: In many organizations, workers are measured by how busy they are and managers are measured by how busy they manage to keep their workers. It may not be expressed in quite those terms, but think back to all of those on-the-job situations where you felt guilty (or downright fearful) if you had an hour at your desk with nothing to do. And think how guilty and incompetent you felt, as a first-time supervisor, if the Vice President happened to stroll through your work-area and notice that one of your subordinates was sitting idle at his desk.[2]

In an attempt to keep busy (or at least provide the external appearance of being busy), managers often assign more than one task to their workers—and the workers accept multiple tasks. There may be some scenarios where this leads to more efficient use of the worker's time and energies, but at the very least, there is some "overhead" associated with switching between one task and another, over and over again. And because of the phenomenon discussed earlier, the worker feels that he dare not finish *any* of his multiple tasks until the very moment they are due; thus, rather than working solely on task A until it is completed, and then task B, and then task C, he'll juggle back and forth between all three—and (if nothing goes wrong), he'll deliver the final results of A, B, and C on the last day of his assigned schedule. And this means that other workers on the project, who required A, B, and/or C as prerequisite inputs for *their* activities, will be unable to start until that particular moment in time. In a more rational world, task A would have been finished at a much earlier point in time; and whoever was waiting for the completion of task A would be able to start *his* task much earlier.

Again, the reaction to all of this often introduces another layer of dysfunctional behavior. Since the workers who are waiting for the completion of tasks A, B, and C are likely to be impatient (and because they are being pestered by *their* boss), they're likely to interrupt the first worker and complain, "Hey! Why are you working on task B, when I'm desperately waiting for task A?" Thus, following the old adage that "The squeaky wheel gets the grease," the first worker stops working on task B, and switches back to task A … until he is interrupted by another worker, who says, "Hey, I thought you were working on task B for me! Why did you stop? Why are you wasting your time—or, in any case, *my* time—by working on task A?" Thus, the task-switching mechanism for the multi-tasking worker is often crisis- or interrupt-driven, which is highly unlikely to be the optimal allocation of time and resources.

# HOW CAN WE CHANGE DYSFUNCTIONAL ORGANIZATIONAL BEHAVIOR?

Changing this kind of dysfunctional behavior is not easy; indeed, it's so deeply ingrained in most organizations that it's virtually impossible. As with the efforts to cope with alcoholism or other substance-abuse problems, it must begin with a deep, sincere, and profound realization and acceptance that the current behavior *is* dysfunctional. It's particularly difficult in today's society, which typically prefers a "quick-fix" solution to serious problems—for example, the equivalent of a "diet pill" that will melt off extra pounds even though we continue to eat too much junk food.

My colleague, Tom DeMarco, likes to tell the story of consulting clients he visits, who ask him, "If we could do just *one thing* to improve our project-management situation, what would it be?" Tom's answer is often simple: "Stop assigning people to work on five or six unrelated projects simultaneously; give everyone *one* project to work on, and leave them alone until they finish that one project." Invariably, says Tom, the response is, "Well, yeah, that *sounds* very rational. But you don't understand, that just wouldn't work in our organization—because in our organization we have constraints A, B, and C, and we have to deal with political problems X, Y, and Z … so give us another *one thing* that could make all of our project management problems go away." Any suggestion that attacks the dysfunctional behaviors in the organization is almost certain to be rejected with the phrase, "Well, maybe that would work in a perfect world—but in the 'real world' where we operate, it could never happen because of X, Y, and Z…" And the organization eventually finds a "pill"—a new development tool, a new systems analysis methodology, a new buzzword—that may bring short-term relief, but rarely attacks the underlying problems.

Even if the organization accepts the notion that its project-management behavior is dysfunctional, it may not understand the manifestations and causes of that behavior in sufficient detail to do anything about it. That should not surprise us, since the same thing is true at the individual level: People who are overweight, or prone to substance-abuse problems, may not understand the psychological, physiological, and sociological forces that led to their current state. It may take months or years of therapy to uncover the details, and not everyone has the patience or resources to undergo that kind of analysis.

The same holds true at the organizational level—especially because the systems dynamics issues underlying the dysfunctional behavior are subtle and complex. Indeed, one of the themes in Chapter 6 is that, until recently, we haven't even had a "language" with which to discuss such issues, let alone study them in a quantitative fashion. The basic concepts of systems dynamics have been discussed for roughly 30 years, but it has been only during the past decade that serious efforts—such as the pioneering modeling efforts of Tarek Abdel-Hamid—have been made to apply them to the field of software development. Alas, these tools and the underlying systems dynamics concepts have received relatively little attention, especially in comparison to the "pills" that the industry loves: new programming languages, new visual programming tools, new buzzword-oriented methodologies (RAD, JAD, XP, OO, UML, and many more). And so the dysfunction continues.

But my goal in this book is not to solve the dysfunctional behavior of entire organizations; nor is it the typical project manager's goal to revolutionize his or her entire organization. The immediate task is to survive and conquer *this* death march project—or, if the dysfunctional forces appear to be too strong, to make the brave decision to walk away from it. Similarly, the spouse of an alcoholic might wish there was a nationwide solution to the problem, but the first priority is to help his or her partner—or, if that proves impossible, then find the strength to terminate the relationship.[3]

For the project manager facing a death march project, two things are necessary. First, determine whether one's own project-management behaviors are dysfunctional—and if so, whether they can be changed. If your attitude at this point is, "The discussion in this chapter is absurd! Our company's scheduling, estimating, and project management behaviors are perfectly sensible!", then either (a) they *are* sensible, and I'm the crazy one, or (b) you and your organization are *so* dysfunctional that you don't even recognize it. In either case, you might as well skip the rest of this chapter, and see whether there's something of value in the chapters to follow.

However, if your attitude is, "Yes, I completely agree that my organization's project-management behavior is hopelessly dysfunctional—and if they left me alone, I would do things in a *much* more rational way!", then you have a potentially simpler problem: How can you get "them" to leave you alone? By "them" I mean whatever organizational and political forces conspire to make you and your team members behave in a dysfunctional way; thus, it might be your immediate boss or other higher level managers who are the problem, or the Methodology Police, or the human resources department, or the end-users and project stakeholders, or *everyone* in the IT organization.[4]

In any case, the trick is figuring out how you can remove yourself and the project team from the surrounding dysfunctional behavior. In my opinion, that's one reason the so-called "skunk works" approach is often so successful: The project team removes itself from the "normal" office environment, and hunkers down in an empty warehouse at the far edge of town. An alternative, in today's networked world, is to let everyone work at home, with weekly (or daily) meetings at the local pub. Another alternative is to have the team work the "graveyard shift" from 10 p.m. to 6 a.m. for the duration of the project; if it's six months or less, it might not pose an intolerable burden on people's personal lives, and it might take the corporate bureaucracy that long to figure out that the entire team has effectively gone AWOL.

Sadly, whenever I suggest strategies like these, the most common response from intelligent, dedicated, earnest project managers is, "Well, yeah, that sounds great—and in a perfect world, we would certainly try something like that. But in the *real* world that I live in, we couldn't possibly do that, because it make the VP of systems development really mad, and it would lead to an official reprimand from the HR department, and it would cause political problems X, Y, and Z…"

And so the dysfunction continues.

# LIFE IN A RATIONAL WORLD

For the remainder of this chapter, let's assume that you've somehow created a small island of sanity in the ocean of dysfunctional behavior surrounding you. What kind of project-management strategies and behaviors would you implement? What would your "rational world" look like?

Before we get into the specifics, let's first discuss the philosophical foundations of such a rational world. As Robert Newbold [5] summarizes it, that foundation would consist of four things:

1. We have an approach to scheduling and logistics that protects us from the effects of Murphy's Law.

2. People are focused on global (system-wide) improvements rather than local ones.

3. Everyone understands and accepts the policies, procedures, and measurements that apply to them.

4. We believe we can make dramatic improvements.[5]

Making certain that everyone understands and accepts the policies and ensuring that everyone believes in the possibility of dramatic improvements are significant tasks unto themselves, of course. But we'll have to leave the details of those tasks for some other discussion—or for your own review of Newbold's excellent book.

As for the first two items on Newbold's list, we've already hinted at two practical strategies: Instead of encouraging every worker to hide a localized "buffer" in his own schedule in order to protect him or herself against worst-case situations, we ask him or her instead to estimate the "average" case—in other words, a task-schedule that has an equal probability of being early *or* late. In a simplistic project, consisting of a single, linear "chain" of sequential tasks, one can hope that the time saved by early-finishing tasks will offset the time lost by late-finishing tasks. For more complex (and realistic) project situations, that won't be sufficient—and we'll want to have a "buffer" to protect ourselves against the unpredictable nature of the tasks, and the "global" instances of Murphy's Law (the most critical, or most complex, of the tasks turn out to be the ones that finish late). But as we'll see in section 7.5 below, the "buffer" should be planned, maintained, and protected by the project manager as an *aggregate*, and doled out only when necessary.

Thus, some localized tasks may finish later than estimated, but others will finish early. To make all of this work, we need to encourage workers to finish their scheduled work as quickly as possible, and we need to remind them not to "create" work when there is none. In the best of all cases, whenever they finish a task, we'll have a new one to give them—and whoever was waiting for them to finish will now be able to start *his* or *her* task. But in a rational world, it's okay to respond to the unpredictable duration of tasks by occasionally sitting idle.

There's a related behavior that we need to have in our rational world: the behavior of honestly acknowledging that we don't have precise answers to fuzzy, complex questions. If someone asks you to estimate how long it will take to perform a complex task that you've never done before, there's no point saying something like, "I estimate that it will require three days, one hour, and four minutes—and there's a 50% change that I might be early by one minute, and I might be late by one minute." Depending on how confident you are, and how honest you are with yourself and your manager, you might say, "I estimate that it will require about three days—and there's a 50% chance that I might be a day early, or a day late," or even "I estimate that it will take about a week—and there's a 50% chance that I could be late by as much as a week, or early by as much as a week." (For example, the latter possibility means that you believe there's a small, but nonzero, chance that, once you actually begin working on the task, you'll find a brilliant solution that will allow the task to be finished instantaneously.)

Eliyahu Goldratt [2] argues that the project manager's strategy should be based on the "Theory of Constraints" (TOC) illustrated in Figure 7.1 below:

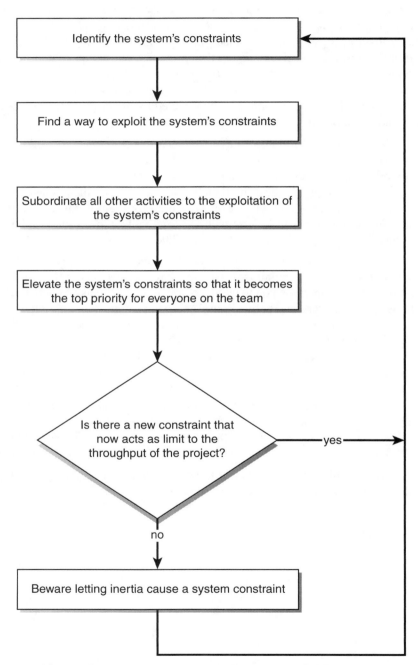

**Figure 7.1**   The steps representing the TOC approach

It's important to realize that the "constraint" represented in the first box of Figure 7.1 may or may not be something as obvious and straightforward as a complex, time-consuming programming task. The constraint might turn out to be a scarce or unavailable resource (e.g., a database designer, or a new piece of hardware, or simply a conference room in which the team can hold meetings). Or it might be a set of organizational policies that inhibits productive work at a critical time, or that motivates project team members to devote time and energy to noncritical activities. All of these need to be identified, exploited, and monitored not only by the project manager, but by all of the team members.

# CRITICAL-CHAIN SCHEDULING

When the organization's dysfunctional behavior has been identified and addressed, and when the project manager has identified the primary constraints that are likely to limit his team's throughput, the final step is to organize a "critical-chain" project schedule. The actual planning and calculations behind such a scheduling activity can be formidable, and as one might expect, software packages are becoming available to carry out all of the "grunt-work" automatically; examples of such packages are ProChain (from ProChain Solutions, Inc., www.prochain.com), and Concerto (from Realization Technologies, www.realization.com).

Critical-chain scheduling algorithms begin by identifying the required tasks, resources, and dependencies in the traditional manner that one would use for creating a PERT (network) chart. What's important is identifying the "critical chain": the longest path (in terms of schedule duration) through the project, taking into account both the resource-related constraints that may exist and also the effort required for the tasks themselves.

If there is any resource contention (i.e., the same resource may be needed simultaneously by more than one task) in the initial network of tasks, it must be dealt with (by resequencing tasks) before the critical chain is selected.[6] At that point, an initial plan/schedule can be developed, based on the so-called 50-50 estimates that we've discussed earlier: rather than asking each worker to develop a worst-case estimate for his or her task, we ask him or her to develop an estimate that has an equal probability of being early or late. To the extent that a buffer is required to cope with unforeseen contingencies, it gets placed at the end of the schedule; thus, Figure 7.2 shows the beginning of such a critical-chain schedule, with three tasks (identified by the resources, X, Y, and Z, who carried) followed by a "project buffer."

**Figure 7.2**   *The beginning of a critical-chain schedule*

Of course, even in a simple project, there are likely to be "threads" of tasks other than the critical chain. Thus, a more complete picture of our schedule might look like Figure 7.3:

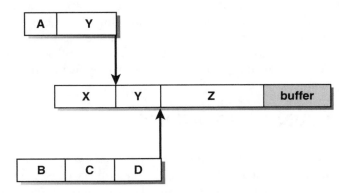

**Figure 7.3**    A more realistic project network

Figure 7.3 poses two risks for our critical chain—and assuming that the critical chain *is* the primary "constraint" that we're concerned about, we need to do whatever is necessary to protect it. At the top of Figure 7.3, for example, we see that resource Y is busy doing something at the same time that resource X is busy on the critical chain. It's essential that Y be available for critical-chain work as soon as resource X is finished; thus, we need a "resource buffer" to ensure that resource Y *will* be available when needed.

Similarly, the task-thread at the bottom of Figure 7.3 "feeds" into the critical-chain thread just before resource Z begins doing his work. To minimize the risk of Z being delayed, we need a "feeding" buffer at the end of that bottom thread. Thus, our revised plan looks like this:

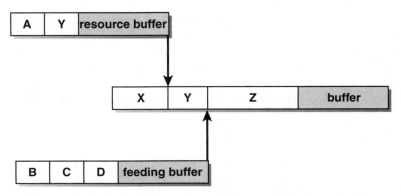

**Figure 7.4**    Schedule with resource and feeding buffers

As General Eisenhower once said, "Plans are worthless, but planning is everything." A plan like the one shown in Figure 7.4 may look realistic at the beginning of the project, but it obviously has to be monitored throughout the project. In terms of the schedule, the project manager can use the project buffer and "feeding buffer" as his primary mechanisms for protecting the overall schedule. Beyond that, if additional sacrifices are necessary, the concepts of "triage" and "good-enough" systems, discussed earlier in this book, provide fallback strategies to help prevent turning the death march project into a failure.

# CONCLUSION

Goldratt's work [4] in critical-chain scheduling strategies are no longer as new and radical as they were in the late 1980s and early 1990s; indeed, they have been widely adopted by several large and reputable manufacturing companies. But the concepts are still largely unknown within the IT industry: Software project managers are barely capable of dealing with Microsoft Project and traditional scheduling concepts.

I have provided only a brief overview of the theory of constraints and critical-chain scheduling approach in this chapter—probably only enough to be dangerous if you attempt to use it on your next project without additional training and study. However, I hope that it has been enough to whet your appetite and to at least make you think more seriously about whether the project management and scheduling "culture" in your organization is counter productive, or downright dysfunctional. If so, you should pursue some of the references at the end of this chapter, as well as excellent Internet resources such as Frank Patrick's "Focused Performance" Web site (www.focusedperformance.com), and the discussion groups at cmsig@lists.apics.org, tocexperts@ groups.yahoo.com, and criticalchain@groups.yahoo.com.

As we've discussed in this chapter, the most important thing we can do is to realize that certain organizational cultures and behaviors doom many death march projects to failure before they even begin. The corporate vice presidents and project stakeholders may have some intellectual reasons for agreeing with such an assertion, but it's not a fundamental, visceral belief: Despite their intellectual agreement and their good intentions, chances are they'll persist in their dysfunctional ways. It's the death march project manager and his or her team who have the visceral involvement: they're the ones who will be working 80 hours per week, they're the ones who will suffer ulcers, and they're the ones whose careers will suffer the most if the project fails.

As a project manager, chances are that you won't be able to change your organization's overall culture. But if you can recognize the organization's dysfunctional behavior for what it is, and if you can isolate yourself and your project team from that culture (at least for the duration of the project), and if you can take advantage of even a few of the critical-chain scheduling strategies summarized in this chapter, you'll have a much greater chance for success.

# NOTES

1.  And this behavior is often imposed upon us at an early age. One of my strongest childhood memories is of a boy who lived next door to me in Omaha in the 1950s, and who came home from school crying bitterly one afternoon. He was in fourth grade, a couple years younger than me, so I had not seen what had caused his distress in the classroom. When I asked, he told me that his math teacher had given his entire class a problem to work on, which the teacher apparently expected would keep the children occupied for the remainder of that school period. But my next-door neighbor, a math whiz-kid who had already astonished me with his skills on more than one occasion, finished the assignment in ten minutes, and proudly marched up to the front of the room to show his solution to the teacher. The teacher took one look at it, tore the boy's paper into small pieces with a dramatic flourish, and said, "Yes, your answer is right—*but you did it too quickly*. Go back and do it again." The boy was outraged and humiliated, but how could he question the authority figure in the classroom? His parents, as I heard subsequently from my own parents, were also outraged; but in the end, they did nothing. And I suspect that that boy has never finished another work-assignment ahead of schedule, ever again, in the 50 years since that incident occurred.

2.  Indeed, the situation is actually far worse in the IT profession, or any other knowledge-intensive profession, where a significant part of the day-to-day job involves *thinking* about the nature of the problem, and/or the nature of the solution. Unfortunately, the externally visible manifestation of thinking—for example, staring at the ceiling with unfocused eyes—is suspiciously similar to that of idle behavior. And sometimes it's even more blunt: The boss will say to you, "We don't pay you to think, we pay you to *do* things!"

3.  To some extent, this contradicts the statements at the beginning of the chapter: If we're trying to solve a "global" problem, we're not going to do it by focusing on "local" solutions. But for the organizational situation, only the CEO and other senior executives have the resources and authority to provide global leadership. While I'm all in favor of that, and while books like the ones at the end of this chapter propose such global solutions, my immediate concern is the project manager facing a death march project.

4.  I have to admit that it makes me a little nervous to suggest, "Everyone else is crazy, and I'm the only sane one around here! "On the other hand, none of this would have happened if "they" hadn't created a crisis by throwing you into a death march project, right? And at some point, you do have to trust your own "gut instinct" and common sense, even if it means you're the only one in the organization with the intelligence, awareness, or strength of character to say, "The emperor has no clothes!"

**5.** Robert Newbold, *Project Management in the Fast Lane,* St. Lucie Press, 1998, page 46.

**6.** If there are no resource constraints, then the initial critical chain is the same as the familiar "critical path" schedule that project managers have traditionally developed using tools such as Microsoft Project.

# REFERENCES

1. Eliyahu Goldratt. *The Goal*. North River Press, 2nd Revision edition, 1992.

2. Eliyahu Goldratt. *Theory of Constraints*. North River Press, 1999.

3. Eliyahu Goldratt. *It's Not Luck*. North River Press, 1994.

4. Eliyahu Goldratt. *Critical Chain*. North River Press, 1997.

5. Robert C. Newbold. *Project Management in the Fast Lane: Applying the Theory of Constraints*. St. Lucie Press, 1998.

6. Lawrence P. Leach. *Critical Chain Project Management*. Artech House, 2000.

7. Peter Senge. *The Fifth Discipline*. Doubleday, 1990.

# *8* Time Management

*Lost, yesterday, somewhere between sunrise and sunset, two golden hours, each set with sixty diamond minutes. No reward is offered for they are gone forever.*

—Horace Mann

In a death march project, virtually all of the critical resources—time, personnel, money, computer workstations, and even office space—are in short supply. Many of the these resources are limited only because of political decisions, and those decisions can be changed: If key stakeholders decide that it's important enough, more people can be assigned to the project, more money can be budgeted, and civilized working quarters can be found.

But *time* cannot be manufactured out of thin air, nor can its passage be slowed. As Horace Mann observes in the opening quotation for this chapter, once an hour has been lost, it is gone forever. While the schedule in a "normal" project may well have enough slack to allow for wasted hours, days, or even weeks, such luxuries do not exist in a death march project. Thus, it's crucial for the project manager to make both *efficient* and *effective* use of the available time that his or her team members are able to contribute to the project.

This has nothing to do with the topic of overtime on a project. Regardless of whether the project team members are working 40-hour weeks or 80-hour weeks, they need to use those hours efficiently and effectively. That doesn't mean we should be looking for hysterically frantic behavior, with people sprinting from one location to another and desperately trying to type 100 words per minute on their computer keyboards.

Indeed, the suggestions in this chapter are simple and straightforward. Having observed many death march project teams wasting vast amounts of time when they could hardly afford to waste a single minute, I believe that for some project managers, the suggestions in this chapter may turn out to be every bit as important as the earlier discussions about software processes and negotiations.

# THE IMPACT OF CORPORATE CULTURE ON TIME MANAGEMENT

*Heck, by the time a man scratches his behind, clears his throat, and tells me how smart he is, we've already wasted 15 minutes.*

—former U.S. President Lyndon B. Johnson

Unfortunately, many project managers are completely oblivious to the amount of time they and their team members are wasting—as they are following the practices and rituals of deeply ingrained social and corporate cultures. A death march project may not be the best excuse for launching a cultural revolution—but it may be appropriate for the project manager to temporarily suspend the time-consuming pleasantries and rituals of the normal corporate day-to-day life.

One of the most common and obvious examples involves the ritual of meetings. In many organizations, meetings habitually start 15-30 minutes behind schedule because (a) everyone expects to spend the first 15-30 minutes socializing with one another (b) coffee and refreshments are provided at the beginning of the meeting, and the refreshments are accessed via a slow-moving, single-file queue of people, (c) the person who called the meeting arrives 15 minutes late, because his/her *previous* meeting ran 15 minutes late, and/or (d) the boss arrives late, and nobody dares start the meeting without the boss.

Even more frustrating is the organization that convenes a meeting to discuss an issue, then spends an hour thrashing over details that could have been resolved by any one of the attendees before the meeting even began, then finally arrives at a decision—only to repeat the same discussion and the same decision-making ritual a week later at a subsequent meeting. Sometimes this happens because the group is so nervous and tentative about making a commitment that they prefer to make a "provisional" or "tentative" decision, in order to have the freedom to abandon it a week later. And sometimes it happens because one or two of the meeting attendees were unhappy with the original decision, and hope that by raising it again, they might be able to achieve a different resolution.

These are just two examples of time being wasted because of inefficient and ineffective meetings; there are, of course, many more such examples. The key point here is that we're not talking about meetings attended by lazy, incompetent, or disorganized individuals; these behaviors reflect the culture of the organization. The culture of an organization is unlikely to be changed in the midst of a death march project—unless the project occupies the entire organization, and is led by the CEO. For most death march projects, though, the most pragmatic strategy is likely to be one of diplomatic avoidance rather than head-on confrontation. Thus, the death march project manager might say to his or her team, "Look, I know that we usually begin our meetings by singing the company song, enjoying some home-cooked pastries from various project members, and passing around the latest photographs of everyone's children—but on *this* project, I'm afraid we'll have to forego these luxuries."

This is not intended to be a book on how to organize and manage meetings effectively; a quick search of the Amazon or Barnes & Noble Web sites will produce a long list of such books.[1] In most cases, focusing on the basics will suffice: Have a purpose and an agenda for every meeting; start the meeting on time; keep the discussion from drifting off-topic; curtail endless repetitions of the same topics and arguments; identify action points at the end of each meeting; and end the meeting on time, so that people won't be late for their *next meeting.*

# TIME SLIPPAGE FROM STAKEHOLDER DISAGREEMENTS

As noted in the discussion of politics and negotiations in Chapter 2, the pressures and demands of death march projects sometimes provoke disagreements between key stakeholders. This is most obvious during the initial discussions of budgets, deadlines, and resource allocations—but it also occurs at various points throughout the project when detailed functional requirements are being documented, when acceptance test criteria are being negotiated, and when details of the user interface are being prototyped.

One consequence, as noted earlier, is that the stakeholders will simply "agree to disagree," allowing the project to muddle onward without any documented agreement or approval of these key issues; or the documented version of requirements, interfaces, acceptance criteria, and other issues will be so vague and abstract that the programmers will be forced to "invent" the details for themselves. An equally common scenario is that the stakeholders will simply refuse to agree to anything at all; it's the political equivalent of a long-term siege, with each camp hunkered down in their trenches, lobbing an occasional hand-grenade at their enemies.

Meanwhile, the project manager is likely to find that progress is stalled. Until they get an agreement on which vendor will provide the hardware for the system, there is *no* hardware; until the stakeholders agree on a particularly contentious aspect of the functional requirements, there is no point attempting to build even a prototype of that functionality. Meanwhile, the clock continues to tick—and if there is one bit of political reality that you *can* depend on, it's that the deadline will continue to remain fixed in place.

The best solution to this problem is to emphasize the problem *at the beginning of the project* to all of the key stakeholders. Of course, they'll all nod their heads, and agree solemnly that it's oh-so-important for them to reach decisions on key issues as quickly as possible in order to avoid paralyzing the project. You can then follow that up with a formal request, *in writing*, that all issues requiring their approval, consent, or review will be resolved in *no more than 24 hours.* Chances are you'll get a lot of hemming and hawing, and a lot of pious excuses about why—even though they would really, truly *love* to provide 24-hour turnaround on all decisions—it's just not possible. After all, people are busy; people are on vacation sometimes; people are traveling; people have other meetings to attend; there are just so many things going on; and the list of excuses goes on…

If you can't get a formal, written commitment to a 24-hour turnaround on all decisions from the stakeholders, then the only other thing you can do is document and publish each day-by-day slippage of the deadline while key decisions are being delayed. As noted above, the stakeholders will almost never allow the "official" deadline to be pushed back in such a fashion; thus, your documented messages need to take the form of, "Notwithstanding the fact that the officially sanctioned deadline has not moved, your failure to reach a decision, during the past 24 hours, on my request for permission to do X, has inevitably delayed this project by one day. Thus, instead of delivering the system on October 10th, as I had estimated in my last status report, I now estimate that it will be delivered on October 11th."

Sometimes there is a valid and legitimate reason that the stakeholders cannot render a decision—for example, they may be waiting for a decision from their outside lawyers or from government regulators. But that doesn't change the reality: If your project plan is predicated on getting answers to all key decisions within a fixed period of time (and if you have indicated that on the PERT charts and Gantt charts associated with your project plan), then regardless of whose fault the delay is, the consequences are still the same.[2] And from my experience, the majority of these delays are *not* caused by external factors beyond the control of the stakeholders; the delays are caused by political infighting among the stakeholders themselves.

Of course, in many political environments, the project manager will quickly be ordered to stop publishing his or her obnoxious day-by-day slippage memos: It's a political response to a political phenomenon and as such, it's politically unacceptable. At the very least, then, the project manager *must* identify the delays as a key risk factor in the overall project—for if the project *does* fail, all of those key stakeholders will experience an amazing bout of amnesia, which will cause them to completely forget that they were the cause of the problem.

Indeed, severe problems in this area should make the project manager re-examine whether he or she really wants to be involved in the project at all. If the key stakeholders aren't sufficiently committed and involved that they *can* put aside their other activities in order to ensure that the project *does* get the rapid response that it needs, then why should the project manager and all of the team members endure the stress and strain? In many cases, the behavior of senior executives and key stakeholders can be predicted in advance: As noted earlier, corporate cultures are involved here and they tend to be fairly consistent over a period of time.

If the project manager suspects that it *might* be a problem, then it may be worth conducting a few simple experiments before officially accepting the role of "captain of the *Titanic*"—for example, send an email message to the key stakeholders that says, "Before I accept this assignment, I'll need to know whether I will have the authority to veto the proposed assignment of technical personnel from other departments to my project team." If all of the stakeholders respond to such an email with an emphatic

"Yes!", or even an unequivocal "No!", within 24 hours, that's fine. But if half of the stakeholders don't even respond to the email, and the others suggest that they'll have to discuss it at their next monthly executive management meeting, then there's not much chance that other key decisions will be forthcoming in a timely fashion.

# HELPING THE PROJECT TEAM MAKE BETTER USE OF TIME

In addition to the ideas suggested above, I believe that a project manager can contribute significantly to the success of a project by helping his or her team members make effective use of their time on a day-to-day basis.

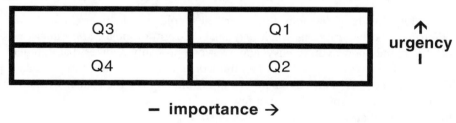

**Figure 8.1** *Prioritizing tasks by urgency and importance*

Meanwhile, managers can use traditional ideas from Stephen Covey's *First Things First* (Fireside Books, 1996). Covey recommends prioritizing tasks on a two-dimensional grid whose axes are "urgency" and "importance." He divides the grid into four quadrants: Q1 (high importance, high urgency) are the "heart attack" tasks; Q2 (high importance, low urgency) are things like regular exercise to prevent a heart attack; Q3 (low importance, high urgency) are office interruptions, email and phone calls; and Q4 (low importance, low urgency) are nonproductive time-wasters.

We've become so "efficient" during the past decade that we've eliminated most Q4 activities during the working day; we save them for the evening, when we relax with TV sit-coms and a glass of wine. But the typical working day is filled with Q3 activities, and they push the Q2 activities aside. Q1 activities can't be ignored because ignoring a heart attack means death, or its project-related equivalent, which is project cancellation or failure. But nobody champions the Q2 activities of planning, thinking, analyzing, and organizing; since such activities have the external appearance of "idle time," they are often frowned upon.

How extensive are the Q3 interruptions? An *NandOTimes* article reported that a typical dot-com marketing director receives 80 to 100 daily emails, 100 to 150 phone calls, 20 to 25 voice-mails, two or three memos, and "face-time" meetings with 10 to 12 people. That's nearly 300 interruptions per day; assuming a 10-hour day with no lunch breaks, that's one interruption *every two minutes*. I marvel at the "productivity" of someone who copes with such an onslaught—but is there any time left for old-fashioned thinking and planning?

IT project teams often have a similar work environment, and managers can help by teaching team members to differentiate between *urgency* and *importance*. For example, filtering one's email is a good discipline, since email is the predominant form of communication in today's high-tech world. I keep four folders in my email program, labeled Q1 to Q4; I've gradually accumulated nearly a thousand "filters" that automatically assign incoming mail to one of these folders. Not only does most junk mail disappear, but email from strangers and busybodies usually ends up in the Q3 or Q4 folder, and less than 10% ends up in the Q1 folder demanding immediate attention.

Here's a slightly devious, but nevertheless cold-bloodedly pragmatic strategy for deferring such interruptions when they take the form of email: *don't answer them at all*. Everyone knows you're busy, and everyone probably realizes that you get a hundred emails a day; thus, the lack of an immediate response to the email message probably won't be seen as a deliberate social affront. And if the sender of that 'urgent' email message doesn't follow up a few days later to see why you haven't responded, then perhaps that 'urgent' message wasn't so 'important' after all.[3]

Managers can also help team members learn to plan their week in advance. Ideally, we would follow the advice offered by Tom DeMarco in his new book *Slack,*[4] and schedule some slack time during the week; we might even encourage team members to schedule time to put their feet up on the desk and think about what they're doing. But if nothing else, we can encourage our developers to ensure that Q2 items are consciously allocated the time they need rather than pushed aside by the immediate pressure of a Q3 interruption. One important reason for doing this is that the Q2-oriented activities of planning and analysis are often necessary to prevent the Q1-related crises and emergencies. And those Q1 crises are usually extremely expensive in terms of time, money, resources, and emotional energy; as we recall from old homilies such as "A stitch in time saves nine," it's usually much more cost-effective to invest a modest amount of time and energy in Q2-related activities in order to prevent the occurrence of Q1 crises.

But this may be overly optimistic: after all, the nature of a death march project is one of constant urgency and dashing about as quickly as possible to deal with all of the tasks that must be accomplished within a compressed schedule. Probably the *most* important thing the manager can do is constantly remind his or her project team members to pause for a moment each time they get a new "urgent" email or phone call from a project stakeholder or end-user; the pause is necessary so that we can consciously remind ourselves to ask, "Yes, I know that this email is 'urgent,' but is it really important? Would *my* deadlines and tasks and priorities be affected if I deferred this new 'urgent' interruption for an hour, or a day, or a week?"

## NOTES

1. For starters, consider *Managing Meetings*, by Tim Hindle, DK Pub Merchandise, April 1999, which has the virtue of being only 72 pages long.

2. Of course, it's possible that the stakeholder decisions are not on the "critical path" for the project, in which case the delay *is* tolerable. But in the majority of cases, the very fact that the stakeholder decisions are required, and the fact that they're stalling or fighting among themselves, is a strong clue that the decision *is* on the critical path.

3. A variation is to file each such Q3-oriented message in a folder that will be examined a week later; at that point, you can decide whether the lack of a follow-up inquiry about that initial message means that it can be ignored. Aside from that, it helps to slow down the "cycle time" of those messages: if you answer an urgent but thoroughly unimportant Q3 message right away, it's likely to prompt *another* Q3 message from the busybody who has nothing better to do than to bombard you with such messages.

4. Tom DeMarco, *Slack: Getting Past Burnout, Busywork, and the Myth of Total Efficiency,* Bantam Books, 2001.

# 9 Managing and Controlling Progress

*The reasonable man adapts himself to the world; the unreasonable one persists in trying to adapt the world to himself. Therefore all progress depends on the unreasonable man.*

—George Bernard Shaw, *Man and Superman* (1903)

It's hard enough to negotiate realistic schedules and budgets with demanding customers, and then staff a project team to build the system, and identify the appropriate processes and procedures with which to do the work. Unfortunately, some project managers believe that once they've accomplished these critical steps, everything else will flow relatively smoothly. Quite understandably, it seems that the most difficult part of the project takes place at the very beginning: negotiating aggressively to acquire the people, the budget, and the calendar-time to carry out the required work, and then convincing skeptical stakeholders that the schedule/budget *is* practical.

Unfortunately, there are two phenomena that occur in death march projects with almost the same certainty as death and taxes: First, it turns out that, notwithstanding the aggressive negotiations and the skeptical scrutiny from stakeholders, the budget and schedule and staffing estimates turn out to be woefully optimistic. Not just optimistic by 10%, but hysterically optimistic by 50%, or 100%, or 1,000%. The reasons for this have already been discussed in earlier chapters—naivete and inexperience, stakeholder negotiations that border on bullying and coercion, and so on—but the *reality* of the hysterically optimistic negotiations often don't become apparent until midway through the project.

Secondly, things do go wrong. Bad things happen to good people despite their best efforts; or as Tom Hanks' character discovered while running across America in *Forrest Gump*, "Shit happens." Managing and controlling the progress of a death march project are not something one can ignore or treat casually; it's a full-time, urgent, demanding job. Indeed, it's what justifies the existence of the project manager after all those hard negotiations in the early days of the project.

To succeed at managing and controlling progress, the project manager has to distinguish between *real* progress and "apparent" progress. Most project managers have long since learned that the "90% done" syndrome can be a dangerous illusion; but in a death march project, they often learn that it's also dangerous to say "we're 100% done with the analysis and design, but we haven't finished writing our code, and we haven't tested any of it." The "daily build" concept, discussed below, is a practical and effective alternative to the classical dilemma.

# THE "DAILY BUILD" CONCEPT

There is often an unspoken assumption that the incremental "releases" or "versions" or "deliverables" planned and scheduled by the project team as part of their prototyping/evolutionary development process will appear at intervals measured in months or weeks. That's what most of us are accustomed to from our past experience with "normal" projects, and it's consistent with the usual pace of business life—for example, weekly staff meetings, monthly status reviews, quarterly presentations to senior management, and so on.

But death march projects, as we've seen throughout this project, typically need a different approach. When it comes to prototyping and incremental development, it often makes sense to organize the entire project around the concept of a "daily build." By this, we mean: compile, link, install, and test the entire collection of code produced by the team *every day*, as if this was the last day before the deadline and you had to ship whatever you've got to the user tomorrow morning.

Realistically, you can't start the daily build on the first day of the project. And while it might be possible to build the equivalent of a "Hello World" subroutine on the second day of the project, it won't impress anyone unless *everything* about the project involves completely new technology. But there's usually a point well before the first "official" demonstration or delivery of a prototype version of the system when the software developers have a reasonable collection of components, subroutines, or modules—at least a few hundred lines of code, and perhaps a few thousand lines—that actually accepts real input, does real calculations or processing, and produces real output. That's the point when the daily build should begin, and a new (and hopefully better) version of the system should be built every day thereafter.

Why is this so important? As Jim McCarthy, Microsoft's Visual C++ product manager and author of *Dynamics of Systems Development* [9], likes to say, "The daily build is the heartbeat of the project. It's how you know you're alive." And there can hardly be a more important priority for the manager of a death march project. If a week goes by while all team members are spinning their wheels and nobody has quite had the nerve to tell the project manager that he or she just can't manage to get the newfangled object-oriented database to communicate properly with the client-server application he or she is working on, the project may have fallen hopelessly behind schedule. As long as the project manager hears status reports delivered in a verbal fashion or documented in written memos (or with data-flow diagrams), it's all too easy to confuse motion with progress and effort with achievement. But if the project manager insists on physically observing the behavior of each day's "daily build," it's much more difficult to hide whatever problems are plaguing the project.

Some project managers will nod their heads and confirm that this is how they've *always* done it; but most will admit that they've settled for weekly builds, or monthly builds, or semi-annual releases of a system. While nobody can rightly claim to have "invented" the concept, many feel that Dave Cutler should be given the credit for popularizing it during the development of the Windows NT operating system; an interesting discussion can be found in Greg Zachary's *Show Stopper!* [10] description of the project. It's also interesting to note that the Windows-95 development project also used the daily build concept; the final beta version before the production system was released in August 1995 was known as "Build 951."

It's important to recognize that an approach like this effectively becomes part of the project team's *process* for developing the system: Imagine what it must be like to be part of a team that has to demonstrate a working version of its software on 951 consecutive days![1] Furthermore, in order to be effective, the daily build should be automated and should run unattended in the middle of the night, when all of the programmers have gone home (or have climbed under their desks and into their sleeping bags!). This implies the existence of automated configuration-management and source-code control mechanisms, as well as automated "scripts" of some kind to carry out the compiling and linking activities. But most important, it implies the existence of an automated test management system that can run all night long, pounding away on the new version of code to see if it still runs yesterday's test cases properly. Thus, to make the daily build concept work, it's almost certain that a reasonable set of tools and technology is already available; we'll discuss this in Chapter 10.

A few small tricks can add even more value to the daily build concept:

- The project manager should move his or her office to the test site or operation center, once the daily build process begins. Dave Cutler did this at Microsoft, and there are apocryphal stories of the tantrums that he threw when he arrived at the office and found that the daily build had crashed in the middle of the night. Tantrums or not, the point is that the project manager wants to be *very* visible and *very* involved in the daily build process, rather than be the commanding general at the rear of the army, receiving daily reports on a battle taking place miles away.

- Since it's likely that the daily build will require at least a small amount of manual supervision while it runs in the middle of the night, it may help to establish the following policy: Any programmer whose buggy code causes the daily build to crash gets the honor of supervising the operation of the (nightly) daily build until the next victim causes a crash. Obviously, there are advantages and disadvantages of such a policy, but at the very least, it makes the whole concept of the daily build much more "real" to the project team!

- Assign one of the programmers who normally comes into the office early in the morning the task of checking whether the daily build ran successfully and then posting the results in a visible place. If nobody is willing or able to show up early, then hire a college student. One company instructed the student to plant a flag outside the building to warn everyone whether it was going to be a good day or bad day upon arrival: a green flag meant the daily build had succeeded, while a red flag meant that it had failed.

# RISK MANAGEMENT

While a "daily build" approach can be extremely effective in gauging and monitoring the progress of a death march project, it doesn't provide any explicit advice for coping with the serious problems that inevitably occur in high-pressure death march projects. It's important here to make a semantic distinction between what some project managers call "issues," which I regard as metaphorically equivalent to mosquito bites, and "risks," which I regard as roughly equivalent to rattlesnake bites. Mosquito bites are annoying, but only in *very* rare cases (e.g., the West Nile virus) do they cause serious health problems. But the problems associated with a rattlesnake bite are immediate and near-certain; they need to be anticipated, monitored, and managed—and if, despite one's best efforts, one does get bitten by a rattlesnake, immediate mitigation efforts are urgently required.

If "risk" weren't such a critical issue, we wouldn't apply the adjective "death march" to the project in the first place. It's interesting to note that one of the breathalyzer test questions identified by the Airlie Council in Chapter 5 is concerned with identification of project risks; and while that question might draw a blank stare from the manager of a "normal" project (even if that normal project has gotten into terrible trouble), it's one that can typically be answered fairly crisply by the manager of a death march project. A manager would be a naive fool if he initiated a death march without having had some serious thought about the primary risks and how they might be mitigated.

Alas, things sometimes get out of hand as the death march project continues. That is, because the risk management activity is addressed in terms of *ad hoc* emotions and instinct rather than a formal process, the manager often misses the emergence of new risks as the project continues. In the best case, the risks that were visible at the beginning of the project will be eliminated; in the normal case, they continue to be worrisome risks throughout the project (e.g., the risk that a key team member will quit). But entirely new risks—things that nobody anticipated—can suddenly emerge and, because the team typically has very little "slack" or "reserve" capacity in terms of schedule, budget, and resources, these new risks can be killers.

If this whole discussion of software risks strikes you as excessive or irrelevant, feel free to skip to the next chapter. My biggest concern is for the project manager who has survived several "normal" projects with an intuitive, *ad hoc* approach; that usually won't work in a death march project. Indeed, it's the existence of an effective formal software risk management (SRM) *process* that makes some organizations willing to "go out on a limb" and take on a death march project that would otherwise be certain suicide.

There is an substantial body of literature on risk management, and it's beyond the scope of this book to cover it all. References [1] through [6] at the end of this chapter will provide as much detail as you need, though it's important here, too, to avoid having the Risk Management Police overwhelm the project with forms, reports, and other aspects of bureaucracy. For example, some death march project managers follow a very simple process of having the team identify and monitor the *top ten* risks in the project; these can be printed on a one-page form, and their status can be quickly reviewed on a weekly basis.

Obviously, other approaches can work just as well; the key is to ensure that it's one that will be understood, accepted, and followed by everyone on the project team—for it's the peons at the bottom of the hierarchy who are usually the first to see the emergence of new risks. In a death march project, we don't have time to let the information trickle up to the top of the management hierarchy by whatever antiquated communication mechanisms are used to convey other forms of political information; the risks have to be pounced on and attacked by the team as a whole in order to prevent them from getting out of control.

The word "control" is crucial here, for the project team has to distinguish between risk *assessment*, risk *control*, and risk *avoidance*. In the worst case, the project team reacts to risks as they occur—for example, by allocating additional resources for additional testing in order to alleviate the consequences of a bug. This kind of "fix on failure" approach, where the risks are addressed *after* they have surfaced, often leads to a crisis-mode form of "fire fighting" that can lead to the utter collapse of the death march project team. Risk *prevention* is usually far better, and it means that the team agrees to follow a formal process of assessment and control in order to preclude potential risks from occurring.

An even more proactive form of risk management seeks to eliminate the root causes of failures and risk; this is often the focus of quality-management initiatives within an organization. It tends to expand the scope of risk assessment to a broader horizon in order to allow *anticipation* of risks; and it can lead to a very aggressive managing culture which incorporates a "risk-taking" ethic by *engineering* the degree of risk that the organization can tolerate. I'm all in favor of such an approach, but it's a more strategic issue that ought to be discussed and implemented outside the context of a death march project. The death march project team has a very tactical perspective: it's not trying to change the culture of the organization, but merely survive and finish the project.

However, this may involve some cultural problems in the organization, especially if there is a perception that *other* projects have not been risky, and that this one is the first, last, and only death march project the organization will ever see. The problem is that the project team is not an island unto itself; if it were, then it could simply focus on the cultural problem of "shooting the messenger" who reports problems to higher level authorities.

But as Rob Charette observes [2], the major causes of project failures often exist in the organizational environment, or in the business environment, which surrounds the project; this is illustrated in Figure 9.1 below. The organizational and business environments are almost always outside the project manager's jurisdiction and political control; but equally important, the project manager often doesn't know about those "external" risks until they come crashing into his project.

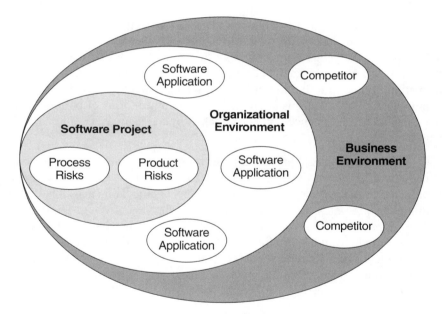

**Figure 9.1**   *The scope of project risks*

Of course, the converse can be true also: The software project creates risks that can affect the organization and the external business environment. But everyone knows that! Indeed, the project manager can expect to be reminded *ad nauseam* that the entire organization—if not the universe and all of civilization!—is imperiled by the death march project. But these same managers, who whine and complain about the fact that the project team is working only 127 hours per week to get the project finished, are often blissfully unaware of things going on in their sphere of control which could derail the death march project.

That's why it's important to have a risk management process that can assess project risks from several different organizational perspectives and balance them appropriately; after all, what engineering (and the software developers) sees as a risk might be seen as an opportunity by the marketing department. This kind of "global" view of risk management is important, but I don't see it as often I would like when I visit death march projects. And as noted above, the project team doesn't have the time, energy, or political clout to change the organizational culture by installing a global risk management process. Thus, the absence of such an organizational process becomes a risk of its own which the team must assess.

Risk *assessment* is usually performed by evaluating the complexity of the system or product being developed, as well as evaluating the client environment and the project team environment. Product complexity can be assessed in terms of size (e.g., number of function points), performance constraints, technical complexity, and so on. Risks associated with the client environment are often a factor of the number of user constituencies involved, the level of user knowledge, the perceived importance of the system within the user's business area, the likelihood that when/if the new system is installed it will lead to a reorganization or downsizing activity, and so on. The risks associated with the team environment include the capabilities, experience, morale, and physical/emotional health of the project team.

Typically, there are a hundred or more risk factors that could be included in a comprehensive risk model; as noted earlier, some project teams will consciously narrow their focus to just the top ten risks. Some of the risks can be quantified in an objective fashion—for example, the response-time performance requirements, or the size of the system in function points. But other factors—for example, the degree of user cooperation or hostility—may have to be assessed on a qualitative basis. As a practical management approach, it's usually appropriate to categorize such risks as "high," "low," or "medium" and to focus on getting a consensus on the state or level of the risk, on the part of everyone involved.

Once the risks have been identified and assessed, the manager and the team can sometimes identify appropriate strategies to minimize or eliminate as many as possible. This is common sense, of course, but it must be remembered that the very nature of a death march project is that there are usually more than the usual risks, and they're more severe, and they *cannot* be eliminated through simple actions. On the other hand, if the risks are extraordinary, sometimes the solutions are too: While the project team might never have dared to ask the CEO or senior vice president to eliminate a project risk on a normal project by spending an extraordinary sum of money or eliminating a severe bureaucratic constraint, it's not unreasonable to ask for such things in a death march project. And if you don't ask—which will often require going around the chain of command, and circumventing several levels of brain-dead middle managers—then you'll never know whether you could have acquired the solution to your problems.

In any case, if there are high-risk factors that cannot be summarily eliminated—which is almost always the situation in a death march project—then they should be documented with a "risk memorandum" that identifies the risk impact, the possible higher level actions, the contingency plans that need to be set in place, and so on. This is not just a "cover your ass" political act, for if the risks do materialize, and if they cause the project to fail, there will usually be dire consequences for everyone involved; after all, that's part of the reality of a death march project. However, *denying* reality is also a common phenomenon on death march projects; it's common for members of the project team, and for the various levels of users and managers surrounding the team, to put on their blindfolds and steadfastly ignore the existence of serious project risks. It's not unreasonable to expect the project manager and the team members to focus on "internal" risks with extreme diligence; but as noted earlier, the "external" risks often can't be controlled by the team members because they're associated with organizational or business issues beyond their jurisdiction. Thus, a risk memorandum is an important *practical* activity in order to force the user and the management community to acknowledge what they would prefer to overlook and ignore.

While I've focused primarily on risk management in this discussion, it's also important to acknowledge the importance of *issue management*. While not all risks are immediately fatal, and while not all risks have a high likelihood of occurring, it's still useful to think of "risks" like "rattlesnake bites": it's something you would very much like to avoid, or, if it *does* happen, there's a good chance of serious injury or death if you don't do something about it right away. An "issue," on the other hand, is more like a mosquito bite: often annoying and distracting, but probably not life-threatening. But if you get bitten by a swarm of mosquitoes, and if some of those mosquito bites get infected, it can cause serious discomfort.

All of which suggests that a death march manager probably won't have the time, energy, or resources to do much about avoiding or preventing the occurrence of issues. But they need to be identified and noted; and they need to be tracked and eventually "closed." Ultimately, they need to be managed, because today's "issue" can become tomorrow's "risk." Thus, at an early stage in the project, one of the developers might casually observe, "Hmmm, I thought someone was supposed to order a testing tool for this project, but it hasn't arrived yet. We'll certainly need it in a couple of months, when we're ready to start doing some serious testing." For obvious reasons, something like this needs to be entered into an "issue log" and tracked properly; if the testing tool still hasn't arrived a couple of months later, when the team is ready for testing and the schedule has no more "slack" time, the absence of that testing tool will be a disaster.

Commercial issue-tracking tools exist, complete with automated notification and escalation mechanism; and that might be one of the categories of "utility" tools that you'll want to include in the "tool bag" that we'll discuss in Chapter 10. For many small and medium-sized projects, though, a simple spreadsheet or Access database will suffice. The technology is typically less important than the management discipline of creating such a list in the first place, and then tracking it on a regular basis.

# ADDITIONAL IDEAS FOR MONITORING PROGRESS: MILESTONE REVIEWS

Traditionally, project managers have used PERT charts and Gantt charts to schedule the progress of their projects; and they have attempted to break the project into small "binary" tasks (i.e., either "done" or "not done") with "quality control gates" to ensure that when team members deliver finished tasks, they will be of a sufficient quality to incorporate into the system being developed. As we've seen above, the daily-build approach helps to operationalize this concept in a very visible fashion: The aggregate of delivered tasks either executes in some demonstrable fashion or it doesn't.

Inevitably, though, the project manager will want to assess the status of the project by holding periodic "status meetings" to review progress, lack of progress, risks and issues (within the context of the risk management discussion in the second section of this chapter). But this is all "water under the bridge"; what the project manager *really* wants is an accurate, realistic assessment of the future. "Given our current status," the project manager wants to say to his or her project team, "when can we reasonably expect to deliver the system to our customers, and what problems should we expect to encounter between now and then?"

This is a difficult enough topic to discuss if the meeting consists of *only* the project manager and the participating team members. If the meeting also includes quality assurance personnel, auditors, senior managers, end-users, and other stakeholders, these project reviews often become highly political events in which the real problems and the real status are hidden in order to avoid political repercussions.

Aside from the disruption and distractions generated by such meetings, these politically-oriented project reviews can be real time-wasters—for example, they can chew up a full day of time on the part of project team members who desperately need that time for the "real" work of analysis, designing, coding, and testing. Thus, in the best of all worlds, the project manager would probably like to prevent such status reviews from happening at all; since that's not usually possible, he or she should try to "buffer" the rest of the project team by excluding them from the meeting so they can get some work done.

At the same time, the project manager should realize that reviews *are* important and can be enormously effective in terms of problem-solving and planning future activities. The trick is to emphasize, as much as possible, informal, *peer-level* reviews, where ideas and suggestions can be shared among people who are actively involved in the project. There are a number of excellent books on this topic; the books listed at the end of this chapter by Gilb et al [7], and by Norm Kerth [8] are good starting points.

Most important: Avoid the bureaucratic tendency of large organizations to save up all of this for a project "postmortem" in which key members of the project team, together with representatives from various groups such as Finance, Quality Assurance, Process Improvement and Training, determine whether the project really did deliver the benefits that were originally promised, within the budget that had been allocated. The postmortem also identifies "lessons learned" from the project in order to help senior management do a better job of authorizing and budgeting future IT projects, as well as help project leaders and developers do a better job of managing projects on a day-to-day basis.

Whether postmortems benefit senior management is debatable; many death march project failures are swept under the rug, and the rapid turnover of senior executives reduces the chances that long-term lessons will be learned and applied from the experiences of recently finished projects. Unfortunately, postmortems rarely benefit project leaders or developers either—because in most companies, the key decisions affecting success or failure are made by people who have disappeared before the project ends. And while those individuals may have documented *what* they decided, they rarely document *why* they made the decisions they made. Alternatives may have been considered, trade-offs may have been evaluated, risks may have been assessed; but the postmortem that takes place a year or two later usually doesn't have this information available.

The survivors who participated in the latter stages of the project are typically too burned out and exhausted to write the kind of memoirs we've come to expect from generals and former presidents. And even if they did, who reads these documents? When was the last time you heard a project leader say to his or her team: "Before we get started, please spend the next few days reading through the postmortem reports of the past 25 projects we've done here at Acme Widget Corp. And then, let's have a meeting to discuss how we can apply those lessons to our new project"?

The solution to the dilemma—and the means for providing real value while the *current* death march project is underway—are quite simple: mini-postmortems, conducted at the end of each project phase, or each prototype, or each incremental "version" of a system delivered to the customer. Depending on the project, this means that the mini-postmortem is likely to cover work carried out during a couple of weeks or months; thus, most of the key players are likely to still be involved, and are likely to remember what they did and why they did it. The mini-postmortem can usually be conducted in a single meeting lasting a few hours—instead of the typical end-of-project postmortem, which can last for days or weeks. Many project teams find that a good strategy is to schedule the presentation of a new prototype or version of a system to their users on a Friday morning, then repair to the nearest tavern for a celebratory lunch before staggering back to the office for an afternoon mini-postmortem, then going home for a weekend's sleep in anticipation of getting started on the next version of the system.

Ideally, the benefits of a mini-postmortem—the "lessons learned"—help the team members themselves rather than some ill-defined community of future IT developers. End-of-project postmortems produce bland aphorisms such as "Be sure to get the users involved throughout your project," while mini-postmortems tend to produce cogent statements such as, "We almost had a disaster with this version of the system because we forgot to invite Mary to our requirements-gathering session; and Fred from Accounting was terrific in helping create acceptance test data, so we should get him involved even earlier for the next version."

# NOTES

**1.** To be honest, I don't know if the Microsoft team actually did this religiously on a daily basis. It's certainly possible that more than one "build" was produced within a single 24-hour period, and it's even possible that the team took a day or two off during its marathon death march.

# REFERENCES

1. Robert N. Charette, *Application Strategies for Risk Analysis*, McGraw-Hill, 1990.

2. Robert N. Charette, *Software Engineering Risk Analysis and Management*, McGraw-Hill, 1989.

3. Tom DeMarco and Tim Lister, *Waltzing with Bears: Managing Risks in Software Projects*, Dorset House, 2003.

4. Capers Jones, *Assessment and Control of Software Risks*, Prentice Hall, 1994.

5. Elaine Hall, *Managing Risk: Methods for Software Systems Development*, Addison Wesley, 1998.

6. Carole Edrich, "Risk Management for e-business," *Cutter Consortium Distributed Computing and Architecture/e-business Advisory Service,* Executive Report, Vol. 3, No. 12, Dec. 2000.

7. Tom Gilb, Dorothy Graham, and Suzannah Finzi, *Software Inspection,* Addison-Wesley, 1993.

8. Norm Kerth, *Project Perspectives: A Handbook for Team Reviews,* Dorset House, 2001.

9.  Jim McCarthy, *Dynamics of Systems Development*, Microsoft Press, 1995.

10. Greg Zachary, *Show Stopper!*, Free Press, 1994.

# 10 Death March Tools and Technology

*#3 pencils and quadrille pads.*

> —Seymour Cray (1925–1996),
> when asked what CAD tools he used to design the Cray I
> supercomputer; he also recommended using the back side
> of the pages so that the lines were not so dominant

*I just bought a Mac to help me design the next Cray.*

> —Seymour Cray (1925–1996),
> when he was informed that Apple Computer, Inc.
> had recently bought a Cray supercomputer
> to help them design the next Mac

Back in the summer of 1992, I had dinner with an amiable group of mid-level Microsoft managers. During the course of the discussion, I asked if it was common for Microsoft project teams to use such methodologies as structured analysis or object-oriented design. The answers ranged from "Sometimes" to "Ummm, I guess so" to "Not consistently" to "What's that?" And when I asked about the use of CASE tools (which were still fairly popular throughout the rest of the industry at that point in time), I was told that the common opinion of Microsofties was that such tools were for "people off the street." This was a term I hadn't heard before, but the rough translation is "ignorant savages who have just emerged from the primeval forest and who are just learning to program, unlike *real* programmers, who don't need no such artsy-fartsy tools."

Somewhat depressed, I asked whether the project teams used *any* tools and was told that in fact, each Microsoft team can choose whatever tools it feels are appropriate for the project it's working on. Seizing on that, I asked, "What does a typical project team consider to be its most *important* tool for a software project?

"I asked one of the project teams the same question the other day," replied one of the managers, "And you know what the answer was?"

"A high-speed C++ compiler?" I asked. "An assembler? A powerful debugging tool for all those bugs in their code, heh heh heh?"

"None of the above," the manager responded, ignoring my lame attempt at humor. "The answer was: *electronic mail*. The average Microsoft programmer gets a hundred email messages a day; he *lives* on email. Take away email and the project stops dead in its tracks."

There's a reason why I began this anecdote by pointing out that it took place in 1992. As I write this second edition of *Death March* in 2003, the year 1992 seems like ancient history—in particular, it was a few years before the explosive growth of the Internet had begun and before the World Wide Web was available. At the time, I was staggered at the thought of anyone getting a hundred email messages a day; in 1992, I was deliriously happy if I got two or three email messages a day. But as you can imagine, if the same question about "most important tool" was raised today, the answer might well be "WebEx," or "PlaceWare" or some other kind of sophisticated, Internet-enabled collaboration rather than email. By contrast, the answer might have been "fax machine" in 1987, "PC workstation" in 1983, "on-line terminal" in 1976, and "my own telephone on my desk" when I began working in the computer field in 1964.

Obviously, we don't expect a death march project team to survive with only one tool. Most teams—even for normal projects—have a wide variety of tools and quite an assortment of technology to accomplish their day-to-day work. But sometimes they have too much, and sometimes they have technology that's too new, and sometimes they have tools they don't want foisted upon them by Dilbertesque managers. And in some cases, they're prevented—for financial, political, or cultural reasons—from getting the one tool they believe critical for accomplishing their objectives.

In case you were worried, let me reassure you that I'm not going to advocate esoteric, advanced software tools that somehow communicate telepathically with the programmer in order to generate well-structured code from disorganized thoughts. But I do want to discuss the notion of a "minimal toolset" for death march projects. I also want to emphasize the critical relationship between tools and processes, especially since the processes in a death march project are likely to be different from those used in the rest of the organization. And finally, I want to issue a warning against introducing completely *new* tools, of any kind, into a death march project team environment.

## THE MINIMAL TOOLSET

In the previous chapter, I strongly recommended the notion of *triage* as a prioritization strategy for dealing with user requirements. The same concept applies to tools and technology for the project team: There are some tools the team "must have," some that they "should have," and a bewildering variety of tools they "could have." And there are some obvious reasons for applying the triage prioritization in a conscious, cold-blooded fashion at the beginning of the project.

The most obvious reason is economics; even if the tools worked and everyone was familiar with them, it would cost too much money to acquire them. And it would take too long to order them: by the time the procurement process in a normal corporate bureaucracy was finished, the project would be finished. In many death march projects, it's important to focus on a few critical tools and then try to persuade senior management (or the Tools Police) to acquire them.

But suppose the team is operating in a large environment that already has hundreds of different tools that have been acquired over the years. Should they all be used? Obviously not! Even if they all work, the mental effort required to remember *how* they work, and the additional effort to make them all work together, usually exceeds the incremental benefit obtained. Consider the analogy of a team of mountain climbers, trying to decide what equipment to take with them as they prepare for an assault on the peak. There are some essentials (tents, drinking water, etc.) they'd better have; and if it's an easy climb, they might want to take along some new-fangled gadgets they read about in their favorite mountain-climbing magazine. But if they're planning to climb Mt. Everest without the assistance of burros or Sherpas to carry everything, then they can't afford the burden of carrying 300 pounds per person of gear on their backs.

Exactly what tools *are* critical, and what should be left behind, is a decision the death march project team should be allowed to make on its own—regardless of whether it conforms to organizational standards. I'm staggered by the number of organizations I visit where the death march project manager tells me sadly that there's an organizational mandate that *all* projects must be done in C++ (or, in other organizations, Visual Basic or Oracle or whatever...), even though that technology is utterly inappropriate for his project. Baloney! Throw it out! Use the tools and technology that make sense! To do otherwise is roughly analogous to someone telling the leader of the Mt. Everest mountain-climbing team, "Our committee has decided that your project team should take along a detailed map of the New York City subway system, because most projects have found it very helpful."[1]

However, I think it's essential that the team members agree on common tools *within* the project; otherwise, chaos will ensue. Obviously, this has to be interpreted with a certain degree of common sense; it probably doesn't matter which word processor the team members use to write their documentation, but it probably *is* important that they all use the same compiler for their C++ code. One of the problems with a death march project is that the software developers believe that it creates a license for complete anarchy at the individual level: If team members want to use an obscure open-source C++ compiler they downloaded from a shareware Web site, they believe it's their inalienable right. Not so: It's the *team* that has the inalienable right, and the project manager must enforce this strictly in any area where incompatible tools could make a significant difference.

This means that unless the team members have worked together on several previous death march projects, they will have to come up with a "minimal" toolset that everyone agrees to use. Thus, triage emerges again: The "must-have" toolset is also the "must-*use*" toolset. Once a consensus has emerged on that set of tools, then the team can discuss the "should-have" tools, where the problems are likely to be a combination of consensus-building within the team and management approval for the purchase of new tools. Beyond that, there may or may not be sufficient time and energy to discuss the merits of the nearly infinite number of "could-have" tools that various team members might be interested in.

I suggested above that the project manager has to be prepared to enforce the consensus; indeed, this could be one of the criteria used by the manager to select potential members of the team. Note that the same could be said about the software processes that we discussed in Chapter 5. And as we'll see below, it's even more important than that, because tools and processes are intimately related to one another.

With all of these caveats in mind, it's impossible for an "outsider" like me to casually enumerate the recommended tools for a death march project. When asked the question, my answer—"It depends..."—is usually confused for the consultant's weasel-worded tendency to avoid giving a straight answer to any question. So, as long as you keep my earlier advice firmly in mind, here is the list of tools I would normally look for:

- *Email, groupware, Web-enabled collaboration tools, videoconferencing, and so on*—Like the Microsoft example above, this is at the top of my list. That's because electronic-interaction tools are not only a means for communicating much more efficiently than memos and faxes, but also because they facilitate coordination and collaboration. Basic email and access to the Internet are things I would insist upon as a project manager,[2] though I would be happy to negotiate as to *which* vendors and products should be used. It matters far less to me whether we're using Microsoft Outlook or Lotus Notes, than the concept that the whole team is on the network and keeps all of its "project memory" on the network. Beyond that, there are some wonderful tools that facilitate document-sharing, "white-board" collaboration, issue-tracking, discussion forums, and other such features.

- *Prototyping/RAD development tools*—As discussed earlier, almost all death march projects use some form of prototyping or incremental development approach; consequently, they need tools to support this effort. It's hard finding a popular development environment today that describes itself as anything else *but* a RAD environment, and the majority of such tools today have a visual, drag-and-drop user interface to help the programmer get more code developed more quickly. Whether the tool should be based on Delphi, Visual C++, Visual Basic, or Java (or a dozen other possible choices) is something I can't recommend on any kind of global basis. But remember the comment above: It's not sufficient to have a consensus that we're all going to use a language like C++ or Java; we have to agree on a common toolset from a common vendor. To have part of the team using Sun's Java environment while the others use Microsoft's Visual J++ product may be technologically feasible, but it's still downright stupid.

- *Configuration management/version control*—Several of my colleagues feel that this should be at the top of the list. As John Boddie, author of *Crunch Mode*, said in a recent email communication to me:[3]

> I would say that a configuration management tool is a real "must have." There is going to be lots of confusion among the pieces of the project and the manager and the team need a way to establish and track versions of the system as they move toward completion, termination or whatever.

There is an obvious benefit to having the CM tools well-integrated with the other primary development tools. Thus, Microsoft's SourceSafe may or may not be the best version-control software, but the fact that it's well-integrated with Visual Basic and other Microsoft development tools is a big argument in its favor. Similarly, many other development tools are integrated with InterSolv's PVCS or other comparable CM tools.

- *Testing, debugging tools*—Many of us would automatically include this with the "basic" development tools that allow us to create code, compile it, and run it. But as we moved from mainframe online applications to GUI-oriented client-server systems, we gradually realized that an entirely new set of testing tools was not only appropriate, but often essential; and tools from vendors such as Rational Software and Mercury Interactive still aren't widely enough distributed in the organizations I visit. Similarly, project teams moving into the world of the Internet and Web-based application probably need a whole new set of testing and debugging tools.

- *Project management (estimating, scheduling, PERT/GANTT, etc.)*—There's a tendency to think of these as the "manager's toolkit," and that may be the case; perhaps it's only the project manager who needs to re-compute the project's "critical path" on a daily basis. But in this same category I would include the estimating tools such as ESTIMACS (developed by Howard Rubin and available from Computer Associates), CHECK-POINT (from Software Productivity Research), and SLIM (from Quantitative Software Management); these are essential tools, in my opinion, because they support the dynamic re-evaluation of schedules and deadlines throughout the project.

- *Toolkit of re-usable components*—If the project team is familiar with the concept of software re-use, and if they regard it as a strategic weapon with which to accomplish high levels of productivity, then a toolkit of re-usable components needs to be on the list of "must-have" tools. This might be a collection of VBX components for Visual Basic, or Sun's Java components, or the STL class library for C++; obviously, it could also include some in-house components developed by other project teams within the organization. The choice is usually language-dependent, and it's another one of those areas that needs to be used consistently by everyone within the project team.

- *CASE tools for analysis/design*—Some project teams regard CASE tools as a "crutch" for novice developers, but others consider them as essential as word processors. My preference is for the CASE tool that's simple, inexpensive, and flexible; aside from that, I won't recommend any particular one or vendor because the real answer to the question of which CASE tool to use is, "it depends..." Indeed, as Doug Scott suggested in a recent email message[4] to me, it might not require any technology at all:

> The best device is a large diagram pinned to the wall. It might contain the (partially complete) E/R diagrams for the system, or the process flows, or whatever. But it give people a focus for discussing the design, and it costs next to nothing.

As I'll discuss below, the biggest problem with CASE tools is that they encourage (and sometimes enforce) a methodology that the project team doesn't understand and doesn't particularly want to use.

## TOOLS AND PROCESS

The issue of CASE tools mentioned above is probably the most obvious example of a truism: Tools and processes are inextricably linked together. There's no point using an object-oriented CASE tool if you've never heard of class hierarchies and use-case diagrams. Such a CASE tool is not only useless, but also an incredible burden, if the project team members sincerely believe that class diagrams are meaningless forms of bureaucratic documentation produced solely to get the Methodology Police off their backs.

The situation is not so black-and-white in many cases: The project team might feel that class-hierarchy diagrams are useful only as an "informal" modeling tool. Thus, a "flexible" CASE tool might be considered a benefit, while a "hard-line" CASE tool would be rejected. Consider the obvious analogy with a word-processor: We all appreciate the benefits of the spell-checker, but we won't want to be forced to use it; and it's quite likely that we *never* use the grammar-checker because it's too slow and clumsy (at least, that's *my* excuse). We would be even more annoyed if the word-processor steadfastly refused to allow the word "ain't" within a document, or required that any phrases it considered racist or sexist be approved in advance by the Political Correctness Committee. A few more "features" like that would be enough to make us all go back to paper and pencil.

What this means, of course, is that the death march project team must *first* agree on the processes and methodologies it intends to follow, and it must decide which of those processes are going to be followed religiously and which ones will be honored in spirit, but perhaps not to the letter of the law. Once this has been decided, the tools and technology can be chosen—or rejected!—accordingly. In this same fashion, the project manager may decide to adopt a particular tool in order to enforce a process that everyone agrees on intellectually, but is likely to practice in a sloppy fashion; a good example is version control and configuration management.

One of the biggest myths about software tools in *any* software project—and a particular danger in a death march project—is that the tool will be a "silver bullet" that will somehow accomplish miracles. Miracles, of course, are what senior management is looking for; and even the project manager may be tempted by the vendors' advertising claims that programming, testing, or various other activities will be improved by a factor of ten through the genius of their tools.

Aside from the problem that such tools are usually brand-new and that nobody knows how to use them (which I'll discuss below), there's a more fundamental point to consider: The only way such a tool *could* be a silver bullet is if it allows or forces the developers to change their process. For example, if I write a program and then compile it, I do so according to a particular process; perhaps I conduct a peer-level walkthrough before the compilation, or perhaps I precede the programming activity with a formal, detailed design process. Now, if you give me a compiler that's 10% faster than the one I've been using before, I'll be happier and somewhat more efficient; maybe the productivity of the overall project will increase by some incremental amount. *But I won't change my process.*

On the other hand, if you give me a compiler that's ten times faster, then it *will* change my process. That's what happened when we went from batch-mode, overnight compiles to online compilation in the 1970s, and then compilation on one's own PC/workstation in the 1980s, and then various combinations of incremental compiling (a la Delphi) and interpretive execution (a la Visual Basic). Because of this, many developers have eliminated detailed design prior to coding on the theory that they can compose programs extemporaneously; the practice of walkthroughs has also been eliminated in many projects on the assumption that the programmer can find and change his own defects efficiently.

Hardly anyone objects to the prospect of using improved technology that permits the *elimination* of processes that were considered boring and tedious. But it's more difficult to introduce new technology that requires us to *add* processes or *modify* processes that we were comfortable with. A good example is the process of re-use and the associated technology of re-use libraries, browsers, and related tools. The project teams that use this technology effectively can raise their level of re-use from approximately 20% (a level that I call "accidental" or *ad hoc* re-use) to 60% or more; indeed, if the technology is matched with a corporate-wide re-use process, then the level of re-use can reach 80–90% or more.

The difference between a 20% level of re-use and an 80% level of re-use is equivalent to a four-fold improvement in productivity. As Paul Bassett points out in an underappreciated book on re-use[2], the subsequent incremental increases in re-use have more profound benefits than you might think. If the level of re-use rises from 80% to 90%, it means that instead of having to develop 20% of the code "from scratch," the project team has to develop only 10%. Thus, their workload has effectively been cut in half.

This is all very exciting—indeed, worthy of being called a "silver bullet"—but it's utterly irrelevant if the project team (and ultimately the entire organization) is unable or unwilling to change its software processes with regard to re-use. The irony is that most organizations will blame their failures on the technology itself: They'll buy an expensive class library, or they'll replace their old software development methodology with object-oriented techniques on the theory that objects are synonymous with re-use; and when they eventually find they've achieved no measurable increase in re-use, they'll blame the problem on objects, or on the vendor of the class library, or on whatever other technology they've depended on. Meanwhile, the process is exactly the same as it was before: The culture of the organization is expressed with the phrase: "Only wimps re-use other people's code; *real* programmers write their own damn code!"

From the perspective of a death march project, there's a very simple moral here: If the introduction of new tools *requires* the team's "standard" process to be changed dramatically, then it will add significantly to the project risk and probably contribute to the failure of the project. This sometimes gets muddled with the issue of training and the issue of learning the mechanics of how to operate the tools; I'll discuss that below. But the more fundamental problem is usually that of changing behavior, which is what software processes are all about. It's hard enough to do under normal circumstances, where we feel that we have lots of time and a supportive environment to slowly become comfortable with the new process. And for obvious reasons it's usually a disaster in a death march project, when we don't have enough time, and we don't have a supportive environment.

# RISKS OF CHOOSING NEW TOOLS

As noted above, some death march projects grab onto new tools and technology as a silver bullet in order to achieve far higher levels of productivity than would otherwise be possible. Let's assume for the moment that we've found some way to solve the cultural and political problems of process-change that were discussed above. What else do we have to worry about?

The two most likely risks are technical and training. In many cases, the silverbullet tool is so new that it's not even available in a commercial form; someone on the project team downloaded the beta version from a shareware Web site. Or the tool can't be integrated with any of the other tools used by the project team; the vendor has made vague promises, but in the meantime, its import-export capability is riddled with bugs. Or the tool isn't supported: it was developed by a graduate student in Iraq, or (even worse!) it was developed in-house by one of the software developers who sees nothing strange about the idea of a bank developing its own CASE tool or an insurance company developing its own DBMS.

Let's assume for the moment that the tool is solid, reliable, and available from a reputable vendor that provides top-notch support. In that case, the problem is likely to be one of training—for if the tool was already being widely used throughout the organization, nobody would have characterized it as a "silver bullet" that would miraculously save the death march team from certain disaster. Occasionally, you'll find a death march project team that begs for permission to use a powerful tool that they've all used in a previous job, but this is rare indeed. In most cases, neither the project team members nor anyone else in the organization has ever seen or used the tool before.

As mentioned before, any nontrivial tool usually has strong implications about the corresponding software process; thus, a new tool often implies a new process. Though such a correspondence should be obvious, it's remarkable how often the vendor's training representative gets half-way through a five-day workshop on how to operate the tool before finding that the students (whose managers are already panicked about falling five days behind schedule as a consequence of attending the workshop!) have absolutely no understanding of the process supported by the tool. It's awfully demoralizing, for example, to spend two days showing a reluctant student how to draw an ERD and then have him ask, "By the way, what *is* an entity? And since I'm gonna program everything in C++, why should I care about all of this stuff?"

But let's assume that the project team members understand the process supported (and automated) by the tool, and that they have enthusiastically agreed that they will carry out the practice in their project; from 25 years of experience spreading the gospel of structured methods and object-oriented methods throughout the wilderness of IT organizations, I know that this is a naive assumption—but there's no point going further unless we do. So, *if* we assume that there are no technical problems with the tool, and *if* we assume that the corresponding software processes won't cause a problem, *then* all that is left is the training and practice associated with the tool itself.

How long does this take? Obviously, it depends on the nature and the complexity of the tool, as well as its user interface, its online help features, and assorted other issues. In the best case, the developers will be able to figure out how to use the tool without any formal training at all; that's what the project manager and the various other managers outside the project desperately want to be true, for they regard *any* training as a waste of time and a distraction from the "real work" of the project. But the more realistic estimate is that it will take an hour, a day, or a week to learn how to use the tool. Whether that takes the form of a classroom session, or reading a book, or just "playing" with the tool, it still takes time.

And the training activity does *not* provide a thoroughly trained, infinitely experienced user of that tool. Training is not a binary phenomenon: The project team members don't go from a state of utter ignorance to a state of sublime mastery of the tool at the end of a one-week training class. This should be obvious, but it somehow baffles senior management, which tends to grumble and complain, "Okay, we spent all that money for those high-priced trainers, and we wasted all that time in the classroom when those lazy, good-for-nothin' programmers could have been programming. Now I want to see some *real* productivity with that silver-bullet tool you talked us into getting for them!" Perhaps it's not so surprising that senior management would be so naive, since no one would know a software tool if he or she fell over one; but sadly, I've seen the same reaction from many technically-oriented death march project managers.

In a wonderful article [4], my colleague Meilir Page-Jones argues that there are seven stages of mastery in software engineering; his article focuses on *methodologies*, but I believe that it applies equally well to tools and technology. In the list below, I've added my own estimates for how long it would take the average software developer to reach various stages, assuming that the tool or technology is of average sophistication and complexity:

**Table 10.1** Page–Jones' Seven Stages of Software Engineering Mastery

*Innocent* (has never heard of technology X)—This obviously requires no time at all.

*Aware* (has read an article about X)—Roughly an hour, in most cases, is enough for a software developer to be in a position where he can voice strong opinions about the advantages and disadvantages of the tool, even though he's never seen it or used it.

*Apprentice* (has attended a five-day workshop)—A week is needed, perhaps compressed into two days because of the pressure of a death march project. Note that at this point, the developer has probably done nothing more than play with canned tutorials provided by the vendor or dabble with a small exercise to illustrate the features of the tool. He hasn't encountered the glitches, shortcomings, and "gotchas" of the tool; he hasn't seen how (or if) it will scale up for large, complex projects. He hasn't tried to integrate it with most of the other tools in his environment.

*Practitioner* (ready to use X on a real project)—A month is probably required to explore the nuances of the tool and become sufficiently comfortable to use the tool on a "real" project.

*Journeyman* (uses X naturally in his job; complains bitterly if it is taken away)—This usually takes six to 12 months. If the tool really is a silver bullet, then the developer becomes an evangelist, doing his best to persuade everyone around him that it's the most wonderful tool on earth.

**Table 10.1** Page–Jones' Seven Stages of Software Engineering Mastery

*Master* (has internalized the details of X; knows when he can break the rules)—This takes usually two to three years, which also means that the developer has survived through two or three new product releases, has found all of the support groups and discussion groups on the Internet, and knows all of the unlisted phone numbers for the technical support gurus at the vendor's organization.

*Expert* (writes books, gives lectures at conferences, looks for ways to extend technology X into new galaxies)—Page-Jones was focusing on methodologies in his paper, and it's not clear that this applies to tools and technology.

## CONCLUSION

Does the gloomy discussion in this chapter mean that we should use no tools at all? Are we supposed to abandon all technology and resort to old-fashioned keypunch machines? Should we assume that technology can *never* save us?

The rhetorical nature of the questions is intended to remind you that common sense should prevail in all such discussions. When the stars and the planets align themselves just *so*, maybe technology *will* save us, at least on one or two death march projects. We should certainly take advantage of as much advanced technology as we can, because it can leverage our intellectual efforts and relieve us of time-consuming, error-prone tedious tasks associated with software development. In the best of all worlds, the software developers will have had a chance to learn, experiment, and practice with high-powered tools in a less-risky environment; indeed, in the best case, advanced tools have already been deployed throughout the organization and are part of the culture and infrastructure of the organization.

And in this case, we wouldn't need to have any discussion about tools and technology at all; we would simply pick up our tools and go to work on the death march project. The reason for the discussion in this chapter—and the reason all of this *is* relevant in most death march projects—is that the organization is using mediocre tools *or* someone believes that a completely new form of technology, announced breathlessly by a start-up vendor just last week, will somehow save the day. The former scenario is depressing but all too common; and the latter scenario is also common, for the simple reason that technology advances quickly and relentlessly in our field.

If new technology could be introduced without any impact on our software processes, and if it didn't require training and practice on the part of the developers, then we would be faced with a simple cost-benefit decision. Since the natural instinct of many higher level managers is to assume that a problem can be eliminated simply by throwing money at it, I find that there tends to be far more brand-new technology used on death march projects than on normal projects. The irony, as I've tried to explain in this chapter, is that the new tool can be the straw that breaks the camel's back; and the project failure is then blamed on the tool. As Sharon Marsh Roberts put it:[5]

> When the team is required to think clearly more than 60 hours per week, it's a bad time to invoke complex logic. Anything that requires a new mode of effort or a more sophisticated way of thinking is a problem.
>
> Doing something new requires the flexibility to "get it wrong" on the first iteration without becoming desperate.

So, use whatever tools make sense for your death march project, regardless of whether the rest of the world thinks they are advanced or old-fashioned. And remember that if you *do* use new tools, it's going to have an impact on the people and the processes within the death march project. As Thoreau put it so eloquently 150 years ago:

> But lo! men have become the tools of their tools.
>
> —Henry David Thoreau, "Economy," *Walden,* 1854.

# NOTES

1. Sometimes the politics can get pretty nasty here. During the mid-1990s, shortly after IBM's acquisition of Lotus, I observed a number of forlorn IBM employees using Freelance instead of PowerPoint and Lotus 1-2-3 instead of Excel, because it wasn't worth the political battles they would have faced otherwise. Similarly, I'm not sure I would want to be part of a project team at Microsoft that decided, circa August 1996, to use Netscape Navigator rather than Internet Explorer. Obviously, political battles of this sort are likely to be the most severe in software product companies; but they can be fairly severe in other private-sector and public-sector companies where the Tools Police have decreed, "We are an 'X' shop! We don't allow no stinking 'non-X' products around here!"—where "X" can be a compiler, a testing product, a configuration management product, or a collaboration tool.

2. Indeed, it's something that we all take for granted these days. And if the death march project depends on distributed teams scattered around the world, or upon the notion that people might do some of their work at home or in a hotel room while traveling, then such tools are mandatory.

3. ```
From: John Boddie, 73757,3311
To: Edward Yourdon, 71250,2322
Date: Fri, Aug 16, 1996, 10:32 PM
RE: Ch6 queries
Ed,
Ch 6 comments follow -
1. If your team had only ONE kind of "optional" or "discretionary"
tool/technology to support them in a death march project, what
would it be? My assumption here is that every project has an abso-
```
```

lute bare-minimum of required things like compilers and debuggers, but there's an awful lot that (a) the project team may not have immediately available, (b) senior management would perceive the acquisition of such new technology as expensive, and (c) one or more managers or kibitzers on the sidelines would say "oh, you don't need THAT tool!".

I would say that a configuration management tool is a real "must have." There is going to be lots of confusion among the pieces of the project and the manager and the team need a way to establish and track versions of the system as they move toward completion, termination or whatever.

2. How important are CASE tools for death march projects? In this context, I mean what we used to call "upper-CASE" tools that support analysis and design-level stuff; depending on how much money you spend, they might also generate code, wash the dishes, and provide various other useful services.

I find them very useful - at the same level as word processors. They allow the team to communicate using a standard format. I've found that inexpensive CASE tools work just fine.

3. How important are "visual" development environments in death march projects? I don't want to be language-specific here, since there are visual versions of most of the high-level programming languages available today. But the issue here is using a "drag-and-drop" kind of development tool for building programs, versus the older style of text editors to type in lines of code, followed by compile, link, test, etc.

In the situations where I have seen these used, I've been impressed.

They appear to remove a lot of the "housekeeping" that takes programmer and analyst time. I have yet to lead a project that uses these tools, but I'm hopeful.

4. How important do you think "groupware" tools are? I don't want to be too specific here, since everyone has a slightly different definition IRA/USPA but I'm thinking of tools similar to Lotus Notes for organizing "threads" of discussions and fostering collaboration, coordination, and communication. I would be interested to know if anyone has used more exotic forms of groupware; if you want to see examples, read Michael Schrage's book "No More Teams!". (And if you've never heard of the book, take a look at my review of his book, which I've posted in the "articles" section of my Web site at http://www.yourdon.com)

E-Mail is critical and document and code libraries are a "must," but the benefits of other groupware functionality might be harder to identify. In a crunch-mode environment, face-to-face working has a lot to recommend it.

5. Are there any tools, or technology-approach, that you consider highly risky or dangerous for death march projects? If you had to

advise a death march project manager to AVOID a particular tool or
technology, what would it be?
The standard rules apply here. You don't pick a technology that is
inappropriate for the task at hand. Using OO and the Web as building blocks for a telephone company's billing system might sound
sexy, but the nature of the job is batch processing and you might
be better off with COBOL.
Hope this helps,
JB

**4.** From: Doug Scott, 100072,1276
To: Ed Yourdon, 71250,2322
Topic: Ch6 queries
Section: The Cutter Edge [14], Forum: CASE - DCI
Date: Tue, Aug 13, 1996, 4:41:06 PM
>1. If your team had only ONE kind of "optional" or "discretionary"
> tool/technology to support them in a death march project, what
> would it be?
I'd get a CASE tool which could enable requirements through to mod-
ule/object definition. Code generation is not IMHO a real problem,
but taking requirements through to low-level models is. And yes, we
still have those who think you can just sit down and write an OLTP
system in assembler.
Failing the CASE tool, then an integrated set of tools such as
Smartsuite or Office, so that we could come up with something similar cheaply and quickly. And we need the spreadsheet.
HOWEVER. The best device is a large diagram pinned to the wall. It
might contain the (partially complete) E/R diagrams for the system,
or the process flows, or whatever. But it give people a focus for
discussing the design, and it costs next to nothing.
> 2. How important are CASE tools for death march projects?
Important, if introduced with appropriate training at the beginning
of the project. A disaster if not.
> 3. How important are "visual" development environments in
> death march projects?
I'm beginning to accept that the "visual" revolution is to do with
right- and left-brainedness, and since programmers are supposed to
be left-brained (or is it right?) they would be quite happy with
command line tools. Analysts, however, and designers, need to be
able to visualise things, and if the tool gives the ability to do
that (some do, but the resultant diagrams simply don't help) then
they're useful.
That wall chart (see above) does help, though.
> 5. Are there any tools, or technology-approach, that you consider
> highly risky or dangerous for death march projects
Most project management tools are, IMHO, a load of rubbish. PERT is
enough to find the critical path, but many tools insist that you do
full resource allocation before the project even starts. I use a

spreadsheet, but I'd love a copy of an old-fashioned PERT diagram-
mer where I could add resources during the project (which is when I
find out what I'm getting) rather than months before.
Doug

5. From: S. Marsh Roberts [ICCA], 70007,4251
   To: Ed Yourdon, 71250,2322
   Topic: Ch6 queries
   Section: The Cutter Edge [14], Forum: CASE - DCI
   Date: Wed, Aug 14, 1996, 7:58:27 AM
   EdIRA/USPA

>> 1. If your team had only ONE kind of "optional" or "discretion-
ary" tool/technology to support them in a death march project, what
would it be? My assumption here is that every project has an absolute bare-minimum of required things like compilers and debuggers,
but there's an awful lot that (a) the project team may not have
immediately available, (b) senior management would perceive the
acquisition of such new technology as expensive, and (c) one or
more managers or kibitzers on the sidelines would say "oh, you
don't need THAT tool!".<<

I'd choose Infomodeler or something similar. Inexpensive tool which
functions to do some elementary things. Feature it, for the CASE-
weary, as a drawing tool, so that we can communicate with the
users.

>>2. How important are CASE tools for death march projects? In this
context, I mean what we used to call "upper-CASE" tools that support analysis and design-level stuff; depending on how much money
you spend, they might also generate code, wash the dishes, and provide various other useful services.<<

Pick one that supports high-level design and communications. If it
happens to also generate code, fine. If not, that's OK. Just don't
pick something that does the dishes, because it will be too hard to
learn and too easy to blame for design delays.

>>3. How important are "visual" development environments in death
march projects? I don't want to be language-specific here, since
there are visual versions of most of the high-level programming
languages available today. But the issue here is using a "drag-and-
drop" kind of development tool for building programs, versus the
older style of text editors to type in lines of code, followed by
compile, link, test, etc.<<

If it works for the programming team, it's important. If the team
is accustomed to text-edited COBOL code, who am I to complain?
At this point there are plenty of experienced VB programmers, for
example.

>>4. How important do you think "groupware" tools are? I don't want
to be too specific here, since everyone has a slightly different
definition IRA/USPA but I'm thinking of tools similar to Lotus
Notes for organizing "threads" of discussions and fostering collab-

oration, coordination, and communication. I would be interested to know if anyone has used more exotic forms of groupware; if you want to see examples, read Michael Schrage's book "No More Teams!". (And if you've never heard of the book, take a look at my review of his book, which I've posted in the "articles" section of my Web site at http://www.yourdon.com)<<
I'll go see your Web site and the review. "I'll be back."
>>5. Are there any tools, or technology-approach, that you consider highly risky or dangerous for death march projects? If you had to advise a death march project manager to AVOID a particular tool or technology, what would it be? <<
Pick one of the following, depending upon prior experience of the team:
a. C or C++
b. Smalltalk
c. AI
d. any new full-lifecycle CASE tool
e. UNIX or any other operating system that's new for the team
When the team is required to think clearly more than 60 hours per week, it's a bad time to invoke complex logic. Anything that requires a new mode of effort or a more sophisticated way of think-ing is a problem.
Doing something new requires the flexibility to "get it wrong" on the first iteration without becoming desperate.
Sharon

# REFERENCES

1. Michael Schrage, *No More Teams! Mastering the Dynamics of Creative Collabo-ration,* New York: Doubleday-Dell Publishing Company, 1995.

2. Paul G. Bassett, *Framing Software Reuse: Lessons from the Real World,* Upper Saddle River, NJ: Prentice Hall, 1996, ISBN 0-13-327859-X.

3. Bo Leuf and Ward Cunningham, *The Wiki Way: Quick Collaboration on the Web,* Reading, MA: Addison-Wesley, 2001.

4. Meilir Page-Jones, "The Seven Stages in Software Engineering," *American Pro-grammer*, July-August 1990.

# 11 Simulators and "War Games"

*War games help you evaluate your relative strengths and weaknesses and help the organization to observe its global strengths and weaknesses... For the purpose of stimulative creative disorder, the most effective form of war game calls for participants to take part in teams.*

—Tom DeMarco and Tim Lister, *Peopleware*

## INTRODUCTION

Earlier in this book, I discussed the issue of training for a death march project team being exposed to new processes and tools. But the traditional training involves methodologies, processes, tools, and technologies which are presumed to be new and unfamiliar to the team members. What about training in the "experience" of participating in a death march project? What about "practice" at dealing with stress and tension and unexpected crises? What about giving the project manager the opportunity to "ruin" one project after another without *really* suffering the consequences of missed deadlines, blown budgets, and burned-out programmers? In short, why not *simulate* the experience of a death march project in order to help both the project manager and the team members prepare for the *real* experience?

When the first edition of this book was being written in 1996, questions like these were considered not just controversial, but utterly radical and unrealistic. And yet the analogies and metaphors with other professions were obvious and familiar: In seminar after seminar, I would simply ask the participants if they would be willing to fly on a commercial airline in which the pilots had *not* had the prior experience of practicing in a simulator. Yes, pilots read books and sit through classroom training; and they do fly in real airplanes with a veteran instructor sitting beside them. But they also spend hour after hour in a simulated cockpit environment, so they can be exposed to both normal and abnormal flying conditions in a "controlled" simulation environment. And they come back to their simulator environment even after years of "real" flying experience, so they can hone their skills and learn about new scenarios. I have yet to find anyone who believes that such an approach is unnecessary or a waste of time and money.

As this second edition of *Death March* was being written in the spring of 2003, the notion of "simulators" is much more familiar and widespread. For example, we've seen news reports of war-game exercises prior to the invasion of Iraq; we'll discuss war games in more detail in the next section. And we've seen numerous examples of "practice drills" for simulated biological, chemical, and nuclear terrorist attacks. Everyone hopes that we'll never have a repeat of the September 11, 2001 attacks; but if something like that *does* occur, it could turn out to be the "ultimate" death march project—and nobody in his right mind wants fire-fighters, police, and emergency medical technicians to respond to such a crisis without prior training and practice.

The theme of this chapter, as you may have guessed, is that the same kind of advance practice is valuable for IT professionals facing a new death march project. If it's important for veteran programmers, database designers and project managers, it's all the more important for new people hired into the organization. Novices—for example, new college graduates who have never had a full-time software development job— don't have to told that death march projects are different from the textbook approach they learned in college (assuming, of course, that they learned *anything* about project management in college!). But they do need to be given the appropriate training in the methods, processes, and tools that the organization has found effective in death march projects. This is likely to be quite different from the older style processes and tools that such recruits previously had to endure; the irony is that as soon as the former recruits moved into their first project, they were often told by their project manager to ignore "all that classroom stuff" and adopt a more pragmatic attitude toward software development. In any case, the new recruits need to understand that the death march processes and tools are being adopted as a matter of proactive choice, rather than reactive desperation.

# THE CONCEPT OF WAR GAMES

Obviously, textbooks and classroom training on project management techniques, processes, and tools are still important and helpful. But rather than arguing whether the classroom is preferable to the "battlefield" of a death march project, I believe that IT organizations should consider a compromise: a death march *simulator*.

Skeptics might argue that such a simulator would not replicate the pressure and tension that one experiences in a real project; airline pilots who have used their simulators to practice emergency situations would strenuously disagree. But if we really need to simulate stress in a software project, we can borrow a familiar tactic from the military: *war games*.

Of course, the phrase "war game" conjures up military images—and in the context of our discussion here, that is both conscious and deliberate. Regardless of your political opinion about war and peace, the fact of the matter is that military strategists, planners, and trainers have long used the concept for multiple purposes: to experiment with different strategies, to anticipate enemy counter-strategies that might not otherwise be readily ascertained, and to train both new recruits and veterans in the most realistic manner possible. Indeed, war gaming has been credited for developing and refining England's strategy for the Battle of Britain in World War II, when its air force was substantially outnumbered by the German Luftwaffe.

Hollywood has become enamored of the war-game concept, as illustrated by such movies as *Top Gun*; and the video-game industry has discovered that sophisticated PC-based war games are among their most profitable products. Indeed, the *real* military has recently gotten into the business of Internet-based "virtual reality" war games; one of the most fascinating examples is www.americasarmy.com created by the United States Army. In the first three months after it was released in the summer of 2002, approximately 873,000 individuals registered their names as "players" in this interactive experience; by the fall of 2002, 4,400 new registrants were signing up *every day* and generating 50,000 Web-site "hits" and 1.5 million file downloads per day. By early October of 2002, 520,000 registrants had competed the equivalent of "basic training" in the Army, which requires three to six hours of playing time.[1]

In a similar way, a software project death march war game could consist of giving several different project teams the same "project scenario"—the same requirements, the same (compressed) amount of time, the same resources to work with—and a well-defined objective to develop a certain amount of working software within a fixed time-frame. If a death march culture hasn't been standardized and formalized within the organization, tell each team that it can use whatever tools and processes it wants to—anything it can beg, borrow, or steal is fair game. The Australian Computer Society has been hosting such a war game at its annual conference since 1994, and several local consulting organizations now use it as part of their own training process.

In order to conduct a war game, or any other kind of "flight simulator" for death march projects, it's helpful to have a simulation model that can mimic the cause-and-effect consequences of various technical and managerial decisions in a project. A good example of such a model is Tarek Abdel-Hamid's system dynamics model, discussed briefly in Chapter 6. A simulation model can be implemented in virtually any programming language, but there are specialized languages and tools for such purposes. Of these, SIMSCRIPT, DYNAMO, and GPSS are perhaps the best known; the model described by Abdel-Hamid is implemented in DYNAMO (and the entire program listing is published in the book's appendix). More recently, though, a number of "visual" modeling tools such as iThink have appeared, most of them modestly priced.

One of the benefits of such models, as mentioned in Chapter 6, is that it provides the team members and the project manager with a good way of articulating and discussing the unspoken assumptions and "mental models" they have about various aspects of the project—especially the "soft" issues like morale, burnout, and overtime. In the context of a death march, a war-game scenario can allow the team to *experience* its mental models and see which ones work and which ones don't; again, it's much less expensive to have such experiences in a simulated environment than a real one.

For example, I once conducted a war game in which each of the competitive teams had nine separate opportunities, during the course of a three-day competition, to assess their own results and the results of the other teams—and then make whatever changes they wanted to their current and future "project parameters" *as well as to past parameters* (i.e., they could rerun the simulation of earlier stages of their projects, with different budget, staffing, and methodology-related decisions). Remarkably, *none* of the competitive teams were willing to make *any* changes to the project-related decisions they had already committed, with one exception: a parameter that governed the size of annual salary increases to be given to team members.[2] Since all of the teams had strongly agreed that they needed to be flexible in the face of unforeseen circumstances, it was a shock for them to see that when given the opportunity to be "infinitely flexible" (even to the point of rewriting their past history), they adamantly refused to do so.

One of the most valuable aspects of a war-game simulator is the ability to conduct a blow-by-blow "playback" of the significant events and decisions in the project. At the very least, it provides a valuable opportunity for discussion—for example, the war-game facilitator can conduct a postmortem and say, "Look what happened at this point, when the end-user introduced three or four 'small changes' to the requirements document. The red team accepted the changes without any revision to the schedule and budget; the blue team refused to make any changes and carried on with its original plan; and the green team accepted the changes, but negotiated with the end-user to remove a slightly greater number of the 'original' requirements in order to provide the necessary resources to accommodate the new requirements. Let's talk about the consequences of those three different decisions..." And, in most cases, the playback mechanism allows the postmortem review to experiment with alternatives: What if we had made *this* decision at a critical point in the simulated project rather than *that* decision?

Even with elegant tools and a wealth of published literature, there's no way of escaping the fact that it requires a serious investment and commitment to build a model that reflects a particular company's environment and allows management to demonstrate the particular death march scenarios it feels are important. Having been involved in several of these simulator projects and war-game scenarios, my experience is that it typically requires at least a few person-months of effort to have a realistic and well-tuned model; and as another illustration, it's interesting to note that the model published in *Software Project Dynamics: An Integrated Approach* [1] was Abdel-Hamid's Ph.D. thesis at MIT.[3]

This means that such an effort is almost certain to be beyond the ability of an individual project manager to develop as part of the training experience for a single death march project. It's clearly a corporate strategic investment—and it may be more than a small 10-person software company can afford to think about. But for the software organizations with hundreds or even thousands of people, it's a modest investment indeed. Keep in mind the context in which all of this occurs: Management is looking for ways of institutionalizing processes and technology that will enable projects to *confidently* promise schedules, budgets, and deliverable functionality two or three times more ambitious than "normal" projects have experienced in the same environment. In planning for such a radical change, management is often prepared to spend vast sums of money—literally millions of dollars in some cases—to equip the developers with new workstations, visual programming tools, and object-oriented methodologies. To complain about the cost of a six-person-month effort to build a simulator is ludicrous; and to deny their project teams the experience of simulating a death march project before they risk millions of dollars on a *real* death march project is pig-headed.

Alas, senior management typically doesn't see it this way. It generally resents the time, effort, and cost of *any* training, and the cost and effort associated with death march simulators are seen as even less justifiable. As a result, the project manger who believes that there may be some merit to this kind of "practice" before the *real* battle of the death march project will probably have to find an "unofficial"[4] way to carry it out. Ideally, this will involve an intense off-site war-game experience with experienced trainers;[5] this is likely to be far more realistic and successful than anything the project manager can cobble together by himself. The war-game seminar/workshop doesn't have to be more than two to three days in length, and if necessary, you can schedule it during a weekend so that the corporate bureaucrats won't be able to complain about the "lost" time.

Alas, none of the video games and Internet-based "virtual reality" games available today are directly related to the field of software project management. As noted earlier, most of them focus on military exercises; and some—like the *Sim City* series of games—focus on nonviolent collaborative efforts (such as being the mayor of a city). For a brief period in the late 1990s, a superb PC-based "game" called "Project Challenge" provided exactly the kind of death march war-game training described in this chapter; but sadly, it disappeared in the aftermath of the dot-com collapse and high-tech recession of the early 2000s. One alternative worth exploring is the collection of consultants and small software companies using tools such as iThink to provide customized "flight simulators" for software project management; one such vendor is Exteco (http://exteco.esmartdesign.com/index2.html), and others can be found by performing Google-searches for terms such as "management flight simulator."

# CONCLUSION

As noted throughout this book, death march projects have become inevitable in today's competitive and chaotic business environment. A few organizations have acknowledged this situation and have begun planning for it in a rational manner. However, the history of the software industry for the past 40 years suggests that most of our organizations don't learn much from their past experiences and are likely to regard each new death march project as a unique and novel experience. Even the organizations that realize death march projects are no longer isolated accidents will have a difficult time, for the established bureaucracy will continue to defend old standards, procedures, methodologies, and tools regardless of how inappropriate they may be.

One cheerful exception to this is the entrepreneurial startup organization. By definition, such organizations have no prior culture to replace and they are likely to regard death march projects as perfectly normal—after all, it's part of the mythos of startup companies that everyone works insane hours while the company takes insane risks in order to compete against the larger, established companies. And if the fledgling company comes to the conclusion that its success is precisely *because* of this behavior, then it will probably try to institutionalize it.

Of course, I'm speaking in generalities here, and there are lots of reasons why such an approach won't succeed. It's interesting, for example, that veteran software developers often bring much of their culture and work-habits with them when they leave a large bureaucracy to start a new software venture. On the other hand, it seems just as common today as it was in the early days of my career for the younger generation of software developers to plunge into new projects on a work schedule that regards 18-hour days as "resting up" while the team gets ready for the *real* work. But among the many things that *have* changed dramatically is the overall pace of work, which many high-tech organizations refer to simply as "Internet time." It's a concept that simply didn't exist for previous generations of software developers, and it's far more likely to lead to death march projects.

Regardless of whether the industry adopts death march projects as the norm, and regardless of whether your company manages such projects in a rational fashion, the fact remains that death march projects are carried out by individuals. I don't have a great deal of hope for the senior management and bureaucratic committees in most software organizations, but I do have a great deal of concern for the individuals who work the long nights and weekends on projects that are often doomed from the beginning. Bringing a death march project to a successful conclusion is obviously important, and I hope this book has provided some practical advice for doing just that; but *surviving* it is even more important! In the best of all worlds, our death march projects should deliver glorious results to the end-user with a schedule and budget that will dazzle senior management, and we should do all of this with our health, our wits, our family, and our sense of humor firmly intact. As E.B. White put it, perhaps in the midst of one of his own death march projects:

> I wake up each morning determined to change the World...
> and also to have one hell of a good time.
>
> Sometimes that makes planning the day a little difficult.

> —E.B. White

# NOTES

**1.** These statistics were provided by retired General Paul Gorman, during an address at the October 2002 "PopTech" conference (www.poptech.org). General Gorman concluded his presentation by saying, "Artificial worlds, carefully constructed and supervised, can be an incredible component for the military. In today's world, there is no other way that we can get ready…"

**2.** This was widely regarded as a key parameter, because it not only affected the overall budget allocated to the team (you can double everyone's salary every year, but you soon run out of money), it also affected the employee turnover rate: If you don't give people competitive salary increases, they're more likely to quit in the middle of the project.

**3.** For those interested in pursuing MIT-related education in this area, explore the one-week short course entitled "Business Dynamics: MIT's Approach to Diagnosing and Solving Complex Business Problems," described in greater detail at http://mitsloan.mit.edu/execed/epp/courses/bus-dynamics.php

**4.** For example, send the team members off for the training they need and *then* apologize to the training department for the fact that you "forgot" to fill out its six-part training-justification form. Or tell the war-game training vendor that you want the first hour of his or her workshop to focus on advanced C++ coding techniques, so that you can describe to the entire workshop to your boss as a course on "hard" coding skills.

**5.** One of the more interesting sources of such training is McCarthy Technologies, (www.mccarthy-tech.com/), which runs a five-day "boot camp" for software professionals; the cost is a few thousand dollars per student and I believe it's well worth the investment. The company is headed by Jim McCarthy, a former Microsoft manager, and author of the highly recommended book *Software Project Dynamics* (Microsoft Press, 1995). More recently, Jim and Michele McCarthy have published *Software for Your Head: Core Protocols for Creating and Maintaining Shared Vision* (Addison-Wesley, 2002).

# REFERENCES

1. Tarek Abdel-Hamid and Stuart E. Madnick, *Software Project Dynamics: An Integrated Approach,* Prentice-Hall, 1991.

2. Tarek Abdel-Hamid and S. E. Madnick, "Lessons Learned from Modeling the Dynamics of Software Project Management," *Comm. of the ACM*, Dec 1989.

3. "The Management Flight Simulator," John Saunders, http://users.erols.com/jsaunders/papers/mfs.htm

4. John A. Byrne, "Flight Simulators for Management," Business Week, Sept. 21, 1998, http://www.businessweek.com/1998/38/b3596135.htm

5. John D. Sterman, "Teaching Takes Off: Flight Simulators for Management Education," http://web.mit.edu/ jsterman/www/SDG/beergame.html

# Index

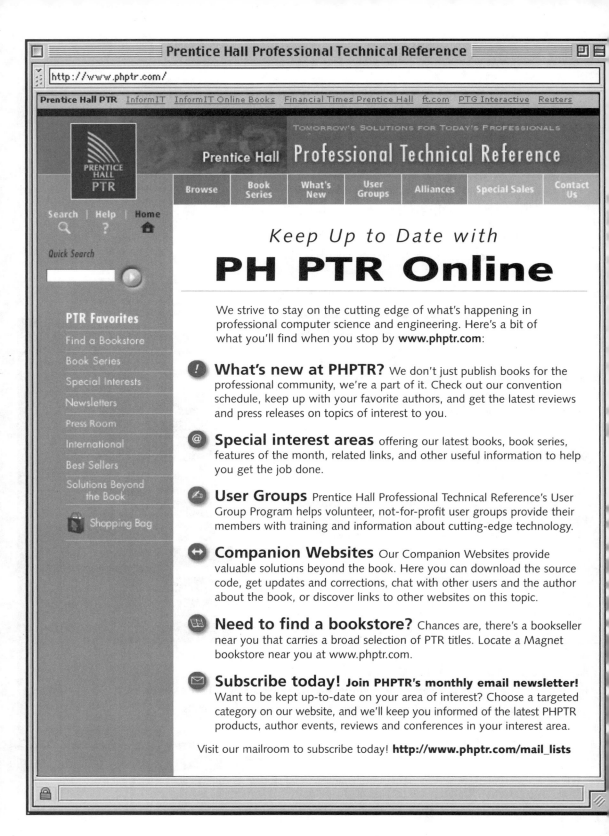